ESTATE PLANNING FOR THE MUSLIM CLIENT

YASER ALI AND AHMED SHAIKH

ABA SECTION OF REAL PROPERTY | TRUST & ESTATE LAW

ABA
Defending Liberty
Pursuing Justice

Cover design by Andrew Alcala/ABA Design

Printed in the United States of America.

23 22 21 20 19 5 4 3 2 1

ISBN: 978-1-64105-326-6
e-ISBN: 978-1-64105-327-3

Library of Congress Cataloging-in-Publication Data
Names: Ali, Yaser, author. | Shaikh, Ahmed, author.
Title: Estate planning for the muslim client / by Yaser Ali and Ahmed Shaikh.
Description: First edition. | Chicago : American Bar Association, 2019. | Includes index.
Identifiers: LCCN 2018047055 | ISBN 9781641053266 (print) | ISBN 9781641053273 (epub)
Subjects: LCSH: Estate planning—United States. | Distribution of decedents' estates (Islamic law) | Inheritance and succession (Islamic law)
Classification: LCC KF750 .A76 2019 | DDC 332.024/0160882970973—dc23
LC record available at https://lccn.loc.gov/2018047055

Discounts are available for books ordered in bulk. Special consideration is given to state bars, CLE programs, and other bar-related organizations. Inquire at Book Publishing, ABA Publishing, American Bar Association, 321 N. Clark Street, Chicago, Illinois 60654-7598.

www.ShopABA.org

Contents

CHAPTER 5
Disposition of Property at Death 91

Introduction

Estate planning involves more than just assisting with the transfer of a client's wealth from one generation to the next. To draft a customized plan that achieves a client's unique goals, an estate-planning practitioner must understand the client's values and convictions and, in many cases, his or her religious beliefs. For many clients, passing on these beliefs and traditions is just as important as, if not more important than, the distribution of their physical assets. As advisors, it thus behooves us to acknowledge and address our clients' religious considerations when conducting their planning.

For Muslims, estate planning is not merely an expression of an individual's love for his or her family, but also an act of religious devotion and a form of worship. Islam, like many other faiths, contains rules relating to the dispositive provisions of a person's wealth that are binding upon members of the faith. Aspects of the faith tradition also inform the decisions a client may make with respect to advance directives and end-of-life healthcare choices.

This book is intended to serve as a practice guide for attorneys interested in providing faith-based estate planning to a large and growing segment of the Muslim population in the United States.[1] Enjoying above-average median household income and roughly $100 billion in disposable income, America's nearly six million Muslims are projected to become the second-largest religious group in the country by mid-century.

Like all clients, Muslims who seek the services of a competent estate-planning attorney are looking for someone to assist them in protecting their loved ones, preserving their assets, and ensuring family harmony.

---

1. *See The Muslim Green: American Muslim Market Study 2014–15*, DinarStandard, http://www.dinarstandard.com/american-market-2014/ (last accessed Sept. 19, 2018); Michael Lipka, *Muslims Expected to Surpass Jews as Second-Largest U.S. Religious Group*, Pew Research Ctr. (Apr. 14, 2015), http://www.pewresearch.org/fact-tank/2015/04/14/muslims-expected-to-surpass-jews-as-second-largest-u-s-religious-group/.

Additionally, however, many Muslim clients are motivated by a desire to comply with a religious obligation to distribute their estate in accordance with a robust set of rules known as the Islamic Law of Inheritance. Others may wish to ensure that end-of-life care decisions be made in a manner consistent with Islamic bioethics, while still others may wish to memorialize their desire that certain funeral and burial rites be administered in accordance with Islamic law. As such, this subfield of estate planning requires unique cultural insight and a foundational knowledge of Islamic law.

Attempting to integrate a complex set of inheritance rules and ethics on top of existing state and federal tax laws might seem like a formidable task. Indeed, prior to the publication of this practice guide, we were unable to identify any other book that filled this purpose. But after years of assisting Muslim clients and counseling other attorneys on how to effectively provide such services to their clients, we are pleased to make this information more broadly accessible. Our goal in doing so is to outline various considerations of Islamic law that are applicable in the estate-planning context in order to provide practical guidance to attorneys who are drafting and administering estate plans for their Muslim clients.

In explaining this subject, we rely on existing scholarship, case law, and statutes in the American legal tradition, as well as rules articulated in classical Islamic religious texts. Since we believe that having a familiarity with a limited amount of Arabic terminology is necessary to attain religious literacy in this practice area, we have retained original Arabic terms in several places throughout this book. Whenever we use a non-English term for the first time, we define it in the immediately corresponding text. Since one need not read this practice manual from start to finish, explanations of all such Arabic terms also appear in the glossary.

We have elected to illustrate various legal principles and concepts through easy-to-understand examples and hypotheticals. The names used in these examples are common names and do not reflect actual cases. Any resemblance to actual persons or events is purely coincidental.

The Kind of Client This Book Can Benefit

In the United States, people are typically free to leave whatever they want to whomever they want after they die, with the exception of a surviving spouse, whose share is protected under most state laws. On the other hand, a Muslim client seeking to plan his or her estate consistent with Islamic law would choose to do so based upon certain rules stipulated in the Quran, the Muslim holy scripture, and the *Hadith*, the normative traditions of the Prophet Muhammad.

Of course, not every member of a faith tradition adheres to all the rules of that tradition all the time. Many attorneys do not ask about the religious background of their clients, and sometimes, even if the topic arises, it may not impact the nature or implementation of a client's stated objectives.

If a client appears to be from the Muslim faith tradition but does not request that any requirements of the client's faith be incorporated into his or her estate plan, the attorney would certainly not be obligated to ask. Some attorneys may choose to inquire, others may not.

But if our own experience combined with the recent spike in demand for Islamic financial products is any indication,[2] an increasing number of Muslim clients are seeking to plan their estates in accordance with their faith and values. This book is intended to address the needs of those clients. Specifically, it will help an attorney answer the question "How can I design an estate plan—including any charitable planning, estate-tax planning, healthcare directives, burial instructions, and other common estate-planning considerations—consistent with my client's religious preferences?"

At first blush, some elements of Islamic inheritance law—which are similar in their level of detail to a state intestacy scheme—may seem unconventional and might give the drafting attorney pause, most notably with respect to the treatment that Islamic inheritance law provides to certain female heirs. While we do not believe that representing clients who voluntarily seek to adhere to a set of constitutionally protected religious principles constitutes an explicit or implicit endorsement of those beliefs, we do suggest that if an attorney ultimately does not feel comfortable drafting an estate plan consistent with the client's faith, he or she should refer the matter to another practitioner who is able and willing to represent the client.

That said, one of our goals in writing this book is to provide solutions for clients who are seeking to adhere to a set of classical religious obligations while recognizing the practicalities of contemporary life in America. Throughout this book we highlight various planning opportunities in this regard and will identify the most common issues that arise when planning for a Muslim client. Since every client scenario is unique, it may

2. Islamic financial assets worldwide shot up to more than $1.3 trillion in 2012 from less than $600 billion in 2007. *See* Mohammed Aly Sergie, *The Rise of Islamic Finance*, Council on Foreign Relations (Jan. 30, 2014), http://www.cfr.org/economics/rise-islamic-finance/p32305.

be advisable in many cases for the drafting attorney to retain a religious advisor or consultant to assist with the understanding and application of Islamic inheritance law to a particular client's situation.

Finally, in addition to benefiting estate-planning attorneys, we hope this book will also serve as a useful reference guide for accountants, financial planners, trust officers, and private fiduciaries serving Muslim clients, as we believe that demonstrating sensitivity to a client's religious concerns and wishes should be an integral component of the estate-planning and administration process.

A Note about *Sharia*-Compliant Estate Planning

There is perhaps no term in today's popular discourse more often misunderstood than the word "*Sharia*," loosely translated as Islamic law. The idea of drafting a *Sharia*-compliant estate plan for a Muslim client may make a practitioner nervous, as the term is routinely associated with negative portrayals of Islam and Muslims. This book is intended as neither a refutation of those accusations nor a rebuttal against such tropes. Rather, this book will provide readers with a basic level of religious and cultural literacy regarding Islam and Muslims in America in order to better serve their clients. We will define the term *Sharia* and explain how Islamic inheritance laws interplay with federal and state laws.

As in all matters of law and theology, there may be a multiplicity of views among religious scholars on any particular issue in the tradition. Since this is fundamentally a book designed for legal practitioners and not one that ventures into theological discussions, we will at times need to make certain legal determinations about what is or is not permissible under Islamic law. In doing so, we will attempt to be as middle-of-the-road as possible. For the most part, we will rely on the Hanafi school of jurisprudence, which is one of the four major schools in the Sunni legal tradition. The Sunni schools of law do not differ significantly in matters of inheritance law, though certain nuances do arise in individual cases. We also separately describe the inheritance rules of the Jafari (Ithna Ashari) school, which is the largest Shia school of jurisprudence as well. Where major differences of opinion exist within the traditions, we will highlight them as well in an effort to provide the practitioner with appropriate tools to counsel the client.

How This Book Is Organized

Estate planning is a complex area of law. We assume the reader has a basic understanding and familiarity with conventional estate-planning concepts and tools. This book is not intended as a replacement to treatises on general estate planning, nor does it purport to cover every scenario that a client may present in one's office. Rather it is intended as a way to provide practitioners with an authoritative "Islamic perspective" on many estate-planning options the practitioner may consider.

In Chapter 1 we introduce the reader to the American Muslim community, one of the most ethnically and economically diverse faith communities in the United States. We will also outline the basic tenets of the Muslim faith, provide an introduction to Islamic law and its sources—including explanations of the terms "*Sharia*" and "*Fiqh*" (schools of Islamic jurisprudence)—and highlight some important Islamic financial principles that are often implicated in conventional estate planning.

Chapter 2 provides an overview of some ethical, legal, and public policy issues that may be applicable when planning for a Muslim client. We will discuss joint representation of a married couple and the use of spousal waivers, address potential Establishment Clause issues, and review certain public policy objections that may be levied by an heir under Islamic law.

Chapter 3 will cover estate-planning considerations during a Muslim client's life. This includes religious practices during life, rules relating to marriage and divorce, ownership and distribution of jointly owned property, investment-related restrictions under Islamic law, retirement planning, and *zakat* and lifetime gifting.

Chapter 4 addresses later life planning and end-of-life care issues, including incapacity planning and Islamic bioethics relating to advance healthcare directives, funeral arrangements, organ donations, and disposition of remains.

Chapter 5 will detail major issues relating to the disposition of property at the time of death, including how the default succession rules under Islamic inheritance law in the Sunni and Shia traditions interplay with state law and federal tax laws.

Chapter 6 provides practical guidance on drafting estate-planning documents for Muslim clients.

Chapter 7 will outline planning opportunities for individuals and assets located outside the United States.

The appendixes will provide detailed tables of heirs under Islamic law and several sample estate-planning documents, including advance health-care directives and a sample will and living trust that can be readily modified and incorporated into a Muslim client's estate plans.

Finally, the glossary provides easy-to-reference definitions for all the Arabic terminology used throughout this guide.

About the Authors

Yaser Ali

Yaser Ali is a wealth-planning attorney in Tempe, Arizona, and counsels individuals and families with their estate, tax, and charitable planning needs. A graduate of the University of Florida, Harvard Graduate School of Education, and UC Berkeley School of Law, and a former law clerk to Judge Damon J. Keith on the United States Court of Appeals, Mr. Ali is also trained as an Imam, having memorized the entire Quran in its original Arabic language and studied Islamic jurisprudence and inheritance law with traditional Muslim scholars.

Mr. Ali's unique background enables him to effectively synthesize issues of classical Islamic law in a contemporary American context. He is a frequent speaker on topics relating to Islamic law and estate planning and routinely advises attorneys around the country on how to design and implement religiously compliant solutions for high-net-worth Muslim clients.

Mr. Ali lives with his wife and two children in sunny Phoenix, Arizona.

Ahmed Shaikh

Born in San Diego, California, Ahmed Shaikh is a graduate of the Indiana University School of Law in Bloomington and a Board Certified Specialist in Estate Planning, Trust and Probate Law by the State Bar of California Board of Legal Specialization. He served as the 2018 Chair of the Trusts and Estates Section of the Orange County Bar Association. He has also served in various capacities in the Muslim community locally and nationally. Since 2006, a large portion of his law practice has focused on Islamic law related to trusts and estates.

Mr. Shaikh's mission is to take challenging stories and with knowledge, understanding, and compassion create better narratives. For families of various levels of wealth and family complexity, this has meant aligning their planning with their values.

Mr. Shaikh lives in Irvine, California, with his wife and three children.

Acknowledgments

We thank God Almighty, without whom nothing is possible, for the ability, knowledge, and patience to complete this work. We also express our deepest gratitude to our families for their enduring love and consistent support.

Surely this book would not have been possible without the help of countless mentors, teachers, colleagues, and friends who have aided us throughout our careers. In particular, we are indebted to Professor Nancy Shurtz, Kashif Mansoor, Shadman Ahmed, Dr. Muzaamil Siddiqi, Bilal Ansari, and Hamza Maqbool for their invaluable assistance in this project. Any errors, of course, are our own.

CHAPTER 1

Meeting the Muslim Client

Islam is the world's second-largest religion. Its followers, known as Muslims, come from diverse countries, cultures, and socioeconomic backgrounds. The largest Muslim populations live in Indonesia, the Indian subcontinent (Pakistan, India, Bangladesh), and Africa, while only about one-fifth of the world's 1.8 billion Muslims hail from the Middle East.[1] Millions more reside in North America and Europe, with Islam currently ranking as the second-largest religion in Canada and Europe in terms of number of adherents.

The United States is home to the most diverse Muslim population in the world, one that is expected to double in size by the year 2050.[2] While the vast majority of American Muslims are concentrated in large urban centers, Muslims constitute the largest non-Christian group in twenty states.[3] This includes Muslims whose ancestors have lived in this country for hundreds of years, converts to the faith, recent immigrants seeking a

1. John Esposito & Dalia Mogahed, Who Speaks for Islam?: What a Billion Muslims Really Think (2007).

2. An estimated 37 percent of voting-age Muslims in America are under 30, and 80 percent are under 50. Emma Green, *American Muslims Are Young, Politically Liberal, and Scared*, The Atlantic (Mar. 21, 2017), https://www.theatlantic.com/politics/archive/2017/03/american-muslims-demographics/520239/; *see also* Michael Lipka, *Muslims and Islam: Key Findings in the U.S. and around the World*, Pew Research Ctr. (Aug. 9, 2017), http://www.pewresearch.org/fact-tank/2017/08/09/muslims-and-islam-key-findings-in-the-u-s-and-around-the-world.

3. Jahnabi Barooah, *Most and Least Muslim States in America* (PHOTOS), HuffPost, http://www.huffingtonpost.com/2012/06/27/most-and-least-muslim-states_n_1626144.html (last updated Dec. 7, 2017).

better life, and their children and grandchildren who are born and raised in cities and towns throughout the United States.

The American Muslim community is also perhaps the most racially diverse in the world. Thirty percent of American Muslims identify as white, 23 percent as black, 21 percent as Asian, 6 percent as Hispanic, and 19 percent as other or mixed race.[4] In terms of education and wealth, Muslims possess the second-highest level of education among major religious groups in this country. A higher-than-average percentage have graduated from college. In fact, an estimated 10 percent of all physicians in America are Muslim.[5]

Globally, Muslim consumer spending on food and lifestyle reached $1.8 trillion in 2014 and is projected to reach a staggering $2.6 trillion by 2020.[6] It is estimated that the American Muslim community enjoys around $100 billion of disposable wealth, a large percentage of which is expected to pass to the next generation in the next 20 to 30 years.[7]

As one examines the diversity of American Muslims, it is easy to recognize how many disparities must exist culturally, economically, and politically within the group. While Muslims follow the same faith, their sheer diversity makes it impossible to paint an image of Muslims with broad strokes. Nonetheless, in the pages that follow, we provide some generally agreed-upon principles of the faith in an attempt to introduce these concepts to the reader.

A. An Introduction to the Islamic Faith

Muslims believe Islam is a continuation and culmination of the Abrahamic faith traditions. Muslims worship one God, *Allah*, and believe that Muhammad is the last and final messenger of God. The word *Allah* is related to the Aramaic and Hebrew names for God, *Allaha* and *Elohim*.

4. *Muslim Americans: No Signs of Growth in Alienation or Support for Extremism*, Pew Research Ctr. (Aug. 30, 2011), http://www.people-press.org/2011/08/30/section-1-a-demographic-portrait-of-muslim-americans/.

5. Hesham Hassaballa, *Muslims Don't Contribute to America? Think Again*, (Jan. 31, 2014), http://www.chicagonow.com/midwestern-muslim/2014/01/muslims-dont-contribute-to-america-think-again.

6. *State of the Global Islamic Economy Report 2015*, DinarStandard, http://www.dinarstandard.com/state-of-the-global-islamic-economy-report-2015 (last accessed Sept. 19, 2018).

7. *The Muslim Green: American Muslim Market Study 2014/15*, DinarStandard, http://www.dinarstandard.com/wp-content/uploads/2014/11/Amercan_Muslim_Executive-Summary-2014_DinarStandard.pdf (last accessed Sept. 19, 2018).

Muhammad is revered as the final messenger in a long line of messengers sent by God, beginning with Adam and including Noah, Abraham, Moses, and Jesus.

There are two major sects in Islam, the Sunni and Shia, whose division is based upon a historic disagreement regarding the successor to the Prophet Muhammad. Although there are a few notable differences between the two sects, particularly with respect to inheritance law, they both agree on the core tenets of the faith.

B. The Pillars of Faith

Islam is founded upon five basic pillars: (1) stating the testimony of faith, (2) performing daily prayers, (3) fasting in the month of Ramadan, (4) giving mandatory alms, and (5) performing a once-in-a-lifetime pilgrimage to Mecca.[8]

1. Stating the Testimony of Faith (*Shahada*)

The foundation of a Muslim's belief is rooted in the *Shahada* or testimony of faith, which states: "I bear witness that there is no god but God [*Allah*] and I bear witness that Muhammad is the messenger of God."

2. Performing Daily Prayers (*Salah*)

Muslims observe five daily prayers to reconnect with God at regular intervals throughout the day: before sunrise, around noon, in the afternoon, at sunset, and in the evening.

3. Fasting during Ramadan (*Siyam*)

Ramadan is the ninth month of the Islamic lunar calendar. During this month, Muslims abstain from all food, drink (including water), and sexual relations from dawn to dusk for thirty days and are encouraged to be increasingly charitable toward those in need. The month ends with *Eid al-Fitr*, or the Feast of Celebration.

---

8. *See* Sahih Al-Bukhari, Vol. 1, book 2, hadith 8, *available at* https://sunnah.com/bukhari/2/1 (last accessed Oct. 4, 2018).

4. Giving Alms or Mandatory Charity (*Zakat*)

The Quran repeatedly instructs Muslims to donate a portion of their wealth to the less fortunate. The term "*zakat*," which literally means "purification" or "increase," is a requirement for financially able Muslims to annually contribute 2.5 percent of their liquid assets to the poor, suffering, or sick. *Zakat* is due each year on the net balance of the following classes of assets, after subtracting basic needs (e.g., a personal residence, furniture, clothing, vehicles, etc.) and debts: (a) gold and silver, (b) cash and liquid investments, (c) business assets, (d) livestock, and (e) agricultural production.

Sadaqah, or voluntary giving beyond the 2.5 percent *zakat* requirement, is also highly encouraged. Notably, for this reason, many Muslim clients will choose to include charitable bequests in their estate plans.

The Ithna Ashari sect of Shia Islam also has an additional charitable requirement of *khums* (one-fifth), which is described further in Chapter 5.

5. Performing a Pilgrimage to Mecca (*Hajj*)

The *Hajj* is a once-in-a-lifetime pilgrimage to Mecca for Muslims who are financially and physically able to make the journey. Estate planning and the pilgrimage tend to be linked. Given its significance, Muslims preparing to embark on the *Hajj* are encouraged to first pay off debts, seek forgiveness from family and community members, and create an estate plan before they depart on the trip.

C. Islamic Law and Its Sources

The term "*Sharia*," often used interchangeably with "Islamic law," literally means "a way to the watering-place" or "a path to seek felicity and salvation."[9] It encompasses the moral, ethical, social, and political codes of conduct for Muslims, ranging from personal acts of devotion and ritual worship to financial ethics, domestic relations, estate planning, and even criminal law.

In many respects, Islamic law is similar to Jewish law. Both religions contain divinely revealed legal systems that govern all dimensions of an adherent's life from the private to the public sphere. Just as devout Jews adhere to kosher laws, observe the Sabbath, and have distinct rules relating

9. Mohammed Hashim Kamali, Shari'ah Law: An Introduction (Ch. 2) (2008).

to marriage and divorce, Muslims observe analogous dietary restrictions known as *halal*, attend congregational prayers every Friday, and follow traditional guidelines pertaining to domestic relations. For Jews, these rules are codified in what is known as the *Halakha*. For Catholics, these regulations are represented by Canon Law. For Muslims, the sacred law is known as the *Sharia*.

At its core, the *Sharia* is comprised of principles that are in consonance with, and protected by, the U.S. Constitution. The recognized *maqasid*, or objectives and principles of the *Sharia*, are debated by religious scholars but include items such as

1. preservation of life;
2. freedom of religion;
3. preservation of mind and intellect, including freedom of conscience and thought;
4. preservation of lineage and family; and
5. protection of private property.[10]

D. Sources of *Sharia*

The *Sharia* is derived from two primary sources and two secondary sources. The two primary sources are (1) the Quran and (2) the *Sunnah*. The secondary sources are (3) *Ijma*, or scholarly consensus, and (4) *Qiyas*, a process of analogical deduction that religious scholars use to derive new Islamic legal rulings.

1. The Quran

Muslims consider the Quran to be the actual word of God, revealed to the Prophet Muhammad in the Arabic language through the angel Gabriel over a period of 23 years.

The Quran contains a few major themes, including the oneness of God, the existence of a life after death and a Day of Judgment, Heaven and Hell, and stories of previous nations and their prophets. It also calls for universal truths such as justice and honesty and contains normative prescriptions for how Muslims should live their lives.

10. See *id.* Chapter 6 for a further discussion of the history and methodology of the *maqasid* of *Sharia*; *see also* Jasser Auda, Maqasid Al-Shariah: *An Introductory Guide* (2008), http://www.jasserauda.net/new/pdf/maqasid_guide-Feb_2008.pdf (last accessed Oct. 5, 2018).

While most religious obligations are described only briefly in the Quran itself, the rules relating to inheritance law are expressly detailed in Chapter 4, titled "The Women." These verses contain explicit instructions regarding how to distribute a decedent's estate and are explained in Chapter 5 of this book.

2. The *Sunnah*

The *Sunnah*, or the normative tradition of the Prophet Muhammad, explains and clarifies the Quran. As a technical term, it refers to the teachings and religious practices of the Prophet Muhammad that his companions transmitted to subsequent generations.

The Quran typically addresses universal principles and contains broad prohibitions and commandments. The practical explanation of most matters of religion is found in the Prophet's *Sunnah*. For instance, the Quran instructs Muslims to establish prayer and give alms, but the details of how and when to pray, and how much one must give in charity and which assets are exempt, are further delineated in the *Sunnah*.

Because the *Sunnah*, at least initially, was transmitted orally, scholars throughout history have held varying opinions as to the authenticity of specific traditions. In fact, disagreements relating to how subsequent generations transmitted and corroborated the *Sunnah* are one of the central causes for the rich diversity of tradition within Islam today.

3. *Ijma* (Scholarly Consensus)

Many discrete points of law are not directly addressed in the Quran or *Sunnah* but attain legal status through the unanimous consensus of Muslim legal scholars at a certain time and place. In early Islamic history, *Ijma*, or scholarly consensus, was critical in formulating the doctrine and practice of the Muslim community.

4. *Qiyas* (Deduction)

Attaining scholarly unanimity on a matter, especially in modern times, is a rare feat. Thus, in many cases, Islamic legal scholars use a process of deductive reasoning, or *Qiyas*, to extend an established ruling to another situation based on a shared legal cause. Legal jurists employ *Qiyas* in deciding many modern religious rulings relating to technology and finance.

E. *Sharia* for American Muslims

The *Sharia* is predominantly concerned with personal religious responsibilities and obligations to God rather than laws enforced by the state. Although various countries have formulated portions of their legal systems on its mandates, these components would not and could not be implemented by U.S. courts under any circumstances.[11]

Rather, for American Muslims, fidelity to *Sharia* in the legal sense means the observance of its norms in private contracts, such as marriage, the distribution of one's estate, and mutually agreed-upon transactions among Muslims—all of which find legal protection within First Amendment jurisprudence.[12] The federal government and states have their own criminal laws that *Sharia* cannot supplant.[13]

Courts may nonetheless consider *Sharia* in civil matters, just as they do with other foreign and religious laws, and in instances where required by comity. For example, American courts routinely honor marriages officiated in foreign countries, uphold binding arbitration agreements by observant Jews before Beth Din tribunals, affirm prenuptial agreements rooted in religious traditions, and recognize the rights of parents to raise children according to their own unique religious beliefs, so long as those contracts and choices do not violate U.S. public policy.[14]

Nonetheless, since 2010, over two dozen states have enacted or considered measures restricting judges from consulting or considering *Sharia*. The anti-*Sharia* movement began in Oklahoma in 2010, leading to a case that actually confirmed the right of American Muslims to plan their estate consistent with their values. In *Awad v. Ziriax*,[15] legislators in Oklahoma proposed a ballot measure to amend the state constitution to ban *Sharia* from state courts. The "Save Our State Amendment," as it was called, represented a high-water mark for an overtly discriminatory campaign

---

11. Eugene F. Scoles & Peter Hay, Conflict of Laws 173–74 (1992).

12. *See* James Sonne, *Domestic Applications of* Sharia *and the Exercise of Ordered Liberty*, 45 Seton Hall L. Rev. 725 (2015).

13. *See* Jeremy Grunert, Note, *How Do You Solve a Problem Like Sharia? Awad v. Ziriax and the Question of Sharia Law in America*, 40 Pepp. L. Rev. 695, 725–26 (2013) (describing statutory and constitutional limitations on the application of *Sharia*-based criminal-law provisions).

14. *See* Sonne, *supra* note 12, at 720 (describing examples of secular courts' deference to foreign authority); Eugene Volokh, *Religious Law (Especially Islamic Law) in American Courts*, 66 Okla. L. Rev. 431, 435 (2014).

15. Awad v. Ziriax, 670 F.3d 1111 (10th Cir. Okla. 2012) (*Awad II*).

that singled out Islam. Though lawmakers conceded they were unable to identify a single case in which an Oklahoma court had ever applied *Sharia*, voters overwhelmingly approved the measure, triggering a firestorm of criticism as well as a number of copycat bills around the country. A federal district court ultimately struck the bill down as unconstitutional, a decision later affirmed by the Tenth Circuit Court of Appeals.[16]

After voters approved the amendment, a Muslim resident of Oklahoma City, Muneer Awad, filed suit, arguing that the amendment singled out Islam and violated his rights under both the Establishment and Free Exercise Clauses of the First Amendment of the United States Constitution.[17] In particular, he argued that the amendment would prevent a court from "probating his last will and testament (which contains references to Sharia law)," which constituted an excessive entanglement between the government and his religion.[18]

A federal district judge in Oklahoma agreed and issued a permanent injunction against the amendment, noting that the issue spoke "to the very foundation of our country, our Constitution, and particularly, the Bill of Rights."[19] The Tenth Circuit Court of Appeals unanimously affirmed the lower court ruling, holding that "the Oklahoma amendment specifically names the target of its discrimination. The only religious law mentioned in the amendment is *Sharia* law" and that, additionally, "[a]ppellants do not identify any actual problem the challenged amendment seeks to solve."[20]

The *Awad* case was not just a victory for advocates of religious freedom; more specifically, it affirmed the right of Muslims in the United States to conduct estate planning consistent with their values.

F. Schools of Islamic Law

Much like judges vary in their interpretation of the Constitution and analysis of applicable statutes and code, the human process of attempting to understand the *Sharia* necessarily allows for flexibility and diversity in its application.[21]

16. *Id.*
17. *Id.* at 1119.
18. *Id.*
19. Awad v. Ziriax (*Awad I*), 754 F. Supp. 2d 1298, 1301 (W.D. Okla. 2010).
20. *Awad II*, 670 F.3d at 1128.
21. Sherman A. Jackson, Islamic Law and the State: The Constitutional Jurisprudence of Shihāb al-Dīn al-Qarāfī (1996).

Within Sunni Islam—the prevailing tradition of approximately 90 percent of the world's Muslims—there are four orthodox schools of *Fiqh*, or jurisprudence: the Hanafi, Shafi, Maliki, and Hanbali schools, named after their respective founders. They differ slightly in their legal methodologies but are considered equally authoritative. Because Islamic inheritance law is mostly taken directly from the Quran, it is one of the few topics in the *Sharia* in which the four Sunni schools are all largely aligned.

As for the Shia tradition, there are two dominant schools of *Fiqh*: the Ithna Asharis, also known as the Ja'faris, which is by far the largest branch of Shi'ism; and the Zaidis. While Sunnis and Shias agree on most of the core principles of Islam, they do have different authoritative texts and, notably, divergent views on several key elements of inheritance law. For instance, Ithna Ashari inheritance law often grants closer female family members a higher position as legal heirs than Sunni law.[22] It also rejects the concept of the extended agnatic family and the superiority of male agnates as legal heirs, both of which are key tenets of Sunni law.[23]

Given the complexity of the field of Islamic inheritance law, Sunni and Shia scholars—and, to a lesser extent, jurists of the various jurisprudential schools within each denomination—naturally differ on a number of rulings. Since this book is intended as a practice guide rather than a comparative treatise on Islamic inheritance law, when referencing the Sunni positions, we have elected to rely on the positions of the Hanafi school of jurisprudence, which has a well-developed corpus of law on the subject. In particular, we rely primarily on one of the most authoritative classical Hanafi texts in the field, *Al Siraji Fil Mirath* ("*Siraji*"), first translated into English in 1792.

When referencing the Shia doctrine, we rely on the prominent positions of the Ithna Ashari school, which are quite similar to the rules for Ismaili Shias. Where notable differences exist between the various schools that may impact a client's planning objectives, we note them as well. In doing so, our purpose is not to advocate for any particular view but to give a practitioner what he or she needs to incorporate a client's values into an estate plan.

---

22. Noel Coulson, *A Comparison of the Law of Succession in the Islamic and British Legal Systems*, 26(2) Am. J. Comp. L. 227, 230 (1978).

23. *Id.*

CHAPTER 2

Ethical, Legal, and Public Policy Issues

Like other areas of law, estate planning presents a set of unique ethical challenges for the practitioner.

A. Joint Representation of Clients

The first question practitioners must always ask themselves when meeting a potential client is "Who is my client?" This seemingly obvious question can be complicated by particularly strong family ties in some Muslim American families. Often assets are jointly owned by family members. Sometimes an adult child may be the one to call or initiate an appointment on behalf of his or her parents—and, in some cases, may even offer to pay for the planning. In some instances, an estate-planning attorney may represent multiple generations of individuals who are exercising differing levels of control in various family businesses.

To comply with the ethical rules that govern lawyers in every jurisdiction, the attorney must make clear his or her relationship to the parties involved.[1] Failure to do so can subject an attorney to disciplinary proceedings.

1. Model Rules of Prof'l Conduct R. 1.7 cmt. 27 (2016).

In particular, the drafting attorney must understand the rules relating to joint representation of a married couple. Estate-planning attorneys commonly represent both husband and wife during the estate-planning process. When representing Muslim clients, however, the counselor must be aware that each spouse will likely have different Islamic heirs and may also have different preferences with respect to successor trustees, personal representatives, and healthcare agents. The RESTATEMENT (THIRD) OF LAW GOVERNING LAWYERS § 130 (2000), illus. 1–3, expressly approves the joint representation where the attorney believes that the couple's overarching planning goals are aligned, or where the attorney obtains informed consent of both parties. If an actual conflict arises during the course of representation that places one client's interests directly adverse to the other, however, the attorney should withdraw from the representation, and both parties will need to obtain separate counsel.[2]

Additionally, and perhaps most importantly, in certain instances Islamic law may provide a surviving spouse less than what he or she is entitled to under a state's intestacy or elective share law. We provide guidance for dealing with such scenarios in section (C)(2) of this chapter.

B. Constitutional Considerations

The recent campaigns to ban the application of *Sharia* are based on a misplaced fear that American Muslims are somehow seeking to supplant the Constitution with Islamic law. As stated earlier, the U.S. Court of Appeals has concluded that such bans violate the Establishment Clause, which requires that "[f]irst, the statute must have a secular legislative purpose; second, its principal or primary effect must be one that neither advances nor inhibits religion; finally, the statute must not foster 'an excessive government entanglement with religion.'"[3]

As a practical matter, the domestic application of *Sharia* may intersect with state and federal law in three areas: (1) domestic relations or family law; (2) estate planning; and (3) alternative dispute resolution.[4] Given the strong presumption in American law for freedom of contract and testamentary choice, long-standing contract-law principles dictate that U.S. courts treat and should continue to treat *Sharia*-based contracts just as

2. MODEL RULES OF PROF'L CONDUCT R. 1.7(a)(1) (2016).

3. *See Awad II* (citing Lemon v. Kurtzman, 403 U.S. 602, 612 (1971)).

4. James Sonne, *Domestic Applications of* Sharia *and the Exercise of Ordered Liberty*, 45 SETON HALL L. REV. 725, 728 (2015).

they would any other contracts. That is, a court should uphold such agreements unless (1) they violate some basic contract-law principles (e.g., in cases of coercion, duress, or unconscionability); or (2) the application of the contract would violate public policy.[5]

C. Public Policy Issues

As basic contract-law principles should be well known to the practitioner, we address the issue of public policy conflicts in this section. In the estate-planning context, there are three primary areas where public policy issues may arise when conducting planning for a Muslim client: (1) restrictions on inheritance for non-Muslim relatives, (2) a surviving spouse's rights and a state's elective share provisions, and (3) unequal distribution to children based upon differences in gender.

1. Restrictions on Distributing Inheritance to Non-Muslims

In most jurisdictions, an individual is allowed to disinherit statutory beneficiaries other than the surviving spouse without explanation. Nonetheless, courts have sometimes disfavored attempts to seemingly control the religious practices of others through the disposition of property.[6] What a court may approve, however, is a moving target. Courts can invalidate a provision "if it is injurious to the interests of the public, contravenes some established interest of society, violates some public statute, is against good morals, tends to interfere with the public welfare or safety, or is at war with the interests of society or is in conflict with the morals of the time."[7]

In the case of non-Muslim relatives, Islamic inheritance law provides that such individuals are not entitled to inherit by right from a Muslim decedent.[8] This raises a question of who qualifies as a Muslim and what individual or entity ultimately makes that determination.

5. *See* Eugene Volokh, *Religious Law (Especially Islamic Law) in American Courts*, 66 Okla. L. Rev. 431, 435–41 (2014) (describing public-policy limits on the application of foreign law); *see also generally* Asifa Quraishi-Landes, *Rumors of the Sharia Threat Are Greatly Exaggerated: What American Judges Really Do with Islamic Family Law in Their Courtrooms*, 57 N.Y.L. Sch. L. Rev. 245, 249–51 (2012) (same).

6. Feinberg v. Feinberg (*In re* Estate of Feinberg), 235 Ill. 2d 256 (2009).

7. E & B Mktg. Enters., Inc. v. Ryan, 568 N.E.2d 339 (1st Dist. 1991).

8. Note that non-Muslim relatives may still inherit through the decedent's *wasiyah* share. *See infra* Chapter 5 for further discussion of the *wasiyah* share.

For example, Ahmad's son Zaki decided that he no longer wants to be Muslim and converted to Christianity. After multiple attempts to change Zaki's mind, Ahmad finally gave up and asked his estate-planning attorney to include a provision in his living trust stating, "I have specifically disinherited my son Zaki because he is no longer Muslim."

It is possible that such a clause may be upheld in court, as an individual is generally free to disinherit any child or relative (other than a spouse, absent a valid prenuptial or postnuptial agreement).[9] As the Oregon Supreme Court has stated, "The right to espouse any religious faith . . . carries with it the cognate right to engage as its champion in the proselytization of followers or converts."[10] Professor Sonne of Stanford Law School explains this point further:

> Provided the will does not require a court to interpret or become unduly tangled in religious doctrine, distributions based on religious status, like a "difference of religion" disqualifier, will be upheld as free religious exercise or under the general right to dispose of one's property as one sees fit.[11]

On the other hand, some courts have found clauses limiting inheritance to members of a certain religious faith to be void as against public policy.[12] Therefore, many practitioners discourage listing the specific reason for disinheritance in the actual will or trust.

Further, complications could also arise where the non-Muslim relative subsequently changes his or her mind and converts to Islam or becomes Muslim again, possibly in order to receive his or her inheritance. For example, if upon Ahmad's death Zaki learns that despite his father's frugal lifestyle, Ahmad left several million dollars of investments that are now going to be distributed to Zaki's siblings, could Zaki assert that he is still, in fact, Muslim? And could Zaki's brothers then—realizing that their share of the

---

9. *See* Restatement (Third) of Trusts § 29 cmt. k (2003); *see also* Shapira v. Union Nat'l Bank, 315 N.E.2d 825, 829 (Ohio Ct. App. 1974) (court upheld clause in decedent's will that conditioned a son's inheritance on marrying a Jewish girl with Jewish parents because the testator was not enforcing religion on the son but only setting conditions on the son's inheritance).

10. U.S. Nat'l Bank of Portland v. Snodgrass, 275 P.2d 860, 863–64 (Or. 1954).

11. Sonne, *supra* note 4 at 737.

12. For examples, see Omar T. Mohammedi, *Sharia-Compliant Wills: Principles, Recognition, and Enforcement*, 57 N.Y.L. Sch. L. Rev. 259, 273 (2012) (citing Drace v. Klinedinst, 118 A. 907 (Pa. 1922)) (holding that a life estate willed to grandchildren on the condition that they remain faithful to a religion was not enforceable).

inheritance is potentially at stake—challenge Zaki's assertion on the basis that they recently saw a cross hanging in the living room of his house?

From an Islamic perspective, a beneficiary's right to inherit vests at the time of the decedent's death. As such, conversion to Islam prior to the decedent's death would qualify a prospective heir to inherit, whereas conversion after death does not. However, a secular court is unlikely to engage in this type of factual determination, as the First Amendment prohibits courts from deciding the "truth or falsity" of religious beliefs or resolving "controversies over religious doctrine and practice."[13]

If required to determine a decedent's beneficiaries in a will contest, a court will employ "neutral principles of law"—which means that they can't use religious or ecclesiastical principles—when determining religious disputes.[14] Needless to say, the result will be uncertain, and the contest will likely consume significant assets of the estate. One option to resolve this quandary would be to authorize an independent Trust Protector to make a final nonreviewable determination of the religious status of any would-be heirs. In such situations, the Grantor should also include an indemnification provision for the Trust Protector, as any disqualified heir may still choose to challenge the determination in court. For this reason, we advise clients who want to disinherit a potential heir to only do so if they are certain of the individual's faith. We also strongly encourage clients to update their estate-planning documents to reflect any changes in a would-be heir's religion that would impact the client's dispositive distribution provisions. As explained in more detail in Chapter 5, clients may also choose to utilize the *wasiyah* share to provide specific distributions to non-Muslim relatives.

2. Surviving Spouse's Rights and Elective Shares

Classical Islamic law presupposes a family structure in which males are primarily responsible for providing for their families.[15] Accordingly, surviving widowers inherit double the share of what a surviving widow would inherit as outlined below:

13. Sonne, *supra* note 4, at 726 (citing United States v. Ballard, 322 U.S. 78, 87 (1944)); *accord* Presbyterian Church v. Mary Elizabeth Blue Hull Mem'l Presbyterian Church, 393 U.S. 440, 449 (1969).

14. Jones v. Wolf, 443 U.S. 595 (1979).

15. Joseph Schacht, An Introduction to Islamic Law 170 (1982).

- Surviving widower if decedent left behind no children: one-half
- Surviving widower if decedent left behind children: one-fourth
- Surviving widow if decedent left behind no children: one-fourth
- Surviving widow if decedent left behind children: one-eighth
- Surviving widow who is not Muslim: no mandatory inheritance rights

In some cases a widow's share under Islamic inheritance law is thus less than what she may be entitled to receive under a state's elective share. In community property states that do not have elective share provisions, this is typically not an issue, as a surviving spouse is free to distribute his or her half of the community assets to beneficiaries of his or her choosing. In separate property states, however, the elective share varies by state and is often one-third to one-half of the decedent's estate, though the amount may be impacted by the duration of the marriage and subject to a minimum dollar amount in some cases.[16] In some states, the elective share applies only to probate property, while in others, it attaches to all assets in the decedent's estate. Even in community property jurisdictions such as California or Texas, for example, a probate homestead or probate allowance could upend the Islamic Law of Inheritance and result in a contrary distribution.[17]

As a threshold matter, if the attorney is representing only one spouse in the preparation of his or her estate plan in a separate property jurisdiction, the attorney must explain that a spouse cannot ensure that his or her assets will be distributed according to Islamic inheritance law without the voluntary consent of the other spouse or an enforceable prenuptial or postnuptial agreement. This is because a surviving spouse will have the option to take an elective share of the deceased spouse's estate regardless of what was stated in the decedent's planning documents.

If a married couple wishes to jointly plan their estate in a *Sharia*-compliant manner and voluntarily waives elective share rights in each other's property, the drafting attorney should prepare an enforceable waiver of an elective share under the particular state's law. For example, under Kansas law, a waiver can be accomplished before or after marriage through a

16. *See, e.g.*, N.Y. Est. Powers & Trusts Law § 5-3.1 (2018) (New York statute providing the surviving spouse with certain cash equivalents plus the greater of $50,000 or one-third of the decedent's net estate); Fla. Stat. §§ 732.201–.2155 (2018) (providing surviving spouse with 30 percent of elective estate or 50 percent of probate estate).

17. *See* Cal. Prob. Code §§ 6520–6528, 6540–6545 (2018).

broad range of means, including "a written contract, agreement, consent to any instrument, or waiver signed by the surviving spouse."[18] Under Florida law a surviving spouse may also waive his or her beneficial rights in the survivor's estate:

> Unless the waiver provides to the contrary, a waiver of "all rights," or equivalent language . . . is a waiver of all rights to elective share, intestate share, pretermitted share, homestead, exempt property, family allowance, and preference in appointment as personal representative of an intestate estate, by the waiving party in the property of the other and a renunciation by the waiving party of all benefits that would otherwise pass to the waiving party from the other by intestate succession or by the provisions of any will executed before the written contract, agreement, or waiver.[19]

When preparing such agreements, practitioners should familiarize themselves with the state's requirements on elective share disclaimers, including disclosure of assets, timing of the disclaimer, and language of the waiver. Rather than declaring a waiver of "all rights," the drafting attorney should expressly state the client's desire to voluntarily waive the elective share, as states may not honor ambiguous waivers.[20] In some jurisdictions, a valid waiver of intestacy rights may also require independent separate counsel for each party, as is often required in the case of prenuptial agreements.

3. Disparate Distributions on the Basis of Gender

The Islamic Law of Inheritance provides that male children shall inherit double the share of female children. Under classical Islamic law, this additional entitlement for male heirs was coupled with a legally enforceable support obligation toward their female family members. Female heirs, meanwhile, did not have any concomitant restrictions as to how they may utilize their inheritance.

In modern times, male heirs who receive an inheritance remain morally obligated to support their female relatives, but such obligations are not required by secular law. Nonetheless, the rules remain equally applicable

18. *See* KAN. STAT. ANN. § 59-6a213(a) (2018).
19. FLA. STAT. § 732.702(1) (2018).
20. *See* Estate of Barrows, 913 A.2d 608 (Me. 2006).

for Muslims today, so many Muslim clients will voluntarily seek to comply with them.

If a client voluntarily chooses to adhere to a distribution scheme that distinguishes among heirs on the basis of gender, that decision itself should not constitute a violation of public policy, as decedents are typically free to plan their estate as they deem appropriate, apart from the rights that are protected for the surviving spouse. Because it is impossible to predict how a particular probate judge may rule on any given matter, however, we typically advise Muslim clients seeking to comply with their faith to avoid the probate process through the use of revocable living trusts in order to ensure a private administration of their affairs.

Most Muslim clients who seek to comply with Islamic inheritance law will, of course, want to ensure that their daughters are adequately supported. This can be achieved through lifetime gifting (outright or in trust) or by designing through contract law an enforceable support obligation in which a male heir's receipt of inheritance could be conditioned.

Example:

Alia has a son, Bilal, and a daughter, Iman. These are her only two Islamic heirs. Bilal is now 31 years old and is a successful neurosurgeon. He has a wife, Sarah, and three children, as well as a home and other trappings of affluence. Iman is 16 years old. She is on the autism spectrum. Alia learned that Iman might not be eligible for disability benefits as her symptoms are not severely limiting enough. Alia fears Iman's condition may hinder future employment and marriage prospects and worries that Iman's sole support structure would collapse if she passes away.

Bilal has been distant geographically as well as emotionally from both Alia and Iman. From Alia's perspective, Bilal does not have a history of showing compassion for his younger sister. Bilal's wife, Sarah, appears to be actively hostile to both Iman and Alia.

Alia would like to make sure Bilal will support Iman. She also does not want to violate Islamic law and does not wish to deny anyone's rights to inheritance.

Alia attempted to discuss the matter of Iman's needs with Bilal but found him unapproachable, and his wife prevented the conversation from going any further.

Alia's attorney advised her to create a revocable living trust that provides that upon her death, one-third of her estate will be allocated to Iman in a discretionary trust. An independent successor trustee shall have the discretion to make distributions for her benefit. The other two-thirds of her estate will be allocated in trust for the benefit of Bilal. The successor trustee shall request Bilal to sign an agreement to support his sister Iman in the event she needs food, shelter, or health care, not just from trust assets but from all of Bilal's assets, whatever the source. If he fails to sign this agreement, Iman will become a permissible beneficiary of his subtrust, and the trustee shall be given the discretion to use funds for the benefit of either Iman or Bilal. Upon Bilal's death, the trust assets will be distributed to Bilal's Islamic heirs.

This plan will give the trustee the discretion to use trust assets to fulfill Bilal's duties of support toward Iman, if necessary. It also gives the trustee discretion to make distributions to Bilal should such a course of action be more appropriate. The terms of the trust also indicate that upon Bilal's death, his Islamic heirs will be the trust beneficiaries, consistent with Islamic inheritance law.

CHAPTER

3

Estate Planning during Life

Counseling a Muslim client requires the practitioner to consider certain Islamic ethics and practices. These include, for instance, an emphasis on traditional family values, particularly with respect to care for elders; financial prohibitions relating to *riba* (interest) and *gharar* (excessive speculation); constraints relating to certain conventional modes of property ownership; and a strong ethic encouraging charitable giving, including both inter vivos and testamentary gifts.

A. Religious Practices during Life

Islamic law encourages a Muslim to live a wholesome life, grounded in strong family values. Respect and care for parents—especially those who reach an advanced age and require assistance—is expressly mandated in the Quran: "Your Lord has commanded that you should worship none but Him, and that you be kind to your parents. If either or both of them reach old age with you, say no word that shows impatience with them, and do not be harsh with them, but speak to them respectfully and lower your wing in humility towards them in kindness . . ."[1]

1. *The Qur'an: English Translation and Parallel Arabic Text* 17:23–24 (M.A.S. Abdel Haleem trans., 2005).

This strong admonition to care for one's parents creates a culture in many Muslim families in which elder parents may live in the home of one of their children. This ethic often stretches beyond parents to other elders within the extended family as well. Often the suggestion that a parent, grandparent, or other relative should live in a nursing home or assisted living facility will be viewed in a negative light. As such, many clients and caretakers would prefer to consider in-home care solutions for their elder relatives if necessary rather than a residential living facility.

Adherent Muslim families also tend to be conservative in many respects. Alcohol, recreational drug consumption, gambling, and premarital and extramarital relationships are all prohibited. Of course, clients may have family members who are engaged in some or all of these behaviors and may wish to address them in their planning documents.

Finally, with regard to family structures and values, Islam only recognizes marriage as between a man and woman. As such, many contemporary issues related to planning for same-sex couples will likely not be implicated in planning for a Muslim couple seeking to design an estate plan consistent with their faith.

B. Marriage and Divorce

The definition of marriage and divorce will sometimes differ under state law and Islamic law. Sometimes, a couple may be married under Islamic law but may not have formally recorded the marriage in state court. In some cases, states may defer to religious officials to confirm certain formalities were observed.[2] If a marriage ceremony was conducted abroad, a state will likely recognize the validity of such a marriage as well, assuming it does not violate public policy in any way.[3] But merely satisfying religious obligations will not qualify a marriage as valid under state law.[4]

Alternatively, a couple's marriage under state law may not be valid under Islamic law. In some cases, even if Islam recognizes a marriage as legally valid, it may nonetheless exclude spouses from inheriting by right for a variety of reasons.

2. *See* James Sonne, *Domestic Applications of* Sharia *and the Exercise of Ordered Liberty*, 45 Seton Hall L. Rev. 725, 731 (2015).

3. *Id.*

4. *Id.*

1. Requirements for a Valid Islamic Marriage

In order for a marriage to be valid under Islamic law, (a) there must be no legal impediments to marriage between the parties, and (b) the couple must partake in a valid Islamic marriage ceremony (*Nikkah*).

a. Legal Impediments to a Valid Islamic Marriage

Islam restricts marriage to that between a man and a woman. It also prohibits marriages between certain close relatives[5] and individuals who were nursed by the same woman, and it applies restrictions based upon religious orientation. For instance, Muslim men can marry women from the "People of the Book," a reference to Christians and Jews, but are not allowed to marry atheists or people of other faith traditions. Muslim women, on the other hand, are prohibited from marrying a non-Muslim, including Christian and Jewish men.

Notably, a valid marriage to a non-Muslim spouse does not necessarily enable that spouse to inherit, as non-Muslims are not entitled to inherit by right from a Muslim decedent. They can, however, inherit through the decedent's discretionary *wasiyah* share. The result of this exception is that under Islamic inheritance law a surviving spouse, if non-Muslim, may either be disinherited or, conversely, receive a higher share than a similarly situated Muslim spouse.

Example:
Khurram is married to Susan, who is not Muslim. They have two children together. Under the Islamic Law of Inheritance, Susan does not inherit by right. However, Khurram may create an estate plan that leaves up to one-third of his estate to Susan, whereas if she were a Muslim, she would have only been entitled to inherit one-eighth of Khurram's estate.

---

b. **Nikkah** *Ceremony*

In addition to ensuring no legal impediments prevent the parties from marrying each other, couples wishing to marry under Islamic law must

5. *See* Qur'an 4:23 (outlining relatives with whom marriage is prohibited).

perform a valid Islamic marriage ceremony known as a *nikkah*. A civil law marriage under state law does not replace this requirement.

The legal formalities of a *nikkah* are fairly minimal. It involves a proposal (*ijab*) by one party and acceptance (*qabool*) by the other in the presence of two male witnesses and a gift to the bride, known as a *mahr*, which is often negotiated in advance by the parties or their families. Various cultures and communities may include additional customary wedding formalities and practices.

Islamic law allows Muslim men to marry up to four wives, so long as all of the women are treated equitably. In the United States, all states prohibit bigamy and hold that marriages by those who are already married are legally void. Because American spouses enjoy several legal, tax, and property-law benefits exclusive to married couples, and because a man cannot legally marry multiple women, as a practical matter, polygamy cannot actually be practiced "equitably."

Nonetheless, though by no means common, some Muslims do engage in polygamy in the United States. Often this takes the form of cohabitation, in which one or more women are not recognized by state law as a spouse and consent to the disparate treatment.

In some cases, Muslims may also be "married" under Islamic law without any legal formalities. This is similar to the way some individuals cohabitate with partners without a formal cohabitation agreement. As with polygamous cohabitants of other faith communities, it appears that the Constitution may prevent criminalization of these types of religious arrangements among Muslims.

As for distribution of inheritance in such cases, the Quran ordains that surviving wives must evenly split the share of their late husband's estate. This raises several potential legal issues and a strong likelihood of litigation if any of the "widows" decide to contest the distribution.

Example:

Abdullah dies while being Islamically "married" (i.e., through a cohabitation agreement and witnesses, but not under state law) to Sarah, Aisha, and Susan. He has two sons, Adam and Idrees, with Susan; one daughter, Khadija, with Aisha; and no offspring with Sarah. Along with his wives and children, Abdullah is survived by his mother, Farrah. Under Islamic inheritance law, upon Abdullah's death, his mother would inherit one-sixth of his estate, his two sons Adam and Idrees get 17/60 each, his daughter Khadija gets 17/120, and his three wives would only inherit 1/24 each.

---

c. Mahr

Mahr is a gift given by a husband to his wife upon marriage that is stipulated in the Quran.[6] This is a significant property right for Muslims, both historically and in the present day. The amount of *mahr* may be negotiated by the parties to a marriage contract. It can be in the form of a pecuniary amount, a percentage of a business or other assets, or an agreement relating to community property. The *mahr* may be paid in full at the wedding as a gift or may also be split into a small immediate gift, known as a *mahr mu'ajal*, and a larger deferred payment, known as a *mahr mu'akhar*, which is to be paid upon either death or divorce. Whatever is agreed upon becomes sacrosanct, and the husband does not have the right to renege on the agreement or take any such property away once the amount has been determined and agreed upon.

Example:
Jahangir, 56, and Firdaws, 35, marry. They both have children from earlier marriages and have agreed to keep their property separate. Firdaws requests a *mahr mu'ajal* of $20,000 at the time of marriage and a deferred *mu'akhar* payment of a seven-unit apartment building Jahangir owns, located in the city they live in, or an equivalent cash value. If Jahangir predeceases Firdaws and he has not already transferred the apartment building or equivalent value to her by the time he dies, she will receive this amount in addition to her inheritance.

In the United States, courts have treated cases involving the enforcement of *mahr* agreements inconsistently. Some courts view the agreements as enforceable prenuptial agreements, while others have held them to be void against public policy and unenforceable.[7]

6. *See The Qur'an, supra* note 1, at 4:24 ("If you wish to enjoy women through marriage, give them their bride-gift—this is obligatory.").

7. *See generally* Tracie Rogalin Siddiqui, *Interpretation of Islamic Marriage Contracts by American Courts*, 41(3) Fam. L.Q. 639–58 (2007); Abed Awad, *Islamic Family Law in American Courts: A Rich, Diverse, and Evolving Jurisprudence*, https://www.americanbar.org/content/dam/aba/uncategorized/international_law/islamic_family_law_in_american_court_8_16_13.authcheckdam.pdf (last accessed Oct. 5, 2018).

2. Divorce under Islamic Law

In classical Islamic law, marriage was considered a contract between individuals that was historically not regulated by the state. This in many respects is like how marriage has been observed in both Europe and the United States.[8] In Islamic law, unlike Christianity historically, divorce has been easy to obtain.

A woman could obtain a divorce either through a process known as *khul*, which involved returning the *mahr* paid at marriage, or by seeking judicial annulment of the marriage. In such cases, judges would typically grant a divorce decree if the husband could not provide support, had a mental or physical disease, deserted his family, or there were some general incompatibility between the spouses.

A man could divorce his wife by making up to three pronouncements that he was divorcing his wife. The first two were considered revocable, during which time the couple may get back together without remarrying, but the third pronouncement was deemed irrevocable. In modern times, many Muslim-majority countries also require court orders for any divorce.[9]

Further, despite the ease with which a Muslim man can divorce his wife, Islam's system of marriage tends to discourage off-the-cuff divorce. This is because the ex-wife is often entitled to a *mahr mu'akhar*, the deferred portion of *mahr* that is paid upon divorce or death. In the case of death, the *mahr* is treated as a debt and must be paid first to the widow before any other distributions are made.

Example:

Haroon, during an argument, tells his wife Aysha that they are no longer married. Aysha and Haroon reconcile three weeks later. They do not require a new Islamic marriage ceremony. If Haroon died during this three-week period, Aysha would have been entitled to inherit from Haroon as his wife. If they had reconciled one year later, they would have needed to contract a new marriage. Finally, if Haroon had told Aysha three times that he wanted a

8. Cynthia Grant Bowman, *A Feminist Proposal to Bring Back Common Law Marriage*, 75(3) Or. L. Rev. 709 (1996).

9. *See* Mohammad Hashim Kamali, *Law and Society: The Interplay of Revelation and Reason in the Shariah*, *in* The Oxford History of Islam 107, 117 (John L. Esposito ed., 1999).

divorce, the divorce would immediately finalize, and Aysha would have no right to inherit from him upon his death.

As a practical matter, oral divorce declarations have historically been contested among Muslim couples in Islamic courts and are frequently invalidated.

Thus, divorce based on mere declaration by the husband in the absence of a formal divorce decree will be subject to a fact-specific inquiry that cannot reasonably be incorporated into a U.S.-based estate plan. In order to avoid such disputes, we recommend defining divorce in a manner consistent with state law.

Example:
Debbie and Jose are Muslims who live in Florida. During an argument about Jose's abuse of painkillers in full view of Jose's adult son Haroon, Jose storms out of the house and tells his wife three times their marriage is over. On his way to a hotel for the evening, he is run over by a truck and dies. The couple had previously created an estate plan with distribution provisions consistent with the Islamic Law of Inheritance. Haroon would like to give legal effect to Jose's declaration that the marriage is over, as he would thus become the sole heir of his father's estate under Islamic law. Unless Debbie consents to this, however, it will not be possible. Debbie may have any number of arguments consistent with Islamic law to keep her inheritance. As neither the estate plan nor state law contemplates declaratory divorce, Debbie would prevail and shall receive her share.

Lastly, the dissolution of a marriage or the death of a husband triggers a waiting period for the woman known as an *iddah* during which she cannot remarry. The time period of the *iddah* may vary from completion of pregnancy to three menstrual cycles or three months, depending on the circumstances. One primary purpose of the *iddah* is to ascertain whether the woman is pregnant and, if so, to determine the child's father.

If a woman's ex-husband dies during her *iddah* after a revocable divorce, she will be entitled to inherit from him. If the divorce was irrevocable, she will not be entitled to inherit.

C. Modes of Property Ownership

Property rights are one of the most distinctive features of any legal system. With a few minor restrictions,[10] Islamic inheritance law does not regulate the specific manner in which a Muslim may own or transfer property while alive. However, a Muslim property owner must ensure that he or she owns a property in such a manner that the property may be devised upon his or her death in accordance with the Islamic law of inheritance.

For an unmarried individual, this restriction poses no issues, as a client may hold title to an asset in his or her personal name or inside a business entity or trust. Married couples, however, must ensure that they hold title to property in a manner that allows the assets to pass upon each spouse's death to the deceased spouse's heirs under Islamic law. In the following sections we evaluate how several conventional forms of joint property ownership relate to Islamic law.

1. Community Property

Community property is the default form of property ownership for married couples in nine U.S. states, including California, where it is a legacy of the transition of the territory from Mexico and the Treaty of Guadalupe Hidalgo. This form of property ownership means that all property earned through the skill, labor, and effort of either spouse while in a "community," i.e., marriage, is owned 50 percent by each spouse.[11] In general, any inheritance, gifts, or assets owned prior to marriage by either spouse will not be considered community property. However, a married couple can alter these default presumptions by preparing a properly executed prenuptial or postnuptial agreement.

Strictly speaking, it is not necessary to be married to own assets as community property. Registered domestic partners in California, for instance, also may own their property as community property.[12] Even unmarried couples who are not domestic partners may choose to own their property as community property through a validly executed cohabitation agreement.[13]

10. For instance, Muslims do not have unlimited discretion to transfer property to others during *maradul maut*, or their "final illness." In such scenarios, people are not free to devise their property as they wish. For further discussion of what constitutes a final illness, see Chapter 4(A).

11. Comment, *For Richer or Poorer—Equities in the Career-Threshold, No-Asset Divorce*, 58 Tul. L. Rev. 791 (1984).

12. Cal. Fam. Code § 297–297.5 (2012).

13. Marvin v. Marvin, 18 Cal. 3d 660 (1976).

Whereas Islamic law has always recognized a woman's right to own and inherit property, community property as a form of property ownership is alien to the Islamic tradition. Nonetheless, this form of ownership does not violate the Islamic Law of Inheritance since couples are free to adopt a "partnership theory" with respect to property acquired during marriage so long as each spouse's share passes to his or her Islamic heirs upon death. Thus, if a married couple agrees—either voluntarily or based upon the default system in their state—to own their assets as community property, doing so would not violate Islamic law.

That said, while Islamic law does not generally restrict how a married couple decides to own their assets, it does require that each spouse's share of the assets pass to his or her Islamic heirs upon death. For this reason, any form of property ownership that includes a right of survivorship—including community property with a right of survivorship, joint tenancy with a right of survivorship, and Tenancy by the Entirety—would violate Islamic law.

2. Tenancy by the Entirety

Tenancy by the Entirety (TBE) is a form of joint ownership with a right of survivorship that is reserved for married couples in several states. Many clients find this form of ownership attractive because of its strong asset-protection features. In general, a creditor of one spouse cannot foreclose on a property or asset owned by the couple as TBE.

Because the right of survivorship automatically transfers the asset to the surviving spouse on the first spouse's death, TBE does not comport with Islamic inheritance law. Assuming that the deceased spouse's portion of the property, which can be clarified through a separate agreement, does not exceed the beneficiary's share of the estate, such ownership may be permissible. But because asset values fluctuate, there is often no way of knowing whether a plan that includes a TBE will conform to the Islamic Law of Inheritance at death. Thus, an estate-planning practitioner may advise Muslim clients seeking asset protection to consider other options, such as a Domestic Asset Protection Trust (DAPT).

In some instances, clients may decide that a DAPT is cost-prohibitive and that they prefer to continue to take advantage of the asset protection benefits afforded by the TBE. In such cases, the practitioner could prepare a property agreement between the spouses stating that the surviving spouse shall compensate the first spouse's Islamic heirs after his or her death in accordance with Islamic inheritance law.

Alternatively, some states recognize a somewhat flexible option known as a Tenancy by the Entirety Trust, which allows for distribution to beneficiaries other than the surviving spouse at death, much the same way a Revocable Living Trust would. For example, a Maryland statute allows for property to be held in trust and retain "the same immunity from the claims of the separate creditors of the husband and wife as would exist if the husband and wife had continued to hold the property or the proceeds from the property as tenants by the entirety."[14] The statute requires the following:

1. The husband and wife must remain married.
2. The property or proceeds from the property must be held by the trustees of the trust.
3. Both husband and wife must be beneficiaries of the trust.
4. The trust instrument, deed, or other conveyance must reference the relevant code section.

Notably, while the statute requires that both husband and wife be beneficiaries, it does not require that they be the *only* beneficiaries. Thus, it may be possible to construct an estate plan that complies with the Islamic Law of Inheritance in states where TBE Trusts are allowed by statute. Of course, because TBE Trusts are predicated on the marriage of both spouses, the death of either spouse will result in the loss of asset protection benefits.

3. Joint Tenancy with Right of Survivorship

Joint Tenancy with Right of Survivorship (JTWRS) is one of the most common forms of property ownership between married couples in the United States. Often referred to as the "poor man's estate plan," a JTWRS allows for automatic transfer of jointly owned property to a surviving spouse (or other joint tenant) outside of probate. From an Islamic perspective, the automatic right of survivorship is generally considered impermissible, as a surviving spouse is entitled to a predetermined fraction of the deceased spouse's estate. Furthermore, the applicable fractions are gender-specific, with the widower usually inheriting twice as much as a widow.

14. Md. Code Ann. Est. & Trusts § 14.5-511 (2018).

Thus, a JTWRS would violate this principle by automatically transferring the entirety of the jointly owned asset to the surviving spouse.

The perpetual remarriage problem is a good example of why the automatic right of survivorship is a poor estate-planning choice.

Example:
Idris and Aliyah have three children: Ali, Bilquis, and Sarah. Idris and Aliyah own their largest asset, their home, as JTWRS so that the entire property automatically passes to the surviving spouse upon the death of the first spouse.

Aliyah dies, leaving the entire property to Idris. He decides to sell the home and move to another city. He meets and marries Aisha, a divorcee who is a single mother with a daughter, Deena. Idris and Aisha combine their assets, including the proceeds from the home Idris and Aliyah owned together, to purchase a new home as a JTWRS, another form of joint ownership.

Idris dies. Aisha assumes full ownership of their estate and marries Bilal. Ali, Bilquis, and Sarah move in with their grandparents. They never inherit from their father or mother.

---

4. Tenants in Common

Another method of joint property ownership available in all states is known as Tenancy in Common, which does not include an automatic right of survivorship. For Muslims, there is no limitation or restriction with this form of ownership, since it identifies the owner and allows the property to be properly devised in accordance with the Islamic Law of Inheritance.

D. Division of Jointly Owned Property

Islamic inheritance law provides fixed shares of inheritance for children, spouses, and parents—and, in some cases, more distant relatives. Thus, as explained previously, any form of property ownership that includes an automatic right of survivorship violates the requirement that a decedent's estate be distributed according to the Islamic Law of Inheritance.

This fundamental planning consideration creates several potential complications, particularly for married couples in a society where many spouses have traditionally followed a variant of the "I love you" estate plan. In such an arrangement, family assets are owned by both spouses and automatically pass to the surviving spouse upon the other's death. All estate-planning techniques can easily lend themselves to the "I love you" plan—simple wills, JTWRS, Revocable Living Trusts, beneficiary designation, etc. This approach is especially prevalent in first marriages where there is a presumption that both parties would care equally about any children of the marriage and would provide for their needs accordingly.

This may also happen in subsequent marriages where spouses each assume the other has lasting goodwill for all the children and that they will be treated fairly. In some jurisdictions, such as Texas, for example, this arrangement is codified into law, at least with respect to the homestead. In fact, the Texas Constitution provides that, on the death of a homestead owner, the surviving spouse is entitled to remain in the property for as long as the survivor elects to use the homestead.[15]

Any arrangement where the surviving spouse receives more than his or her entitlement is not permissible in Islam. To resolve this issue, a planner may need to provide creative solutions that can enable a client's goals that may, at first blush, appear to contradict the Islamic Law of Inheritance. For example, a goal that the surviving spouse own the family home outright despite the home representing 90 percent of the family's wealth would be difficult to square with the injunction that a widow is entitled to only one-eighth of her husband's estate. The drafting attorney has a few options to address these scenarios.

1. Severing the Automatic Right of Survivorship

Where a married couple jointly owns a primary residence, we often recommend transferring title to a joint revocable living trust. The trust should include a provision that if any joint tenancy property or community property with right of survivorship is transferred to the trust, the clients will be considered to have severed the joint tenancy immediately before transferring the property, and no right of survivorship shall exist with respect to the property.

This should only be done if all parties understand the consequences of the transfer, particularly with respect to asset protection. Doing so will

15. Tex. Const. art. XVI, § 52.

ensure that each spouse owns a current 50 percent interest in the property. Upon the first spouse's death, the surviving spouse will then be entitled to inherit one-half, one-fourth, or one-eighth depending upon the scenario, from the deceased spouse's share of the property.

2. Use of a Deed of Trust

If a married couple wants the surviving spouse to remain in the family home, the attorney can draft a plan that allows for the surviving spouse to do so, and even own the home outright even if there is no cash to pay for the home, without violating the Islamic Law of Inheritance through the use of a deed of trust. This method allows for the rights of the deceased spouse's beneficiaries to be protected through a recorded instrument that is attached to the property. In order to comply with Islam's prohibition on interest, the deed of trust should not carry an interest rate, and the surviving spouse need not make any monthly payments. The revocable living trust should authorize such a process.[16] Note, however, that this technique may result in imputed income for the surviving spouse.

A deed of trust may not be a good solution for certain blended families and in second-marriage situations. While it is not necessary for assets to be liquidated upon a decedent's death, if the decedent left behind heirs who are not related to the surviving spouse, they may not want to consent to such an arrangement. Thus, in order to maintain family harmony, this arrangement should be coupled with a trust instrument that includes sprinkling powers that would allow for the trustee to compensate individual heirs who may want their inheritance earlier.

3. Use of Business Entities

Ownership is not the same as control. Business ownership can be held in a variety of entities that confer different rights. For example, in a limited liability company, an individual may be a minority owner but maintain control as a manager. In a corporation, there may be voting shares and nonvoting shares.

As far as the Islamic Law of Inheritance is concerned, any business-ownership technique is acceptable so long as it is structured while the owner or partners are alive and not in their final illness. Partnerships

16. *See* James P. Lamping, *A House Divided: The Purchase of an Interest in the Family Residence Following Its Allocation to a Credit Trust*, 14(3) Cal. Trusts & Estates Q. 42 (2008).

should have well-drafted operating agreements, shareholder agreements, and/or buy-sell agreements stipulating the equity interests and rights and responsibilities of each owner along with a mechanism for calculating the value of the partner's share in the event of the death of an owner or dissolution of the partnership.

If a couple wants to ensure that a surviving spouse continues to control a business that provides him or her a source of income and employment, it is possible to preserve this arrangement without sacrificing inheritance rights through a carefully drafted operating agreement for a limited liability company. Under such an arrangement, membership units of a limited liability company could be divided upon the first spouse's death, but the surviving spouse would remain a manager and distribute profits as he or she deems appropriate.

4. Use of Disclaimers

Islamic inheritance law guarantees that certain heirs are entitled to inherit from the decedent but also concurrently allows for those heirs to disclaim their shares should they choose to do so. Thus, it is possible through a family settlement agreement for heirs to make various arrangements, including additional distribution to family members who need more than what they are entitled to inherit.

An heir must have legal capacity in order to disclaim his or her share. A trustee or personal representative may not disclaim a share on behalf of a minor or incapacitated person.

Further, under Islamic law, consent to disclaim inheritance is enforceable only after the passing of the decedent. Any consent given during the decedent's life may be revoked prior to distribution of the decedent's estate.

Example:
Akbar's daughter, Basma, has a learning disability. She can work at a job that requires unskilled labor and is reasonably responsible with her money, but Akbar fears she won't have enough to live a comfortable life after he dies. He asks his two sons, Babur and Shah Jahah, to consent to give up their inheritance shares to Basma. Under Islamic law, such consent is revocable while Akbar is alive and must be ratified by the sons upon Akbar's death.

---

5. Gifting Strategies

A Muslim is free to make lifetime gifts to others at any time, provided the donor is not in a condition known as "final illness" (*maradul maut*).[17] For instance, a married couple that owns a property jointly may choose to transfer the property solely into one spouse's name. This should be done only after careful consideration of both the tax and nontax consequences of the gift, as it is of course unknown which spouse will die first. It is also, of course, impossible to guarantee that a marriage will not end in termination.

For these reasons, while gifting is certainly a valuable tool in the estate-planning attorney's toolbox, it can be fraught with potential family conflicts, particularly in blended families, and, in the case of the elderly, could invite allegations of elder abuse.

6. Establishing a Family *Waqf*

Under classical Islamic law, assets could also be owned through the use of a *waqf* (plural, *awqaf*). The term "*waqf*," often translated as "endowment" or "trust," is an Arabic word that refers to assets that are donated, bequeathed, or purchased for the purpose of being held in perpetual trust as an ongoing charity (*sadaqah jariya*) for a general or specific cause that Islam regards as socially beneficial.

The defining characteristics of a *waqf* are that it must be perpetual and irrevocable. Historically, *awqaf* were utilized extensively in the creation and maintenance of mosques, hospitals, universities, and libraries throughout the Muslim world. They were also employed to protect natural resources, for instance to preserve an easement or land for grazing.

Often, *awqaf* were also used as a means of preserving an asset within a family. This can also be accomplished today when a family member designates property as a *waqf* for the benefit of the family. Since this gift is donated during the donor's life, the assets would be governed by the *waqf*'s governing documents and would not be subject to the Islamic Law of Inheritance.

17. See Chapter 4(A) for an additional discussion of *maradul maut*.

Example:
Afzal owns 300 acres of ranch land. He would like to place this asset into an LLC, which is in turn owned by an irrevocable trust sited in a jurisdiction that has abolished the traditional rule against perpetuities, so that his descendants can enjoy the ranch and benefit from it in perpetuity. Descendants can use the ranch property's designated guest quarters for family reunions or vacations and use the lands for hiking, fishing, and camping. A self-sustaining board of directors composed of family members will regulate the property. Profits from the ranch's substantial business operations shall be made available for the benefit of the most deserving among the descendants, determined by the board of directors. If there are no needy family members, then profits shall be distributed to a charitable family foundation for the purpose of providing recreational and fitness opportunities, particularly soccer fields, basketball courts, indoor swimming pools, and gyms, for children in impoverished communities, as determined by the board of directors. Immediate family members, defined as children and spouses of the board of directors, shall not be eligible for cash benefits but may be eligible for use of the ranch property.

Although this type of *waqf* may not immediately appear to be "charitable" by conventional standards, it satisfies the Islamic requirements, as Afzal's family members are entitled to enjoy the use of the property in perpetuity. Once the property has been donated to a *waqf*, it is not directly owned by a beneficiary but rather is subject to the beneficial enjoyment by a class of individuals. Since *waqf* assets are not subject to the Islamic Law of Inheritance, Afzal's gift would not violate the rule prohibiting gifts to nonascertainable beneficiaries that would otherwise apply had he not transferred the property to the *waqf* prior to his death.

E. Financial Issues Relating to Investments

Muslims believe that God is the ultimate owner of all property and that wealth is simply a trust from God.[18] Unlike certain ascetic religious

18. The Quran explains this point in several verses. *See The Qur'an, supra* note 1, at 3:109 ("Everything in the heavens and earth belongs to God; it is to Him that all things return.").

traditions, Islam neither condemns nor discourages the acquisition of wealth. Muhammad himself was a successful trader and was married to one of the wealthiest merchantwomen of Mecca. At the same time, Islam differs from modern laissez-faire capitalism in that it does not allow considerations of profit maximization or efficiency to dictate all of an individual's economic decisions.

Three principles govern all Islamic financial ethics: (1) wealth must be acquired and invested in an ethical manner; (2) debt is discouraged while trade is encouraged; and (3) *riba* and *gharar* are prohibited.

1. Wealth Must Be Acquired and Invested in an Ethical Manner

Islam requires that the acquisition of wealth should be achieved through lawful means that promote mutual consent and goodwill. As such, investments in illicit industries, such as alcohol, pornography, and gambling, are deemed impermissible. Where a company has a permissible primary income source but also has certain ancillary businesses or business units that are engaged in impermissible activities, such activities must only constitute a de minimis component of the company's overall revenue.

Many Islamic investment firms and mutual funds have developed Islamic screens in order to resolve these complex issues. Because compliance with strict Islamic law principles may cause a trustee to violate the Prudent Investor Rule, which requires a fiduciary to manage a trust portfolio in a manner that balances risk and often requires a diversification of investments, estate-planning documents should waive this obligation and instruct the trustee to adhere to Islamic finance principles when considering how to invest trust assets.

2. Debt Is Discouraged

Islam discourages the voluntary assumption of debt. In fact, Islamic inheritance law prioritizes payment of debt over inheritance distribution. Under Islamic inheritance law, all types of mortgages, including those regarded as *Sharia*-compliant, are considered a form of debt.[19]

As a result of the significant hardship posed by mortgages, particularly for unemployed or underemployed surviving spouses, one of the most common ways to satisfy such debts is purchasing life insurance products.

19. Certain mortgage contracts allow spouses and other beneficiaries to inherit a property subject to the mortgage. As long as the beneficiaries assume all liability of the debt and the decedent's estate does not retain any liability, such agreements are valid and permissible under Islamic law.

As described below, this raises problems for Muslim clients since such products are considered impermissible by many Muslim scholars.

Example:
Elyas passes away, leaving behind a wife, Khadijah; son, Ahmad; and mother, Sarah. Elyas had named his trust as the beneficiary of his $1 million term life insurance policy. Elyas's only debt is an outstanding mortgage of $400,000 on the couple's home, which is currently worth $1 million. Upon Elyas's death, his trustee uses the proceeds from Elyas's life insurance policy to pay off the mortgage, rendering his estate debt-free. The trustee distributes the remaining $600,000 in proceeds pursuant to the Islamic Law of Inheritance, including a share to Khadijah.

Note that if Khadijah owned the home with her late husband as community property or as tenants in common, the payoff of her 50 percent share of the mortgage constitutes "extra" inheritance beyond her entitlement. Because $200,000 from the life insurance proceeds was used to pay off Khadijah's share of the debt, the trustee should decrease her share of Elyas's remaining estate to account for the distribution.

3. *Riba* and *Gharar* Are Prohibited

Islamic law also contains a set of financial ethics by which observant Muslims seek to organize their businesses and financial transactions. Today, the Islamic finance industry is one of the fastest-growing segments of the global economy, expanding at a rate of almost 20 percent a year, with total assets estimated at around $2 trillion.[20]

a. Riba

The prohibition against dealing in *riba* lies at the heart of Islamic finance.[21] *Riba* includes the earning and paying of money at a predetermined rate on a loan and is considered an exploitative form of social injustice.

---

20. Kuala Lumpur, *Big Interest, No Interest,* The Economist (Sept. 13, 2014), http://www.economist.com/news/finance-and-economics/21617014-market-islamic-financial-products-growing-fast-big-interest-no-interest.

21. For a further discussion of Islamic financial ethics and its prohibitions, see generally Mufti Muhammad Taqi Usmani, An Introduction to Islamic Finance (1998), *available at*

For estate planners operating within a financial system that heavily relies on the exchange of interest between debtors and creditors, and a tax code that provides significant deductions for interest payments, a categorical prohibition against dealing with interest may seem impossible to reconcile. Nonetheless, the prohibition is rooted in an understanding that money has no intrinsic value; it is simply a medium of exchange. Because lending is considered to be a charitable act wherein a lender is not undertaking any risk (beyond the extension of the loan), he or she is not permitted to charge a profit on the loan.

The prohibition on *riba* in the estate-planning context will impact a Muslim client's ability to purchase annuities and life insurance products, issue certain interfamily loans, and engage in various planned giving techniques.

b. Gharar

Gharar is a concept in Islamic finance that refers to unduly speculative transactions. While every transaction involves some amount of risk (i.e., minor *gharar*), a transaction is prohibited on the basis of *gharar* when there is significant uncertainty regarding components of the deal, such as the specific characteristics of an item, quantity of the object, price, payment period, etc. While gambling is the most common form of transaction prohibited on the basis of *gharar*, many conventional financial and estate-planning products such as insurance potentially fall into this category as well. We will address many of them throughout this book.

For now, we simply wish to point out that the prohibitions on interest and excessive speculation can significantly impact a client's estate-planning objectives and desires. Fundamental estate-planning tools such as life insurance, annuities, and bonds all contain *riba*- and *gharar*-based components that the drafting attorney must be aware of when designing an estate plan for Muslim clients.

F. Retirement Planning

The subject of retirement planning is vast and largely outside the scope of this book. However, we will endeavor to address the issues associated with such plans to the extent that they raise concerns for Muslim clients and their estate-planning goals.

---

http://muftitaqiusmani.com/en/books/PDF/An%20Introduction%20To%20Islamic%20Finance/An_Introduction%20_to_Islamic_Finance.pdf (last accessed Oct. 5, 2018).

As a primary matter, retirement accounts must be invested in a *Sharia*-compliant manner, and the beneficiaries of such accounts should be named in accordance with the Islamic Law of Inheritance. Historically, many employers have not allowed employees to select investments inside a defined contribution plan in a religiously compliant manner. Nonetheless, many employers that do not have *Sharia*-compliant options in their menu of funds will now typically offer them upon request. In the context of Individual Retirement Accounts (IRAs), some clients may opt to open self-directed IRAs to control their own investments inside a real-estate investment LLC or in another manner they deem to be *Sharia*-compliant.

For the purposes of this book, there are three areas where retirement plans pose challenges for Muslim clients. The first is the joint-and-survivor annuity payment that is required under the Qualified Joint-and-Survivor Annuity (QJSA) and the Qualified Preretirement Survivor Annuity (QPSA). The second is owner-employee issues associated with a defined benefit plan. The third is the consequences of preferential tax treatment of distributions for a surviving spouse in a defined contribution plan and the concept of a stretch-out for other beneficiaries.

There are two primary categories of retirement plans: (1) qualified plans and (2) nonqualified plans. A qualified plan simply refers to a plan that meets the legal requirements set forth under the Employee Retirement Income Security Act of 1974 (ERISA), the Internal Revenue Code (IRC), and various regulations that confer special tax treatment on such plans. Qualified plans—which include defined benefit plans such as traditional employer-provided pensions, defined contribution plans such as 401(k) plans, 403(b) plans, and other such plans—are funded with pretax money, and the funds invested in these accounts can grow in a tax-deferred manner.

Any retirement plans that do not meet these requirements are deemed nonqualified. In an employer-provided nonqualified plan, for instance, contributions would generally be tax-deductible by the employer as compensation but would count toward the employee's gross income. This may include deferred income, unless certain requirements are met.

While the distinctions between plans can vary widely, all employer-provided plans must inure to the benefit of employees and their beneficiaries. All plans include nondiscrimination provisions, minimum participation and coverage rules, vesting standards, and other regulations. For the most part, these regulations should not impact a Muslim client's estate plan.

1. Joint-and-Survivor Annuities

One possible source of contention that arises between retirement planning and Islamic inheritance law is that certain qualified retirement plans provide a Qualified Joint-and-Survivor Annuity (QJSA) for the participant and the participant's spouse. The plan may allow for a QJSA if the participant has been married (even for less than one year). If the participant dies before retirement, the plan must allow for something called a Qualified Preretirement Survivor Annuity (QPSA), which must pay the surviving spouse at least 50 percent of what would have been distributed to the participant.[22] If the participant would like to waive the QJSA and the QPSA requirements, the spouse must consent.

The QJSA and QPSA are not required in every qualified plan. For example, in the case of a profit-sharing plan and stock-bonus plan, the QJSA and QPSA are not required if the participant's entire vested benefit is payable in full to the participant's spouse and the participant makes an election to not receive benefits as a life annuity.[23] Any arrangement where the survivor is not a beneficiary of a Joint-and-Survivor Annuity (JSA) will require the consent of the surviving spouse.

One major distinction between a defined benefit plan and a defined contribution plan is that in the former, the participant does not control an account that fluctuates in value based on market performance. In a 401(k) plan, for instance, the participant receives a statement that has an account value, just like a bank or brokerage account. In a defined benefit plan, however, a statement will include an employee's accrued benefit. For example, the benefit may be stated as $3,500 per month of which 100 percent is vested, meaning, if the employee continues working, the employer is obligated to provide a certain type of benefit—in this case, $3,500 per month once the employee reaches a "normal" retirement age. The statement may or may not include additional details. For example, it may not answer the following questions:

- What, if any, monthly payment can the participant expect should he or she decide to retire early?
- Can the employee withdraw a lump sum of the accrued pension?
- Is there a death benefit available for the beneficiaries? If so, how much?

22. 26 U.S.C. § 401(a)(11) (2018).
23. 26 U.S.C. § 401(a)(11)(B)(iii) (2018).

These additional details are not required by the IRC. Indeed, it is common for there to be no early retirement, no lump sum, and no death benefit for beneficiaries. The only benefit promised may be a monthly payment, with a JSA for the surviving spouse.

In general, it is permissible for an employee to include a JSA as part of a qualified or nonqualified plan without violating the Islamic Law of Inheritance. The JSA is treated as a contract with a third party to take care of a surviving spouse through a series of regular, monthly payments. Therefore, it is unnecessary for the participant and spouse to opt out of the joint-and-survivor pension benefits.

Example:
Dawud is a university professor. He is married to Yasmin and has three children. His university offers a pension with a JSA. He also owns a home and has some savings. He may, if he desires, opt to make Yasmin the beneficiary of his JSA. He can then create an estate plan that distributes his other assets consistently with the Islamic Law of Inheritance. The pension distribution to his wife would not be regarded as inheritance. Upon his death, Yasmin would receive her one-eighth share of Dawud's inheritance, which is not to be reduced by the pension benefits.

Practice Pointer: Social Security Benefits
The same analysis described previously applies to Social Security survivor benefits that may be provided under federal law. This includes both lump sum and continuing benefits for the surviving spouse, an ex-spouse under certain circumstances, and surviving minor dependents.[24]

The lump sum benefit, which would be consequential for Islamic inheritance benefits, is only $255. Survivor benefits that are meant for specific beneficiaries, such as a surviving spouse, are not required to be distributed pursuant to the Islamic Law of Inheritance, as such assets are not treated as inheritance. This is akin to the JSA discussed previously.

24. *See* Social Security Administration Publication No. 05-10084, *Survivors Benefits* (Mar. 2018), https://www.ssa.gov/pubs/EN-05-10084.pdf.

2. Owner-Employee Pensions and Defined Benefit Plans

A defined benefit plan is an employer-sponsored retirement plan that provides a fixed benefit upon retirement. While many employers have moved away from defined benefit plans or traditional pension plans due to their high cost and onerous reporting obligations, such plans remain attractive to certain small business owners, especially among small, privately owned physician practices, due to their significant tax advantages. If the business owner is older, for instance, he or she may be able to make large contributions to the pension plan, which allows the business to take large tax deductions.

A defined benefit plan set up by owners of a small business primarily for the benefit of themselves and their family will usually include a death benefit. There is no requirement that a surviving spouse receive a survivor annuity as there would be in a qualified plan. However, given the strong similarities between an employer-provided pension and an owner-employee pension, Muslim business owners do not need to include the pension benefit as an asset subject to distribution under Islamic inheritance law. Thus, as in the prior example, a Muslim client may designate a surviving spouse as the recipient of a JSA. If a death benefit is paid after both spouses die, however, it should be distributed to the beneficiaries of the original participant, consistent with the Islamic Law of Inheritance.

Example:
Abid is a plastic surgeon for a corporation of which he is the only employee. He creates a defined benefit plan with a JSA. Abid further designates that any remaining cash balance be distributed to his living trust, which mandates that his assets be distributed consistent with the Islamic Law of Inheritance.

---

3. Spousal Rollover and Required Minimum Distributions

Many financial advisors advise clients to name a surviving spouse as the primary beneficiary of various types of retirement accounts. This is because the surviving spouse can elect a spousal rollover, while other beneficiaries must either withdraw all assets within five years or take Required Minimum Distributions (RMDs) consistent with actuarial tables published by the IRS beginning at year one of the plan holder's death.

A spousal rollover enables the surviving spouse to roll assets over to a new or existing IRA in her name and treat them as her own. This provides her with creditor protection, enables her to name her own beneficiaries, and allows her to avoid having to take any distributions until she is 70½, thereby allowing the account to grow tax-deferred over the intervening years.

Qualified retirement plans and IRAs offer asset-protection benefits, but these benefits may not be available for inherited plans.[25] Beneficiaries of inherited plans can either take a lump sum distribution, liquidate all assets within five years, or, if the beneficiary qualifies as a "designated beneficiary," utilize the life expectancy method and withdraw required minimum distributions each year based upon IRS tables.

Specific distribution rules for inherited IRAs are beyond the scope of this book. What is important for purposes of Islamic inheritance law is that the preferential tax treatment of certain beneficiaries over others does not alter the rights of the beneficiaries. If a Muslim client intends for his surviving spouse to enjoy the benefits of the spousal rollover (rather than splitting each account consistent with the Islamic Law of Inheritance for each), the couple's plan will need to include a property agreement stating that the surviving spouse will compensate other trust beneficiaries so the overall distribution of the estate is consistent with the Islamic Law of Inheritance. If sufficient assets are not present in the estate, this option would not be consistent with Islamic law.

Finally, many practitioners advocate for the creation of special-purpose trusts for retirement plans to provide asset-protection benefits and enable a beneficiary to stretch out the tax-deferred benefits.[26] These trusts are an exception to the general rule that the designated beneficiary of a retirement account must be an individual person by allowing the trust beneficiaries to enjoy the same advantages. The mechanics of such planning are comprehensively addressed in detail in Natalie Choate's *Life and Death Planning for Retirement Benefits* and other similar titles. We simply note here that, so long as beneficiaries are apportioned based on Islamic inheritance law, such trusts can be a component of a Muslim client's estate plan.

25. Clark v. Rameker, 134 S. Ct. 2242 (2014).

26. 26 U.S.C. §§ 402(c)(11), 401(a)(9)(B) (2018).

G. Gifting, Lifetime Transfers, and *Zakat* Obligations

Islamic inheritance law limits the amount of a Muslim's discretionary bequests, or *wasiyah,* to one-third of his or her estate, with the remainder (at least two-thirds) passing by right to the decedent's Islamic heirs. A Muslim client may not use such bequests to disproportionately enhance the shares of one or more of the Islamic heirs without the consent of the other Islamic heirs.

Because of these restraints on testamentary power, many Muslims will engage in both charitable giving and intergenerational wealth transfers while they are still alive. Such lifetime transfers, also known as inter vivos gifts, are often structured for asset protection or tax planning purposes in order to support a beneficiary who may otherwise be entitled to a smaller share under Islamic inheritance law, or as a means of transferring ownership of a family business to the next generation. This section addresses many of the ways in which an estate planner can facilitate such gifts outside the mandatory distribution scheme of Islamic inheritance law but nonetheless within the parameters of Islamic law and Islamic financial ethics.

While this section will cover a variety of gifting and estate-planning tools, it is not intended as a comprehensive practice guide on such topics. Each topic has a substantial body of laws and regulations and cannot be accorded comprehensive treatment here. For the most part, our coverage concerns the Islamic permissibility of each of these estate-planning techniques.

1. The Current Federal Estate and Gift-Tax Regimes

The estate tax has become far less relevant to the middle class in the United States since the passage of the American Taxpayer Relief Act (ATRA) of 2012 followed by the Tax Cuts and Jobs Act of 2018. ATRA set the estate-tax rate at 40 percent with a $5 million exemption per person, indexed for inflation. In 2018, the exemption was increased to $11.18 million. The far more generous estate-tax exemption of 2018 will revert back to ATRA exemption amounts in 2026 absent further congressional action.

The estate tax is different from the federal income tax in many important ways. First, unlike the income tax, the estate tax applies to a vanishingly small number of American families—only a fraction of 1 percent of the

U.S. population.[27] Second, the federal government has included enough exemptions in the IRC that a savvy taxpayer will almost never have to pay the federal estate tax, regardless of his or her net worth at death.

While estate-planning attorneys engage in painstakingly technical and creative work to achieve the goals of their high-net-worth clients, estate-tax planning is often an exercise in combining various federal tax exemptions with the time value of money. The following are a few of the most important provisions contained within the IRC for estate-planning practitioners.

a. *The Annual Gift-Tax Exclusion*[28]

Section 2503 of the IRC permits taxpayers to make "under-the-radar" gifts of a specified value to an unlimited number of individuals without reporting them on their tax returns. In the case of a married couple, each spouse can give up to the exclusion amount to the same individual. In 2019, the annual gift-tax exclusion was $15,000.[29] The IRS adjusts this number annually for inflation.

The annual gift-tax exclusion is widely used in estate planning and, despite its seemingly miniscule scope, can work to transfer large amounts of wealth from a taxable estate during a client's lifetime. While estate planners often utilize the annual exclusion in the context of life-insurance planning, it is also useful for business-succession planning and other purposes.

b. *The Unlimited Marital Deduction*[30]

Section 2056 of the IRC allows a taxpayer to transfer unlimited sums of money to his or her surviving spouse, free of the gift and estate tax. This unlimited marital deduction functions as a delay mechanism rather than a true, tax-free transfer, however, as the tax is simply deferred until the death of the second spouse. Surviving spouses of course may survive for decades.

---

27. *History, Present Law, and Analysis of the Federal Wealth Transfer Tax System, Hearing before the Subcomm. on Select Revenue Measures of the House Comm. on Ways and Means*, 114th Cong. 1 (2015).

28. 26 U.S.C. § 2503 (2018).

29. *What's New: Estate and Gift Tax*, IRS, https://www.irs.gov/businesses/small-businesses-self-employed/whats-new-estate-and-gift-tax (last updated May 16, 2018).

30. 26 U.S.C. § 2056 (2018).

c. *The Unified Credit against Estate Tax*[31]

As mentioned in our previous discussion of ATRA, section 2010 of the IRC contains a unified exclusion that effectively removes the vast majority of Americans from the ambit of the estate tax. In addition to minimizing estate-tax liability, this exclusion is also useful for leveraging gifts and sales to transfer substantial wealth from a client's estate.

d. *Estate Tax Charitable Tax Deduction*[32]

The charitable tax deduction under IRC section 2055 is substantially different from the income-tax charitable deduction of IRC section 170. The latter limits a taxpayer's deduction to a percentage of his or her adjusted gross income.[33] There is no comparable limit on the estate-tax charitable deduction, however. This means the estate of an individual who donates all his or her assets to charity at death will not be subject to the federal estate tax. By contrast, giving away all your annual income will certainly not result in total income-tax forgiveness.[34] While many charitable-planning techniques are also designed to remove assets from the donor's taxable estate and thus can be characterized as estate-tax planning, some of the most prominent charitable-planning techniques do little or nothing at all to reduce estate-tax liability. Nonetheless, these techniques remain popular as financial-planning vehicles for increasing family wealth and facilitating charitable giving.

e. *Split-Interest Techniques*

Split-interest techniques are useful for both charitable and noncharitable transfers of wealth outside the testator's estate. These methods generally allow for the gifting of an asset at an effective discount (such as with a Qualified Personal Residence Trust, or QPRT)[35] or effectively transfer the growth of an asset to future generations (as with the Grantor Retained Annuity Trust, or GRAT, discussed next).

31. 26 U.S.C. § 2010 (2018).
32. 26 U.S.C. § 2055 (2018).
33. 26 U.S.C. § 170 (2018).
34. White v. Commissioner, T.C. Memo. 2016-167.
35. 26 U.S.C. § 2702 (2018).

2. No Religious Restrictions on Gifting While Alive

Charitable giving is highly encouraged in Islam, and the Quran and *Hadith* of the Prophet are replete with verses and traditions extolling the virtue of voluntary charity. Islamic law does not restrict how much a person can give to charity during his or her lifetime—the only exception being if a person is in the stage known as his or her "final illness."[36] In other words, people are free to give all of their wealth away during their lifetime if they so choose.

A gift, or *hiba*, is defined in Islamic law as an immediate and unconditional transfer of the ownership of some property or right to another. The donor must relinquish control of an asset, and the recipient must take possession. A completed gift, even if made in trust, will become part of the recipient's estate and should be distributed, upon the death of the recipient, to his or her Islamic heirs. Where a person intends to gift only a limited interest in the usufruct or *manf'ah* of a property, Islamic law does not treat the transfer as a completed gift, and the donor retains "ownership" of the property for the purposes of Islamic inheritance law and ongoing *zakat* obligations.

Under Islamic law, gifts are generally revocable with the consent of the beneficiaries. That is, the recipient of a gift may voluntarily return it to the donor. This is one example of an instance where Islamic law, various state laws, and IRC rules may differ. For example, 529 higher education plans allow an account owner to reclaim his or her assets or transfer them to other children without the consent of plan beneficiaries. The IRC treats 529 plans as gifts. Because these assets have not left the account owner's control, however, they do not constitute completed gifts under Islamic law.

One important category of gifts is the split-interest transfer, which splits property rights into a present and future interest in a single asset. Split-interest transfers are common in charitable planning where there is an income interest, such as an annuity or unitrust payment from a charitable remainder trust, and a residual interest that vests either after the donor's death or at the completion of a stated period. The Qualified Personal Residence Trust (QPRT) is an example of a split-interest gift that may appeal to certain high-net-worth Muslim families wishing to transfer

36. See Chapter 4(A) for an additional discussion of *maradul maut* in the context of incapacity planning.

their wealth outside the mandatory distribution system of Islamic inheritance law while still complying with Islamic law.

One of the primary estate-planning objectives of lifetime gifting is to exclude the value of an asset—as well as any appreciation—from the decedent's estate. In fact, many estate-planning transactions would not occur but for the existence of the transfer tax regime. This ability to "freeze" or even reduce the value of an asset in an estate can reduce or even eliminate significant estate-tax liability.

But while most estate-planning clients desire a reduction in their tax liability, many may have difficulty relinquishing control of their assets in the process. As a result, some clients may seek to engage in purported transfers of wealth while still retaining control of their property. The IRC contains various regulations inhibiting the tax benefits of such transactions.[37]

Example:
Iqbal owns a rental home. He places the home in a trust for the ultimate benefit of his children but retains the right to all income from the home during his life and may revoke the trust at any time. Because of Iqbal's continued control over the property, his purported gift would be incomplete for IRS purposes and would form part of Iqbal's gross estate at his death. Similarly, under Islamic inheritance law, the rental home would need to be distributed to Iqbal's Islamic heirs (and not just his children) in accordance with Islamic inheritance law.

Unlike the revocable trust in the preceding example, irrevocable trusts are not subject to unilateral termination by the grantor. Rather, under the Uniform Trust Code and various state codes, the undoing of an irrevocable trust requires unanimous consent by the trust beneficiaries.[38] In the case of charitable trusts, it is frequently necessary to obtain a court order. Apart from these restraints, there are also financial costs associated with terminating such trusts. The fact that they may end prematurely, however, does not present any Islamic law concerns.

37. *See, e.g.*, 26 U.S.C. § 2036 (2018).
38. *See, e.g.*, Cal. Prob. Code § 15403 (2018).

3. Utilizing the *Wasiyah* Share to Make Bequests upon Death

While Islamic law does not generally restrict lifetime gifting, a Muslim may dispose of only up to one-third of his or her net estate through a *wasiyah*, or discretionary bequest, upon his or her death. The rest must pass based on the *faraid*—Islam's mandatory rules of succession. The term "*wasiyah*" is often translated and understood by Muslims to refer to a "last will," but these terms are not entirely interchangeable due to the different limitations they involve. For example, while the *wasiyah* can dispose of a maximum of one-third of the decedent's net estate, a will can dispose of the entire net estate. In addition, whereas Islamic law enables the testator to use his or her *wasiyah* share for bequeathals of nonprobate property, such as life insurance proceeds, a last will and testament has no such legal effect if those assets have designated beneficiaries. The rules governing *wasiyah* are discussed in detail in Chapter 5.

4. Transfer-on-Death and Pay-on-Death Accounts

Transfer-on-Death (TOD) or Pay-on-Death (POD) accounts offer a way to transfer wealth to a named beneficiary outside the probate process. Such accounts, along with beneficiary deeds, comprise an alternative method of distributing a decedent's property.

To provide some flexibility to those who wish to pass property on to their children after death without creating traditional testamentary documents, certain states recognize a "revocable TOD deed," or a "Ladybird Deed" as it is known in Florida, which transfers property to the beneficiary upon death without the need for probate.

Unlike a comprehensive estate plan, TOD-based planning only addresses individual assets without regard to other assets and liabilities or changed circumstances. While the simplicity of this type of planning is often attractive to clients, it lacks the flexibility needed by administrators to distribute assets in an efficient and Islamically compliant manner and is thus generally inadvisable for Muslim clients.

Example:

Abed has an estate that consists of \$200,000 in a 401(k) account, a residence worth \$400,000, and a \$20,000 bank account. He would like to create an estate plan consistent with Islamic inheritance law, primarily for the benefit of two children: his 30-year-old son, Waris, and 32-year-old daughter, Wafa. These are Abed's only Islamic heirs. He makes his children TOD beneficiaries of the bank account and home and designates them as beneficiaries of the retirement account in proportion to their Islamic shares.

From the perspective of Islamic inheritance law, there is nothing overtly wrong with Abed's plan. It may cease to comply with the rules, however, if an unexpected event occurs. This could include premature death of a beneficiary, incapacity, or creditor concerns. For this reason, we generally recommend a revocable trust-based plan that inherently allows for a mechanism to recalculate beneficiaries in accordance with Islamic law.

H. Charitable Trusts

There are two primary types of charitable trusts that we address in this section: (1) Charitable Remainder Trust and (2) Charitable Lead Trust.

1. Charitable Remainder Trusts

A Charitable Remainder Trust (CRT) is one of the most effective ways for high-net-worth families to invest appreciated assets, decrease taxes, and benefit various charities. While a CRT is not technically an estate-planning trust, it represents an important tool—or rather a series of related tools—in the tool kit of the estate-planning attorney and provides several important benefits:

1. An immediate charitable income-tax deduction upon transferring assets into the CRT
2. Trustee-donor retains control over his or her own investments
3. Ability to sell and diversify investments inside the trust in a tax-free environment (similar to an IRA)
4. No capital-gains taxes on the sale of appreciated assets inside the trust[39]

At its heart, a CRT is a "split-interest" trust comprised of an income interest to be paid not less than once a year to the grantor and a remainder interest donated to charity at the expiration of a fixed term or upon

39. *See generally* Thomas J. Ray, Charitable Gift Planning 201 (2nd ed. 2007).

the death of a grantor or another individual. The grantor often transfers an appreciated asset into the trust, thereby removing the asset from his or her estate and earning an immediate charitable income-tax deduction. The trustee sells the asset at full market value and reinvests the assets in income-producing assets. The trust can be structured to pay a percentage of trust assets, called a Charitable Remainder Unitrust (CRUT), or a fixed amount, called a Charitable Remainder Annuity Trust (CRAT). Upon the death of the grantor or the expiration of a term, remaining trust assets are distributed to the charity.

Because the appreciated asset can be sold by a CRT with no immediate imposition of the capital-gains tax and the grantor receives an income-tax deduction, the practical economic impact of creating a CRT is often to increase the overall size of the estate. Thus, not only is the CRT a gift to the charity, but the charitably inclined donor is often better off financially after creating a CRT than before.

Example:

Elias and Zarina are both 60-year-old California residents. Anticipating retirement, they seek to transfer $2 million in appreciated stock from their medical device company, EZhearts Inc., to income-based investments. The couple wishes to transfer their funds to investments they believe will provide a reliable annual return of 8 percent. Elias and Zarina's federal capital-gains tax rate in 2018 is 20 percent plus the net investment income tax of 3.8 percent and an additional 13.3 percent in California state taxes, totaling $742,000 in tax liability. Once reinvested, an 8 percent annual return on their investment of the remaining $1,258,000 would amount to $100,640 each year, taxed at ordinary income-tax rates. A better option for Elias and Zarina would be to transfer the $2 million worth of shares to a CRT that pays 8 percent a year. There would be no immediate imposition of the capital-gains tax, so the entire amount would be available for investment. Thus, the trust would earn $160,000 per year. Furthermore, the couple would receive an immediate income tax deduction in the year of the donation. If that amount exceeded the deductibility limit for the first year, they could carry it forward for the following five years.

While the CRT income in the preceding example would be taxable, a portion of it would be taxed at a relatively low capital-gains rate due to the unrealized gain from the initial sale of the couple's stock. And so long as funds remain inside the CRT, Elias and Zarina could sell assets tax-free for the purpose of making other investments within the CRT.

a. CRT Distributions

As described previously, the income beneficiaries of the trust are paid either a fixed percentage of the trust principal, recalculated annually (unitrust), or a fixed dollar amount (annuity trust). The annuity amount is a specific number stipulated at the creation of the trust and does not change regardless of the trust's performance. In either case, the payout must be between 5 percent and 50 percent of the trust's assets annually.

In the preceding example, a $2 million trust paying 8 percent annually is an annuity trust. If the investment increased in value several times over, the grantors would not receive more than 8 percent of the initial contribution annually. The benefit of the successful investment would automatically pass to charity upon the second spouse's death.

A Muslim client may view this as problematic, as the 8 percent fixed payout resembles an unlawful *riba*-based payout commonly found in most commercial and charitable annuities. However, there are substantial differences between the CRT income and *riba*. First, a CRT is not a transaction in the form of a loan, but rather a transaction between the grantor as an individual and the grantor as a trustee of an irrevocable trust (in most cases). Because it is not possible to engage in a *riba* transaction with oneself, the CRT income cannot be classified as *riba*.

The other potential concern a Muslim client may have with CRTs is excessive speculation, or *gharar*. Where the term of a CRT is set as the grantor's life, one aspect of the trust is inherently speculative—namely, the timing of the grantor's death. If the grantor lives for as long as projected in the actuarial tables, the creation of the trust was certainly a good deal for the grantor. If, however, the grantor dies soon after creation of the trust, there is little tax benefit to the grantor, if any at all.

While the grantor's untimely death is certainly a risk in the CRT, this fact does not render CRTs unduly speculative, as there is no transaction with an outside party. The gift to charity and income to the grantor for life are part of the bargain. The CRT is not typically intended as a speculative financial bet but a tax-advantaged charitable gift.

b. CRTs and Islamic Inheritance Law

CRTs present two important considerations from the perspective of Islamic inheritance law. The first relates to the way CRT income passes to a surviving spouse or other beneficiary. The second relates to *zakat*.

c. CRT Survivorship Benefits and Islamic Inheritance Rights

In the example previous, when Elias dies, Zarina could continue to be the income beneficiary of their CRT. This financial arrangement resembles that of a JSA benefit in a pension or annuity. The key issue for married couples is whether such an arrangement is Islamically permissible if the assets of the first spouse to die are not distributed consistent with Islamic inheritance law.

A surviving spouse's JSA proceeds are not subject to Islam's mandatory succession rules upon the death of the decedent due to the existence of a contract with a third party for the survivor's support. In the case of CRT, however, there is no third-party contract. Because Elias and Zarina's joint CRT is designed to benefit the surviving spouse without consideration of the decedent spouse's Islamic heirs, it would likely violate Islamic law.

To address this problem with CRTs, the drafting attorney has three options when drafting a CRT for a married couple.

The first—and most practical—option would be to draft two CRTs, one for each spouse. This would ensure that the surviving spouse continued to receive income after the death of the first without deriving that income from the decedent spouse's estate (which should be apportioned consistent with Islamic inheritance law).

The second option would be to create a joint CRT but with distributions proportional to the inheritance rights of the decedent spouse's Islamic heirs. If the spouses contributed equally to the trust, the surviving spouse would be the beneficiary of half the trust income, while the remaining Islamic heirs would be beneficiaries of the other half. The latter group could include a wide range of relatives. As a result, this second option may be unmanageable if the income is to be paid based upon the lives of individuals as opposed to a term of years. Further, if the grantor creates a CRT to benefit Islamic heirs for the duration of their lives, each of the beneficiaries must currently be living.[40]

The third option is that the CRT can combine terms of years so long as no combination exceeds the IRC's 20-year limit. Note, also, that one

40. 26 U.S.C. § 664(d)(1)(A), 664(d)(2)(A) (2018).

trust cannot combine life benefits for some individuals and term-of-years benefits for others.[41] More importantly, though, such combinations are incapable of being made equitable under Islamic inheritance law.

In light of the impracticality of intertwining Islamic inheritance law and a joint CRT, we recommend the first option, in which Muslim spouses create individual CRTs. This option will better serve the goals of the Islamic inheritance law while avoiding potentially impermissible distributions to the surviving spouse or other beneficiaries.

d. Why CRTs Are Permissible in Islam

Unlike other assets, such as life insurance, for which the distribution is connected to death, CRT assets are irrevocably gifted during the client's life and thus not subject to Islamic inheritance law. Thus, upon the expiration of the term or death of the final income beneficiary, a CRT remainder interest will pass to charity without taking into consideration the rights of the grantor's Islamic heirs. Specifically, the distribution of CRT assets to charity may exceed one-third of the grantor's estate, which is the limit on a Muslim's discretionary bequests, or *wasiyah*. In addition, the testator may have completed a separate living trust or will that already donated one-third of his or her wealth to charity upon death consistent with the rules of the *wasiyah*.

Though the grantor retains an interest in CRT income, the charitable remainder is permanently allocated to charity. While it is theoretically possible for the grantor to undo the trust and receive the noncharitable portion back based upon the actuarial tables, the charitable gift portion cannot be undone. If the grantor undoes the noncharitable portion of the CRT, that portion of the trust will revert back to his or her estate and should be distributed upon his or her death pursuant to Islamic inheritance law.

e. Wealth Replacement Trusts

A wealth replacement trust is a tool in which the grantor uses the income from a CRT to buy life insurance to replace the assets that he or she is giving away. Because the life insurance policy belongs to an irrevocable trust, the proceeds are not subject to the estate tax. While a wealth replacement trust is not per se impermissible, most Islamic scholars take the opinion that conventional life insurance products are prohibited in Islam as they

41. 26 C.F.R. §§ 1.664-2(b)(5)(i), 1.644-3(b)(5)(i) (2018).

contain unlawful amounts of *riba* and *gharar* and would thus regard a wealth replacement trust as impermissible.

Example:
Bilques funds a CRT with $2 million in cash. According to a formula provided by her advisor, about $2 million would be distributed to charity upon Bilques's passing. In addition to making this charitable donation, Bilques would like to leave her children with the same amount. Bilques's advisor suggests she use her CRT income to purchase a permanent life insurance policy. In doing so, Bilques's investment would not only benefit herself and her chosen charities, but her children would also receive $2 million in proportion to their Islamic shares after her death, free of both income tax and estate tax.

As explained previously, while a CRT itself does not violate any element of Islamic law, the impermissibility of life insurance would render a wealth replacement trust generally inapplicable for Muslim clients.

2. Charitable Lead Trusts

A Charitable Lead Trust (CLT) is essentially the inverse of a CRT. That is, rather than donating the remainder interest to charity, a CLT pays either a unitrust or annuity interest to charity for a period of years, after which the remainder passes to one or more noncharitable beneficiaries. If the trust income is insufficient to pay the guaranteed annuity interest, the trustee must utilize trust principal to make up the difference.

A CLT can be designed to reduce income taxes or reduce or eliminate the estate and/or gift taxes on assets transferred to the trust as well as any corresponding appreciation of those assets and also creates a substantial stream of income for the charitable beneficiaries of the trust.

CLTs can be designed as grantor trusts or nongrantor trusts. In a grantor trust, the donor is entitled to a charitable income-tax deduction in the year the trust is created and is subject to income tax on all income incurred by the CLT. In a nongrantor trust, the donor is not subject to income tax on the trust's income but also is not entitled to an income-tax deduction in the year of creation. While most CLTs are structured as nongrantor trusts, donors are still entitled to a charitable-gift tax deduction based on the section 7520 rate and actuarial assumptions in the IRS tables.

CLTs are often utilized to pass substantial wealth to grandchildren or even more remote descendants free of the federal generation-skipping tax. However, because Islamic inheritance law provides fixed inheritance shares to particular individuals who will often not be "skip persons" under the code,[42] the utility of this provision may be limited.

This is because the assets inside a CLT will be treated as belonging to the grantor unless the grantor has no ability to influence a change in distribution of the trust principal. Because this is generally not the case, the fact that a CLT is irrevocable will not remove the trust assets from the grantor's estate as far as Islamic inheritance law is concerned. In other words, unless the CLT irrevocably gifts its residue to one or more specific beneficiaries, the trust assets must be distributed according to the Islamic Law of Inheritance upon the death of the grantor.

Example:
Azhar creates a CLT that includes a "supergrantor" provision, a hybrid instrument with both grantor and nongrantor trust provisions in which Azhar is subject to all of the income and gain incurred by the trust (a grantor trust for income-tax purposes), but the CLT assets are not includable in Azhar's estate for estate-tax purposes. This allows him to create a CLT with either a unitrust or annuity interest flowing to charity for a period of years, with the remainder passing to his family. As the grantor, Azhar retains the right to reacquire any property in the trust by substituting property of equivalent value. He also appoints a trust protector with the power to modify the CLT's distribution provisions if necessary to comply with Azhar's intent. Azhar incorporated this flexibility into his CLT to protect against potential breakdowns in his children's marriages. While the future interest would pass outside Azhar's estate for tax purposes, the assets would remain within his estate for the purposes of Islamic inheritance law and thus be subject to its mandatory distribution scheme.

---

a. Use of CLTs for Zakat Payments

One possible use of the CLT is for planned payment of *zakat,* the annual obligation to donate a percentage of one's assets to charity. *Zakat* is assessed

42. 26 U.S.C. § 2613 (2018).

on 2.5 percent of the value of one's assets, with various exceptions. For high-net-worth Muslims, the obligation to pay *zakat* can represent a substantial financial consideration.

Depending on the financial and tax-planning goals of the client, a CLT can take the form of either a "grantor-style" or "nongrantor-style" trust. A benefit of the grantor-style CLT is that it generally results in a large tax deduction in year one. A disadvantage, however, is that the IRS will treat all trust income as the grantor's income, even though it is going to charity. A nongrantor-style CLT, on the other hand, will not be taxed to the grantor but will rather be taxed as a "complex trust," which can distribute corpus, accumulate income, or make donations to charity.

b. Charitable Lead Annuity Trust

A Muslim client wishing to make *zakat* contributions through a CLT can use a Charitable Lead Annuity Trust, or CLAT.

Example:
Bilal funds a CLAT with $1 million with a 7 percent annual annuity for a 20-year term. The trust will be used to fulfill most of Bilal's anticipated annual *zakat* obligations. The trust states that the $70,000 annual payment will be shared equally among three public charities that support poor Muslims in the United States and in his native country of Egypt, where he maintains another home and has extended family. The guarantee ensures that this amount will be paid to the charities regardless of the CLAT's gains or losses. Thus, if income and capital gains are less than the guaranteed $70,000, Bilal's trustee will cover the balance from the CLAT's principal. Any growth in the account will pass to the CLAT's remainder interest, an irrevocable trust, free of gift or estate taxes.

If Bilal creates a CLT that gifts the residue irrevocably to another trust for the benefit of his daughter, Sarah, without leaving any options for a change in this designation, even by an independent third party, the distribution provisions upon Sarah's death would be to her Islamic heirs under Islamic inheritance law. Since Bilal created his CLT for the purpose of paying *zakat*, he would be able to treat the CLT assets as his own for *zakat* purposes, but not for inheritance purposes.

c. Charitable Lead Unitrusts

A CLT may also be structured in the form of a unitrust, known as a Charitable Lead Unitrust (CLUT). A unitrust interest is a charity's irrevocable right to receive payment of a fixed percentage of dividends or interest on the assets of a CLT, determined annually. It is possible to take the average valuation appraised on multiple dates throughout the year, but the method of valuing the trust assets must remain uniform from year to year.[43]

In the preceding example, if Bilal dies during the term of his CLT, the charitable contributions continue to be paid until the term is completed. However, since Bilal would no longer be obligated to pay *zakat,* the charitable contributions could count toward the *zakat* obligations of the CLT's beneficiaries as assigned by Bilal upon the CLT's creation.

I. Charitable Gift Annuities

A Charitable Gift Annuity (CGA) is similar to a commercial annuity, except that the transaction occurs between a donor and a charity. Specifically, the CGA is a transaction in which an individual transfers cash or property to a charity in exchange for a tax deduction, and the charity promises to pay one or more annuitants a lifetime stream of income, guaranteed by the charity's assets. The payout on the annuity is lower than it would be on an insurance product, so it is a variant of a "bargain sale"—the difference in payout represents the "gift" to charity. Thus, the IRC "bargain sale" rules govern CGAs.[44] Many charities utilize the services of insurance companies or community foundations, which in turn use insurance companies to facilitate these types of gifts.

CGAs are generally considered impermissible, as they violate the Islamic prohibition against *riba* and *gharar.*

Example:

Aisha, an 80-year-old widow, owns $2 million in publicly traded securities with a basis of $500,000. She would like to retire from the income of this investment, but the stocks do not pay much in dividends. Lately, Aisha has been thinking of reinvesting her $2 million in a CGA at her alma mater. If Aisha were to do so, the

43. 26 U.S.C. § 664 (2018).
44. 26 C.F.R. § 1.1011-2 (2018).

charity would receive the $2 million in exchange for its promise to pay Aisha a guaranteed 6.8 percent, or $136,000 per year, for the rest of her life. The charity could then use the money however it wished, subject to the continuing financial obligation to Aisha.

If Aisha were to purchase the CGA in the preceding example, she would qualify for a substantial income-tax deduction, which she could carry forward to the next five years, if necessary. In addition to the deduction, Aisha would receive an annual $136,000 payment consisting of a mix of ordinary income, capital gains, and tax-free return of capital.

The preceding transaction would be regarded as prohibited in Islam, as the annual payments of a CGA are regarded as *riba* under Islamic financial ethics and therefore impermissible. Second, the prohibition on *gharar* applies because the annuity is guaranteed by the assets of the charity. If Aisha lives to be 110, for example, the charity will have had to pay her a total of $4,080,000 by that time. Similarly, if Aisha dies soon after the contract is signed, the obligation of the charity ends.

1. Differences between a CGA and a CRAT

You may be wondering why a CRAT, which is very similar to a CGA, is permissible under Islamic law while a CGA is not. In fact, not only does a CRAT qualify the donor for a tax deduction, provide a fixed rate of return, and provide significant value to a charity, it also avoids the pitfalls of *riba* and *gharar*.

There are two important differences between a CGA and a CRAT for the purpose of Islamic estate planning. The first relates to the charity's access to funds, and the second is that donors cannot engage in a *riba* transaction with themselves.

First, a charity can utilize the funds from a CGA right away, but it must wait until the death of the final income beneficiary of a CRAT to receive the trust's assets. In addition, there is a possibility that the grantor of a CRAT may replace the original charitable beneficiary with another one before the CRAT terminates, which is not possible in a CGA.

Second, as explained previously, an individual cannot engage in a *riba* transaction with him- or herself, and for Islamic financial ethics purposes, a CRAT is a transaction between the grantor and the grantor as trustee of an irrevocable trust. Moreover, the annuity from a CRAT is guaranteed with funds in the trust, all of which were contributed by the grantor. If the funds run out, payments stop. Although this is unlikely (as the income beneficiary of a CRAT typically invests in assets that produce income at or above the annuity amount), there remains the important distinction from a CGA, where the charity itself is legally obligated to make fixed payments to the donor, regardless of the financial condition of the charity.

J. Irrevocable Trusts

Irrevocable trusts are used for a variety of reasons, including tax planning, asset protection, gifting, and Medicaid planning. From an Islamic law perspective, if an asset is genuinely being given away, it will not be subject to Islamic inheritance laws upon the grantor's death. On the other hand, if the grantor does not truly relinquish control, the trust assets should ultimately pass to the grantor's beneficiaries upon his or her death in accordance with Islamic law.

1. GRUTs and GRATs

The Grantor Retained Unitrust (GRUT) and the Grantor Retained Annuity Trust (GRAT) are two forms of irrevocable-trust planning that allow a grantor to make gifts on a discounted basis while minimizing estate and gift taxes.[45] In either case, a donor gifts assets to the trust while retaining an income stream for a specified period of time. At the end of this term, the trust terminates and is distributed to remainder beneficiaries.

The trustee of a GRAT must make annuity payments to the grantor at least annually. If there is insufficient income to pay the annuity, the trustee must withdraw the difference from trust principal. In the case of a GRUT, there is a fixed rate of return based on the market value of the trust assets as determined on a yearly basis.

Despite its simplicity, a GRAT can dramatically reduce or even eliminate the taxable value of a gift. It may be used as a mechanism to transfer large amounts of wealth to future generations with minimal to zero gift tax or even burning of gift-tax exemption.[46]

GRATs are more attractive as an estate-planning tool when interest rates are low. This is because the underlying investment must outperform

45. 26 U.S.C. § 2702 (2018).

46. Walton v. Commissioner, 115 T.C. 589 (2000).

the IRC section 7520 interest rate for beneficiaries to receive anything at the end of the GRAT term. The section 7520 interest rate—calculated monthly—is used for discounting present values, future interests, and annuities.[47] If the property gifted does not appreciate at a rate greater than section 7520, the GRAT will not serve its ultimate purpose of transferring wealth to remainder beneficiaries.

Example:
Fareed transfers a $1 million commercial real estate property, which he expects to appreciate significantly over time, to a GRAT structured to pay a 5 percent annuity for a term of 20 years. If Fareed dies during the 20-year period, the trust will continue to pay the 5 percent annuity to his estate. At the end of the term, the GRAT will terminate, and the property—including any appreciation above the section 7520 rate—will be distributed to Fareed's beneficiaries free of any transfer tax.

Under Islamic inheritance law, Fareed made a complete gift of the remainder interest in his GRAT property during his lifetime. This means that the gift is exempt from distribution upon his death to his Islamic heirs.

Practice Pointer: Allocating *Zakat* Obligations
In designing a Grantor Retained Trust for a Muslim client, it is important to decide how *zakat* will be paid on the assets involved. The client can also decide who will pay it—the grantor or the trustee of the GRAT or GRUT.

2. Qualified Personal Residence Trust

A Qualified Personal Residence Trust (QPRT) is an estate-planning tool for high-net-worth clients that enables a grantor to make a lifetime transfer of a personal residence to one or more beneficiaries (often children) in exchange for rent-free use of the residence for a fixed number of years. The donor accomplishes this by creating an irrevocable trust and transferring

47. 26 U.S.C. § 7520 (2018).

his or her interest in a residence to the trust. The trust provides the donor with a right to live in the residence rent-free for a fixed period, typically ten to 20 years, after which the asset is transferred outright or in trust to the donor's beneficiaries.

Only the value of the remainder interest in the QPRT will be subject to the gift tax under IRC section 2702. The QPRT is generally considered a safe way of transferring wealth to family members while reducing the taxable value of the gift, as the IRC specifically authorizes the transaction.[48]

The value of a QPRT gift—which is deemed to have occurred at the time of transfer to the trust and not when the retained interest expires—is calculated using valuation tables provided by the IRS. These tables, in turn, utilize the section 7520 rate to calculate the value of the gift. Estate-planning attorneys can also utilize various software programs to calculate this value. Note that the donor should never retain a lifetime power of appointment over the remainder interest, as doing so would render the gift incomplete.

Example 1:

Altaf, 60, transfers his $3 million home to a QPRT in July 2018. He anticipates living another 20 years or more. He figures he is unlikely to continue to live in the home after he turns 80, and if he does, he will be able to pay fair-market-value rent.

Altaf's goals are twofold. First, he would like to reduce his taxable estate. Second, he would like to provide more financial support to his daughter, Kauther, than she would receive were Altaf's entire estate to pass according to Islamic inheritance law. In order to achieve this, he must give it away during his lifetime. Altaf's QPRT provides that he can continue to live in the residence for 20 years. Since he is gifting his daughter only the remainder interest in the home, his taxable gift would be calculated at $891,780.

As Altaf has not used his $11.18 million lifetime gift-tax exemption (in 2018), he would pay no gift tax.

If Altaf dies during this 20-year term, his QPRT assets will be included in his gross estate.[49] This would render the gift of the home to his daughter incomplete and require that the distribu-

48. Rev. Proc. 2003-42, 2003-1 C.B. 993.
49. 26 U.S.C. § 2036(a) (2018).

tion of the home conform with Islamic inheritance laws. In this scenario, Altaf's goal of benefiting his one daughter would be frustrated.

On the other hand, if Altaf survives the 20-year QPRT term, his home would either pass outright to Kauther or transfer to another trust for her benefit. He would then pay rent to Kauther or to the trust at fair market value until he decides to move or passes away.

Example 2:
Altaf, instead of creating one QPRT, creates five QPRTs for the same residence, each with a different term of five, ten, 15, 20, and 25 years. By dividing his interest in the home into five-year increments, Altaf increases the likelihood that he will survive at least some of the QPRT terms. With the passage of each five-year period, one-fifth of Altaf's home transfers to his daughter. Each 20 percent interest transferred this way serves as a completed gift under Islamic inheritance law. As such, these individual gifts would not be considered part of Altaf's estate upon his death, neither by Islamic law nor by U.S. tax law.

The sale of a home in a QPRT can convert the trust to either a GRAT, or, if the beneficiaries are not close family members, to a Grantor Retained Interest Trust (GRIT), though the latter is less typical.

3. Grantor Retained Interest Trust

The Grantor Retained Interest Trust (GRIT)[50] is a less common planning tool because the technique benefits only persons outside the donor's immediate family, such as a niece, nephew, or life partner. For Muslims, however, a GRIT may suit certain gifting arrangements, such as the transfer of wealth to an unregistered spouse.

For federal gift-tax purposes, the beneficiary's interest in a GRIT equates with the right to own an asset after a specified period of time, such as 20 years. The grantor's right to income from the gift is subtracted from the value of the asset in the hands of the beneficiary. This discount

50. 26 U.S.C. § 2702 (2018).

is also based on the applicable federal rate in effect the month the GRIT is created.

Example:
Dawud married Ishal in a religious ceremony not legally recognized in any state in the United States. He and Ishal instead create a written cohabitation agreement. During the wedding, Dawud gifts Ishal a *mahr* (akin to a dower) of $2.5 million. To avoid "burning" his lifetime estate-tax exemption for that amount, Dawud makes the gift in the form of a GRIT through which he will pay himself 3 percent of the principal value over 20 years. Since he is paying this from his own funds, this arrangement does not violate the prohibition on *riba*. The income value of the gift he will retain as grantor amounts to $1.5 million based on a calculation made by his estate-planning attorney. If Dawud dies during this 20-year period, the entire $2.5 million is included in his estate, but if he survives the initial term, the gift will pass to Ishal at a reduced gift-tax value and outside his estate.

Though the GRIT may become part of Dawud's taxable estate (i.e., if he dies during the 20-year term), so long as the $2.5 million principal is an irrevocable gift, his successor trustee can still distribute this money to Ishal after his death. This is because Ishal's *mahr* is considered a debt upon Dawud under Islamic inheritance law. Thus, only after paying Ishal her *mahr* will the remaining principal and capital growth pass to Dawud's other Islamic heirs for the balance of the GRIT term.

---

4. Sales to an Intentionally Defective Grantor Trust

Another popular estate-planning tool for high-net-worth individuals is the Intentionally Defective Grantor Trust, or IDGT, which is commonly used to freeze certain assets for estate-tax purposes but not for income-tax purposes. The IDGT is made "intentionally defective" for income-tax purposes, meaning the grantor, rather than the trust, continues to pay income tax on trust income.

The grantor funds the trust by selling highly appreciated assets to the IDGT. The sale generally takes the form of an installment note to be repaid to the grantor over several years at a low rate of interest. The interest is not recognized as taxable interest income, though any income generated by the assets would be taxable to the grantor. Since selling something to oneself cannot result in income, there would be no income tax on the sale itself, and all transactions between the grantor and the IDGT are free of any income tax.

The assets in the trust, along with any future appreciation remaining, will be outside the grantor's taxable estate while the grantor continues to pay income tax on trust income.

Example:
Abdullah, a wealthy businessman, creates an IDGT designed as an irrevocable trust. He intentionally violates one or more of the Grantor Trust Rules found in IRC sections 671–679 to trigger tax treatment that requires him to pay income tax on all trust income but that avoids inclusion of the IDGT's assets in his estate under section 2037. Specifically, Abdullah elects to have the power to borrow from the IDGT without adequate security, which triggers grantor-trust treatment of the irrevocable trust. To ensure there is economic substance to the transaction (a requirement), in creating the IDGT, Abdullah gifts $1 million to the trust to be distributed in equal shares to his two daughters and two sons. Because he is making the distributions during his lifetime, it is not inheritance. The IDGT then purchases a stake in the limited partnership units that Abdullah owns, valued at $8 million, with a note payable to his Revocable Living Trust (RLT) with interest at fair market value. This transaction is not *riba* (impermissible interest), as will be described below. The limited partnership interest is appraised at a discounted value, accounting for restrictions on transfer and ownership. The same assets, if outside the partnership, would be worth $12 million.

Abdullah's estate-planning technique in the preceding example compresses (through the limited partnership) and then freezes (through the sale) the value of an asset for estate-tax purposes. Abdullah is giving away only the $1 million gift to the IDGT. Any increase in value of the limited partnership interest would be transferred to the children free of estate tax, since the entire asset is being transferred in exchange for a note that remains in Abdullah's estate.

Under Islamic financial ethics, Abdullah's interest payments are collected on his own asset. As such, the interest income he has reserved for himself and his estate is not considered unlawful.

5. Beneficiary Defective Grantor Trusts

A Beneficiary Defective Grantor Trust (BDGT) is similar, in many respects, to the IDGT, though it has a few important differences.[51] The trust is created by a parent or a third party and seeded with a gift. This is typically the only gift to the trust, of which the beneficiary is the owner for income-tax purposes but not for estate-tax purposes. After this minimal funding, the beneficiary begins to conduct transactions with the trust in a manner similar to the grantor of an IDGT.

The "beneficiary" of a BDGT refers to the client who is utilizing a small gift from a parent to establish the term. Another reason for the name is that the beneficiary of a BDGT maintains complete investment control and can serve as an investment trustee. Finally, while the distribution trustee is typically a different entity to maintain the BDGT's asset-protection benefits, the beneficiary has the full ability to replace this trustee. Overall, the BDGT presents a remarkable potential for estate- and asset-protection benefits.

As one may expect, distribution of the assets within a BDGT must be consistent with Islamic inheritance law for the principal beneficiary, who maintains effective control and beneficial enjoyment of the assets. The beneficiary must also pay *zakat* on all assets inside a BDGT.

6. Domestic (and International) Asset Protection Trust

Several U.S. states have enacted laws that enable a grantor to create a trust for asset protection, known as a Domestic Asset Protection Trust (DAPT).[52] If the grantor of such a trust were to get divorced, lose a future lawsuit resulting in a judgment, or even file for bankruptcy (if the trust is at least ten years old),[53] assets inside the trust would be protected for the

51. Richard A. Oshins, *The Beneficiary Defective Inheritor's Trust ("BDIT")*, N.A.E.P.C.J., https://www.naepc.org/journal/issue07h.pdf (last accessed Sept. 5, 2018).

52. *See Eleventh Annual ACTEC Comparison of the Domestic Asset Protection Trust Statutes*, http://www.actec.org/assets/1/6/Shaftel-Comparison-of-the-Domestic-Asset-Protection-Trust-Statutes.pdf.

53. 11 U.S.C. § 548(e) (2006).

benefit of the trust beneficiaries, who may include the grantor, his or her spouse, or other family members.

Several international jurisdictions also recognize asset-protection trusts. The advantage of utilizing offshore trusts is that they are often domiciled in jurisdictions that do not give full faith and credit to U.S. judgments. That is, if an individual loses a lawsuit in the United States, the foreign jurisdiction will not necessarily recognize the verdict, and the judgment creditor would likely have a difficult time collecting against the defendant in the foreign jurisdiction.

The grantor of a DAPT, which is generally a self-settled trust, is generally not the same entity as the distribution trustee. However, the grantor—and potentially other individuals close to the grantor—may serve as a trustee for other purposes, for example as an investment trustee.

For Muslim clients, DAPTs as well as offshore trusts are acceptable estate-planning tools. However, the final distribution of assets from these trusts—where the grantor is a permissible beneficiary or maintains any intent to potentially benefit from the assets—must follow Islamic inheritance law.

Example:

Abdullah is a successful neurosurgeon. He is married to Nura, a radiologist. In addition to their general estate-planning goals, they would like to obtain extra asset protection to account for their high-risk professions, which could result in malpractice liability beyond available insurance coverage.

Their attorney recommends they create foreign and Domestic Asset Protection Trusts. The couple follows this advice and creates two offshore trusts in the Cook Islands, which are funded with $1 million each. They also create two $500,000 DAPTs in Nevada.

Abdullah and Nura leave their personal residence and $600,000 of savings outside their asset protection trusts, instead using these assets to fund an RLT or various qualified plans to avoid being insolvent at the creation of their asset protection trusts. They have no intention to use the assets for their own personal needs in the near future (three to five years) but do hope to invest the assets as a nest egg.

Abdullah and Nura authorize their trustees to make discretionary distributions to the grantors of their asset protection trusts. If anyone other than the grantor, such as a judgment creditor, requests funds, the distribution trustee is obligated to refuse the request.

While Abdullah and his wife lack full control of the assets inside the asset protection trusts, the assets are plainly their own for Islamic inheritance purposes. As such, the couple must design the trusts to require final distribution consistent with Islamic inheritance law and be cognizant of the *zakat* obligations due on such assets.

K. Self-Canceling Installment Notes

The Self-Canceling Installment Note (SCIN) is an estate-planning technique to transfer value out of an estate that involves the sale of an asset from one party to another that is typically structured between family members. The asset is sold in exchange for an interest-bearing promissory note for a term that is shorter than the seller's life expectancy. If the seller dies before the end of the term, the note is canceled and is thus not part of the decedent's estate. To survive scrutiny, the technique must constitute a sale that avoids all appearances of a gift. There is a premium paid for the self-canceling feature. This often means a higher purchase price or higher-than-market interest rate.

While Islam generally prohibits transactions involving interest, asset-backed financing is one of the principal features of Islamic finance.[54] Accordingly, installment sales are generally considered permissible, even where there is a built-in increase in the price to account for the delay in payments. Given Islam's categorical prohibition on dealing in *riba*, however, a practitioner should carefully draft the terms of the SCIN in a manner that ensures there are no unlawful terms or payments.

54. *See generally* Usmani, *supra* note 21.

L. Educational Savings Plans

1. College Savings Plans

Ensuring access to quality higher education for one's children is often a paramount goal for parents. But given the dramatic increase in the cost of higher education and the fact that many parents are still paying off their own student loans, planning for a child's education needs can be a daunting task. Fortunately, there are a few tax-advantaged methods to assist with such planning. For Muslim clients, each plan must be evaluated carefully for compliance with Islamic finance rules and the laws of inheritance.

2. 529 Plans

IRC section 529 was established in 1996 under the Small Business Job Protection Act to provide a tax-advantaged mechanism for families to set aside funds for future college costs. Since that time, these programs have become popular, and every U.S. state sponsors at least one plan.

There are two types of 529 plans: prepaid-tuition plans and college-savings plans. Under the prepaid-tuition plan, which is typically offered by individual qualified higher educational institutions, payments made to in-state public colleges will be credited against future qualified higher education expenses. The plans also lock into place the current cost of tuition, which typically provides significant savings over future costs.

A college-savings plan, on the other hand, is a savings program administered by the state for the purpose of paying qualified higher educational expenses at any eligible educational institution. It functions much like a 401(k) or IRA in that contributions are invested and will increase or decrease depending on the performance of the fund.

Participation in a 529 plan can provide substantial benefits but also involves some costs with respect to control of one's assets.

A contribution to a 529 plan account on behalf of the designated beneficiary is treated as a completed, present-interest gift for tax purposes. A donor may contribute the full annual exclusion gift amount ($15,000 in 2019) every year to the 529 account free of any gift taxes and may choose to take a special election that allows him or her to make five years' worth of annual exclusion gifts in one year free of any gift taxes. If the donor dies during this five-year period, the donor's gross estate will include a portion of the 529 contribution allocable to the tax years after the donor's date of death.

Example:
Haroon invests $70,000 in a 529 plan for the benefit of his daughter, with $14,000 (in 2018) allocable to the present year and the balance to four future years. Haroon dies that year. Four years' worth of his gifts, or $56,000, would be included in his estate for gift-tax purposes.

In the above example, if Haroon had lived the entire five-year period, the funds would be excluded from his estate for estate- and gift-tax purposes.[55]

For the generation-skipping tax, contributions made will be considered a present-interest gift. Similar to the gift-tax treatment described previously, five years of annual exclusion gifts may be considered gifts so long as an election is made in a timely filed gift-tax return. Generation-Skipping Transfer (GST) tax issues may arise, however, if contributions exceed available GST exclusion amounts, or when a beneficiary is changed to one who is two or more generations below that of the donor.

While there is no federal tax deduction on contributions to 529 plans, some states may offer state income-tax deductions or credits for such contributions. The major income-tax benefit is that income and gain within the accounts are not taxable so long as distributions are made for qualified educational expenses. These distributions are tax-free to the owner and beneficiary.

One remarkable feature of 529 plans is that they typically constitute a completed gift for transfer-tax purposes. At the same time, the owner maintains a significant level of control over the account and can change beneficiaries at will. Furthermore, the owner can designate a successor owner and can even withdraw his or her money, albeit subject to penalties on the earnings (not the principal). Thus, unlike with other completed gifts, the owner of a 529 plan continues to control the account in important ways. Upon death, the account transfers to the individual designated by the plan owner. If no successor is designated, the 529 plan may become a probate asset.

55. 26 U.S.C. § 529(c)(2)(B) (2018).

3. Planning with a 529 Account

As a practical matter, educational expenses are not always allocated equally among children within a family. One child may never attend college while another might go on to graduate or professional school. Perhaps one child attends an expensive private school while another earns a full scholarship at an in-state institution. Fortunately, 529 plans are flexible enough to allow for parents to change their beneficiaries based upon a child's need. If there are no educational expenses or if need is greater somewhere else, the funds do not need to be used for qualified educational purposes and can simply be withdrawn after payment of applicable taxes and penalties.

For most clients, 529 plans are a desirable asset, with some significant caveats. For Muslim families seeking to ensure that their assets are invested in a manner consistent with Islamic principles, these state-sponsored plans unfortunately do not have enough investment flexibility to allow for this. Individuals who contribute to 529 plans are prohibited from retaining full investment control of 529 plan assets. That is, the owner cannot dictate to the trustee how to invest the monies he or she has deposited. Rather, most 529 plans offer a limited range of mutual funds from which account owners can choose. Choices that meet all the stringent Islamic financial ethics rules are never included. Because investments cannot be made consistent with Islamic financial ethics, many Muslim families will choose not to participate in 529 plans.

Nonetheless, under Islamic inheritance law, the account owner of a 529 plan is the owner of the assets, and these assets must be distributed in a manner consistent with Islamic inheritance law upon the owner's death. Furthermore, the account owner must pay *zakat* on the asset while he or she is alive.

If the 529 plan allows, the successor account owner should also serve as the trustee of the plan owner's RLT. This will permit the most efficient distribution of plan accounts so that plan assets are used for qualified educational purposes while conforming to Islamic inheritance law.

4. Coverdell Savings Accounts

A Coverdell Education Savings Account, formerly known as an "education IRA," is established to fund "qualified educational expenses" for a beneficiary under 18 years or with special needs.[56] The standards for what constitutes a qualified educational expense under a Coverdell account are very

56. 26 U.S.C. § 530 (2018).

similar to the 529 account requirements described previously. Like a 529 plan, contributions are not tax-deductible. The key advantage is that these accounts can grow tax-free.

Coverdell accounts are less popular than 529 plans due to their annual contribution limit of $2,000. This limit may be further reduced or completely phased out depending on the income of the donor.

When the beneficiary of a Coverdell account reaches the age of 30, he or she will be entitled to any unused amount remaining in the account, unless the beneficiary has special needs. The owner of the account can also change the beneficiaries to other family members under 30 or to a special-needs beneficiary, though with less flexibility than a 529 plan. Importantly, unlike a 529 plan, a donor cannot withdraw his or her funds once they are deposited in a Coverdell account. Thus, assets inside a Coverdell account belong to the beneficiary and need not be distributed at the donor's death in a manner consistent with Islamic inheritance law.

M. Life Insurance and Annuities

For many Americans, life insurance is a vital component of financial and estate planning. Not only does it provide immediate liquidity to an estate for payment of taxes and debts, but it also bestows an "instant estate" on beneficiaries who may not have significant assets of their own.

Life insurance products can range from very simple to incredibly complex and can be difficult for clients to understand. They come in many varieties, some of which are branded and trademarked by commercial insurance companies; others may include components specifically designed for individual clients.

Most Muslim jurists hold that the majority of conventional life insurance products are impermissible because they contain aspects of *riba* (interest or usury) and *gharar* (excessive speculation). We will expand on this a little later. Nonetheless, because many American Muslims do own such products, one must include them in the Islamic estate-planning calculus. Accordingly, we will discuss the process for distributing life insurance proceeds to a client's Islamic heirs as well as the use of irrevocable life insurance trusts under Islamic law.

1. An Introduction to Life Insurance

Life insurance is a contract between an insurance company and an insured under which the insured agrees to make regular payments (or premiums) to the insurance company in exchange for the company's promise to pay a sum of money to the insured's beneficiaries upon his or her death. Life insurance differs from other forms of conventional insurance such as property, medical, and casualty insurance in that the latter are not intended as part of a financial-planning portfolio but simply to insure against a specific form of loss. Life insurance, meanwhile, is marketed as an effective investment product and a means to provide for one's family after death.

There are two basic categories of life insurance: (1) term life insurance and (2) permanent (or whole) life insurance, which includes a savings component.

2. Term Life Insurance

Term life insurance is a common type of insurance policy: The insurance company promises to pay the insured's beneficiaries a fixed payout if the insured dies within a specified period or term (usually five, ten, or 20 years). This payment is known as the face value or death benefit of the policy. If the client outlives the term, the policy lapses and the beneficiaries receive nothing. The premiums in a term life insurance policy are typically less expensive than in a whole or permanent life insurance policy, though the relative affordability will depend on certain factors, such as an insured's age and health.

3. Permanent/Whole Life Insurance

As the name suggests, permanent (or whole) life insurance policies extend over the policyholder's lifetime rather than expiring after a fixed term. That is, so long as the insured continues to make premium payments, he or she will remain insured despite any changes in his or her health. Further, the premiums in a permanent/whole life insurance policy are invested, and the policy develops a cash value that appreciates over time through the accrual of interest, dividends, or variable investment income. The interest and earnings on such policies are generally not taxable, and the policyholder can opt to use this money as security for a loan, to pay policy premiums later in life, or to transfer wealth to his or her heirs at death. This ability to grow wealth and pass it income tax–free to one's beneficiaries is perhaps the greatest appeal of such policies, particularly for high-net-worth clients.

Permanent life insurance policies come in many varieties, including (a) traditional whole life, (b) universal life, (c) variable life, and (d) variable universal life.

a. Traditional Whole Life Policies

This is the simplest form of permanent life insurance. A traditional whole life policy contains both a savings component and a death benefit. Because the annual premiums and death benefit remain the same for the duration of the insured's life, the cost of the premium is often higher than other types of policies.

b. Universal Life Policies

Universal life policies are often described as a hybrid between term and whole life policies. The savings component generally earns a stipulated rate of interest that adjusts annually. Once there is sufficient cash value in the account, the insured may use funds from the account to pay the annual premiums. An insured also has the option to adjust premiums and death benefits based on his or her financial situation.

c. Variable Life Policies

Variable life policies allow an insured to invest his or her savings component in stocks, bonds, and money-market mutual funds. To account for the inherent risk of these policies—investments can depreciate rather than appreciate over time—insurance companies may adjust the death benefits they pay.

d. Variable Universal Life Policies

A variable universal life policy is a hybrid of a variable and universal life policy, meaning there are lots of moving parts. Under such a policy, an insured can choose how and where to invest and adjust both premium payments and death benefits.

4. Irrevocable Life Insurance Trusts

As previously indicated, one of the biggest advantages of life insurance is that proceeds pass to beneficiaries free of income tax. Nonetheless, for estate-tax purposes, the entire death benefit is still considered part of the policyholder's taxable estate.

In the case of a potentially taxable estate, clients should place their life insurance policies inside an Irrevocable Life Insurance Trust, or ILIT, to remove the death benefit from the estate. Since the ILIT will serve as both the owner and beneficiary of the life insurance policy, it will not be considered part of the client's estate.

To make premium payments using an ILIT, the grantor makes a tax-free gift to the trustee of the ILIT for the benefit of each of the trust beneficiaries. The trustee then issues notices known as Crummey letters to individual beneficiaries of the trust, informing them that a gift has been made for their benefit, and unless they elect to withdraw the gift within a fixed number of days, the trustee shall use these gifts to pay the insurance premium.

Upon the death of the insured, the trustee of an ILIT collects the insurance proceeds and distributes them to the beneficiaries per the grantor's instructions.

5. Life Insurance in Islam

While Islamic law does not prohibit risk pooling, most conventional insurance products contain two problematic components, namely *riba* (interest) and *gharar* (excessive speculation, often in the form of the sale of an undefined or unspecified product), that have caused most Muslim jurists to deem them impermissible in Islam.[57]

The prohibition against dealing in *riba* and *gharar* lies at the heart of Islamic financial ethics. Conventional insurance products contain various manifestations of *riba*, including the possibility of a contractually guaranteed payout as well as investment of premiums and insurance funds in certain financial instruments, such as bonds, which themselves may contain *riba*.

Insurance contracts also contain *gharar* because payouts are based on the occurrence of a contingency. For instance, when an insured outlives the period of time specified in a term life insurance policy, or when the policy lapses due to unpaid premiums, the insurance company acquires all the profit and the insured receives nothing. On the other hand, if the contingent event occurs shortly after the initiation of a policy, the insurance company is at a significant disadvantage. The speculative nature of this contract mimics that involved in other transactions forbidden in Islam, such as lotteries or other forms of gambling (*maysir*).

While Muslim jurists have sanctioned various forms of conventional insurance where legally required (e.g., health insurance and car insurance) or where the risk of exposure from not insuring may be catastrophic (e.g., professional liability insurance and property insurance), with few

57. *See generally* Frank E. Vogel & Samuel L. Hayes, III, Islamic Law and Finance: Religion, Risk, and Return 150 (1998).

exceptions, most scholars still assert that life insurance products are impermissible for Muslims.

A minority view holds that all forms of conventional insurance, including life insurance, are permissible, while others hold that they are permissible provided the insurance company invests proceeds in a *Sharia*-compliant manner. This requirement renders this third view illusory, however, as it does not appear any such products currently exist in the United States. For instance, any life insurance product that includes an interest-earning component or relies on interest-bearing investments as part of an investment contract (such as universal life and variable universal life insurance policies that invest in ways that violate Islamic ethics) would still be regarded as impermissible. While it is theoretically possible to create a variable or variable universal life policy that invests in *Sharia*-compliant investment vehicles, insurance companies in the United States do not generally structure their investments in a manner that complies with Islamic financial ethics, and we are not aware of any such products currently being marketed as acceptable for American Muslim investors.

Nonetheless, a blanket prohibition on life insurance runs the risk of overlooking the important social function it serves in abating the significant financial loss families and businesses face when an individual dies. Recognizing these realities, certain jurists analogize the purchase of life insurance to hiring a security guard to protect valuables from being stolen. Though the likelihood of theft may be low, hiring a security guard is not seen as a speculative gamble but rather as a necessary form of precaution.

As a practical matter, notwithstanding the disputes over its permissibility among Muslim scholars, life insurance continues to serve as an important component of many financial plans—not just for families but for businesses as well. For this reason, practitioners serving Muslim clients should keep themselves apprised of the ways in which such financial strategies intersect with Islam.

6. Life Insurance and the Islamic Law of Inheritance

The death benefit of a life insurance policy must be distributed to the policy owner's heirs according to the Islamic Law of Inheritance. If the policy is owned by an ILIT, the trust beneficiaries must be the grantor's Islamic heirs. Because distribution is tied to the death of the grantor, one cannot evade the Islamic Law of Inheritance, even where the policy is owned and distributed through an irrevocable trust. For this reason, life insurance policies may not be useful for Muslim clients who wish to name an individual, such as a spouse, as a sole beneficiary, unless the other heirs are compensated through other assets as memorialized in a separate property agreement.

7. Specific Examples of How Life Insurance Is Used

a. Payment of Debt and Taxes

One of the most significant benefits of life insurance is its potential to pay off a decedent's debts. In places such as California, debts incurred by either spouse during a marriage are owed by the "community" rather than by the borrowing spouse alone. This means that a surviving spouse in a community-property state will often be personally liable for the decedent's debt. Similarly, both spouses are equally liable for any jointly held debt in non-community-property states. An important consequence of these arrangements is that the burden of the decedent's debt is left entirely on the surviving spouse rather than being distributed among the decedent's beneficiaries.

Additionally, life insurance can be an effective tool to cover state or federal estate taxes that may be due on a decedent's death.

b. Funding Special Needs Trusts

Special-needs beneficiaries can present exceptional issues in Islamic estate planning. While Special Needs Trusts (SNTs) are acceptable estate-planning devices for the purpose of Islamic inheritance law, parents of special-needs children often prefer to fund SNTs through life insurance. Since clients often have multiple Islamic heirs, the requirement that life insurance be distributed consistent with the Islamic Law of Inheritance may conflict with the goal of benefiting one particular beneficiary.

There are, of course, ways to fund an SNT other than life insurance, such as lifetime gifting. For example, if the client has adult children, he or she can invite them to donate to the SNT of their sibling without altering their status as beneficiaries of their parents' trust.

c. Buy-Sell Agreement Financing

Business partners often use life insurance to fund buy-sell agreements. In general, such agreements are either entity-purchase agreements or cross-purchase agreements. The purpose behind such agreements is to pass the decedent's business assets on to his or her beneficiaries while enabling the enterprise to operate within its own succession plan according to the aspirations of its owners. While life insurance is nonessential to a buy-sell agreement, many Muslim clients will have acceded to such an arrangement through the course of their business dealings or may otherwise view life insurance as an appropriate way to fund such an agreement.

Buy-sell agreements generally seek to serve the interests of both the business and the decedent's family by aspiring to fairly evaluate the decedent's business interest and fund distributions to the decedent's family accordingly. Assuming the estate-planning and relevant agreements are properly documented, this inheritance can easily be distributed pursuant to the Islamic Law of Inheritance.

8. *Takaful*—A *Sharia*-Compliant Alternative to Conventional Insurance

In its purest form, insurance is not an investment contract but rather a contract with an organization that pools risk. An agreement to insure a building against the risk of fire, for example, is just that—a contract stipulating that, in exchange for the payment of regular premiums, the insurance company will compensate the claimant in the event of a certain contingency, in this case, the building's catching on fire. Unlike life insurance, however, such products are not sold as investment products or marketed as part of a financial-planning portfolio but rather are touted as an intelligent mechanism for decreasing liability exposure and protecting the claimant from a specific form of loss. The problem from an Islamic perspective, however, is that such policies still contain impermissible elements of *gharar* and *riba*.

To resolve this problem, financial institutions in many Muslim-majority countries have developed an Islamically permissible form of cooperative insurance known as *takaful* (literally, "solidarity").

Based on the Islamic concept of *ta'awun*, or mutual assistance, *takaful* is a true risk-sharing mechanism in which participants (i.e., policyholders) pool resources (i.e., premiums) to subsidize each other's risk and assist one another in the event of casualty or loss.[58] The insurance company, which functions more like a fund manager than a conventional insurance company, invests each policyholder's premium in a *Sharia*-compliant manner. In the event of a loss or qualifying contingency, each policyholder agrees to make a gift to the impacted individual to cover the associated costs.

58. *See generally* Hania Masud, *Takaful: An Innovative Approach to Insurance and Islamic Finance*, 32 J. Int'l L. 1133 (2014).

Although there are currently no widely marketed *takaful* products in the United States, given the rapid growth of the Islamic finance sector internationally, we anticipate such products will eventually make their way to U.S. markets in the coming years.

9. Annuities

Annuities are another popular component of long-term financial and estate planning. Commercial annuities are essentially the opposite of life insurance. Whereas life insurance is intended to protect one's family against financial loss incurred upon death, annuities are designed as a safety net against financial loss from outliving one's wealth by providing a guaranteed income stream for life or a number of years in exchange for a lump sum payment up front. Annuities are frequently marketed to older individuals as a better investment than life insurance, as they may be relied on for funds throughout retirement and not just for when no other money exists.

There are several types of annuity products on the market. Variable annuities, for instance, are used as an investment tool offering tax deferral, though often with higher fees than other investment products. Fixed annuities are designed to provide a lifetime payout or payments for a fixed number of years at a predefined interest rate.

In general, annuities are considered impermissible under Islamic law, as the guaranteed payment is a form of *riba*. Even where the underlying investment is invested in a *Sharia*-compliant manner, the annuitization of payments renders the product impermissible.

Nonetheless, many Muslims will have annuities in their financial portfolio that must be accounted for in their estate plan. In the case of an income stream for life, payments will cease upon the death of the annuitant, and the beneficiaries will receive nothing. In the case of a joint-and-survivor annuity, payments will continue to be made to the survivor, even after the death of the spouse. This does not violate Islamic inheritance law since the contract is signed with a third party while the deceased spouse is still alive to take care of the surviving spouse. Finally, where no annuity payments have begun, any proceeds should be distributed to the annuitant's beneficiaries in accordance with the Islamic Law of Inheritance. Because insurance companies offer numerous variations of payments in the event an annuitant passes away, the annuitant and planner should carefully review the rules to ensure compliance with Islamic inheritance law.

CHAPTER 4

Planning for Incapacity and Death

Powers of Attorney, Advance Healthcare Directives, and Funeral Arrangements

A comprehensive estate plan accounts not only for a client's physical assets and heirs but also his or her very body and life. As advances in medicine and technology now enable people to live longer than ever before, the likelihood that an individual will face some period of diminished capacity during his or her lifetime is similarly increased. At the same time, the cost of healthcare continues to rise, and outstanding medical bills are now one of the greatest causes of bankruptcies in the United States.[1]

For this reason, it is imperative for clients to have a financial plan in place to prepare for incapacity or long-term illness. In addition, clients who wish to exert influence during a period of incapacity may do so by preparing advance directives and appointing individuals whom they trust to make important financial and healthcare decisions on their behalf.

1. Dan Mangan, *Medical Bills Are the Biggest Cause of US Bankruptcies*, CNBC (June 25, 2013), https://www.cnbc.com/id/100840148.

Muslim scholars, physicians, and bioethicists have provided guidelines with respect to end-of-life care, organ donations, funeral instructions, and disposition of a decedent's body, all of which come into play when developing a Muslim client's advance healthcare directives. Just as cultural competency is a critical component of a physician's care, an estate-planning attorney must also familiarize him- or herself with these rules and preferences in order to draft a plan that effectively encapsulates the client's wishes.

A. Incapacity Planning

1. Medicaid Planning and Long-Term Care

Muslim families, like other Americans, may have to contend with long-term medical expenses that can sometimes have a catastrophic impact on their finances. Nursing-home care can easily deplete a lifetime of savings. Options for families include exhausting personal savings, long-term care insurance, or Medicaid—a government program that covers some long-term care costs.

Since Medicaid is a needs-based program, many middle-class families have turned to legal strategies to qualify for Medicaid and preserve exempt assets from Medicaid recovery after death.

In general, Medicaid—or similar state programs, such as Medi-Cal in California—requires an individual to own less than $2,000 in assets to qualify.[2] Because Medicaid is administered by individual states—though funded with federal support and mandates—there is some degree of diversity as to how each state's program is administered.

The most obvious method of qualifying for Medicaid is to purposefully impoverish oneself by giving away property in advance of qualification. The Deficit Reduction Act of 2005 resulted in substantial changes to Medicaid qualifications and extended a series of look-back and estate-recovery rules to discourage the giving of gifts to obtain Medicaid qualification. Other Medicaid-planning techniques, such as the use of annuities and life estates, were severely hampered as well. In practice, however,

2. *Medi-Cal General Property Limitations*, Cal. Health & Human Servs. Agency, http://www.dhcs.ca.gov/formsandpubs/forms/Forms/MC%20Information%20Notices/MC007ENG(0414).pdf (last accessed Sept. 5, 2018).

some states have chosen to closely follow federal mandates while others have not.

As a general rule, impoverishing an individual without his or her consent is impermissible in Islam. Medicaid qualification is not an adequate purpose by itself. It would be acceptable, however, to transfer an incapacitated grantor's assets to irrevocable trusts so long as the trust beneficiaries are the grantors' Islamic heirs and the assets are not immediately transferred for use by the beneficiaries but rather made available after death.

Further, some clients who would benefit from Medicaid planning lack legal capacity to make dispositions of property to qualify for the program. It may therefore be necessary to address Medicaid qualifications through a conservatorship, a successor trustee, or an attorney-in-fact under a power of attorney.

The following section is far from a primer on Medicaid planning but rather seeks to highlight the implications of Islamic inheritance law for such planning.

a. ABLE Act

Many individuals with special needs require public assistance. The income threshold for these needs-based services is often very low. This criterion often prevents individuals dependent on public benefits from accumulating savings of any kind, as doing so would hamper their ability to receive government benefits. In many cases, savings too meager to cover even one month's expenses are enough to render an individual ineligible for needed services.

The Achieving a Better Life Experience (ABLE) Act is a notable exception to this rule. It allows individuals disabled at the age of 26 or younger—or their families—to establish an ABLE savings account that would not affect the disabled party's eligibility for certain government benefits.

If an individual state has adopted the ABLE Act, a person's Medicaid benefits will never cease, regardless of the size of his or her ABLE account, though Social Security disability benefits would cease after the first $100,000.

Many state programs are tied to Social Security disability eligibility. After the death of an account owner, Medicaid would have to be reimbursed for medical expenses. If the account is large enough that Medicaid is satisfied without taking the entire balance, the rest is distributed to the beneficiary's heirs. For Muslim clients, the beneficiaries of the account should be designated in accordance with Islamic inheritance law.

b. Special Needs Trusts

A Special Needs Trust (SNT), or Supplemental Needs Trust, as it is sometimes called, is a trust intended to provide supplementary benefits to a beneficiary without rendering the beneficiary ineligible for public assistance. There are two types of SNTs: first-party trusts and third-party trusts.

First-party SNTs are created by the beneficiary and are designed to benefit individuals with special needs who qualify for—or expect to one day require—public benefits available only to people with limited resources. Upon the death of the beneficiary, the state Medicaid agency must be reimbursed for its expenditures on the beneficiary's behalf.

On the other hand, third-party SNTs—the more common of the two trusts—are created by the beneficiary's family members. These trusts are typically designed as part of a parent or relative's estate plan to help a family member with special needs receive gifts or inheritances without disqualifying him or her for government assistance. A key advantage of third-party SNTs is that the government need not be reimbursed for Medicaid payments on behalf of the beneficiary. This is because, from the government's perspective, the assets in the trust never truly belonged to the beneficiary.

From the perspective of Islamic inheritance law, however, assets inside an SNT do belong to the beneficiary and thus would be subject to distribution in accordance with Islamic inheritance law. Regardless of how the trust is structured (i.e., first-party or third-party), if there are any assets remaining in the trust after the government has been reimbursed (if necessary), the assets must be distributed to the beneficiary's Islamic heirs upon death.

Example:

Ali and Rizwana create a third-party SNT to assist their autistic daughter Sultana. Although Sultana lacks any direct control over how the funds are spent in order to protect the assets from becoming an available resource for public assistance eligibility, the trust should, nonetheless, name Sultana's heirs under Islamic law as the beneficiaries of the trust upon her death.

---

2. Gifting in a Final Illness (*Maradul Maut*)

Islamic law does not generally regulate inter vivos gifting. There is no need to gift assets in a manner consistent with Islamic inheritance law, as completed lifetime gifts remove an asset from the donor's estate.

One notable exception, however, is that a person may not gift more than one-third of his or her estate during his or her final illness, known as *maradul maut*. The term "final illness" is not synonymous with "terminal illness." Rather, Hanafi jurists define *maradul maut* either as a period in which a person is on his or her deathbed and unable to perform routine daily functions or as a situation in which a healthy individual is facing the possibility of imminent death.

Under this definition, a patient with cancer or Alzheimer's would not automatically be considered to be in *maradul maut*, whereas a soldier in the thick of battle or a convicted criminal facing execution by the government might be. Because people routinely survive near-death experiences, whether a gift was given during a donor's *maradul maut* is often a post hoc determination. To this end, jurists have provided certain guidelines to determine what is not considered *maradul maut*:

- An illness that does not impede daily activities, such as prayer or leaving the home
- An illness that lasts longer than one Islamic calendar year (355 days)

B. Powers of Attorney

Incapacity planning can also involve the preparation of a springing power of attorney, which comes into play upon an official declaration by physicians that a person is no longer competent to make decisions for him- or herself. From an Islamic perspective, there are no specific issues unique to a power of attorney.

That said, due to advances in medicine and technology, people may now live for an extended period of time in an incapacitated state where they are unable to make independent volitional choices. For this reason we recommend memorializing many of the client's financial preferences in the power of attorney form in order to guide the agent's actions. A few examples of such clauses could include an instruction outlining the Islamic prohibition on dealing with interest, a requirement that the agent only invest in *Sharia*-compliant securities, and an express statement of a principal's desire to continue supporting certain charities that the client supported when he or she was healthy.

C. End-of-Life Care

Advances in modern medicine have created situations in which individuals may frequently be kept alive in minimally conscious states. Determining whether medical interventions are appropriate and necessary in a given situation and when to forgo further treatment are some of the most challenging and sensitive decisions for clients and medical providers alike.

Often these preferences are dictated by religious considerations.[3] In Islam, there is a delicate balance between seeking to fulfill the *Sharia*'s objective of preserving human life and the notion of patiently enduring and accepting God's will. Under classical Islamic law, jurists in four Sunni schools of law all held that seeking medical treatment in the case of illness or injury was not obligatory, unless there was certainty that forgoing treatment would cause death.[4] Modern juristic bodies meanwhile have held that Muslims are required to do all they can to ensure the survival of a viable life in danger[5] but should also cease the provision of life-sustaining medical treatment where there is no hope of revival.

Central to the determination of whether to prolong life through artificial means is the Islamic definition of death itself. Keeping pace with modern scientific norms, most of today's Islamic scholars recognize two forms of physical death: (1) permanent cessation of cardiopulmonary activity and (2) permanent cessation of brain activity.[6] The latter definition

3. *See generally Views on End of Life Medical Treatments*, Pew Research Ctr. (Nov. 21, 2013), http://www.pewforum.org/2013/11/21/views-on-end-of-life-medical-treatments/ (last accessed Oct. 5, 2018).

4. Aasim Padela & Omar Qureshi, *Islamic Perspectives on Clinical Intervention near the End-of-Life: We Can but Must We?*, 20(4) Med., Health Care & Phil. 545, 550 (2017), *available at* https://doi.org/10.1007/s11019-016-9729-y (last accessed Sept. 5, 2018).

5. See *Resolutions and Recommendations of the Council of the Islamic Fiqh Academy 1985–2000*, https://uaelaws.files.wordpress.com/2012/05/resolutions-and-recommendations-of-the-council-of-the-islamic-fiqh-academy.pdf (last accessed Sept. 5, 2018), a meeting of Sunni and Shia jurists, which held that seeking medical treatment is obligatory when neglecting treatment may result in the person's death, loss of an organ, disability, or (if the illness is contagious) harm to others.

6. Aasim Padela & Afshan Mohiuddin, *Ethical Obligations and Clinical Goals in End-of-Life Care: Deriving a Quality-of-Life Construct Based on the Islamic Concept of Accountability before God (Taklif)*, 15(1) Am. J. Bioethics 3, 5 (2015).

is particularly important in light of advancements in medicine that could potentially sustain the body of a brain-dead person indefinitely. Because most Islamic scholars view brain-death as death itself, the prevailing view is that Muslims may cease life support in such cases. Similarly, if a patient is in a permanent vegetative state, defined as "a clinical state of unconsciousness in which there is no evidence of self- or environmental awareness and no evidence of movement requiring planning or cognition," Islamic bioethics dictates that a physician is under no obligation to initiate or continue providing care.[7] According to jurists who hold these views, "prolonging mere physiological life—or more appropriately the physiological functions of the body—is not consonant with Sunni Islamic bioethical values."[8]

There are times when life-saving medical intervention is less urgent than where an imminent failure of the circulatory, respiratory, or neurological functions is involved. While the patient's quality of life must always be taken into consideration—namely whether further treatment would "uphold an individual's ability to perform deeds that can attain God's pleasure (such as worship)"[9] in these nonemergency situations—the focus of the patient, his or her caretakers, and/or the attendant physician(s) is likely to center on the safety and efficacy of the treatment.

Finally, with respect to the various forms of life support, Islamic law is concerned primarily with the potential byproducts of such measures rather than their particular modality. Specifically, Islam prohibits treatments that would result in undue harm to others, as well as those that involve wrongful profiteering. For example, blood transfusions are permissible so long as the donor is not harmed and there is no buying or selling of the blood. This moral imperative to protect the interests of others and avoid commoditizing physically necessary treatments carries over into the Islamic view of organ donations, which is discussed in more detail in the coming pages.

D. DNR and Euthanasia

Individuals may decline life-saving medical treatment in advance by executing a Do Not Resuscitate (DNR) order. This legal document empowers the client to prospectively refuse resuscitation—specifically CPR or

7. *Id.* at 10.
8. *Id.*
9. *Id.* at 7.

Advanced Cardiovascular Life Support (ACLS)—if his or her life became dependent on it.

Here, again, a Muslim is able to take matters into his or her own hands and prevent intervention in situations where there is no doubt he or she would fail to fully recover from the underlying cause (i.e., illness, injury, or other extreme weakness) or where an intervention would have "marginal utility and cause great disruption to the body."[10]

To the contrary, however, third parties (such as family members and close friends) are unable to impose a DNR order on the client unless the client is incapacitated and suffering from a chronic, untreatable medical condition at the time of the incident, giving rise to the need for resuscitation, as verified by a proper medical authority or authorities.

Finally, while Muslims may decline life-saving interventions on their behalf, they may not proactively seek life-ending ones. The Islamic proscription on euthanasia (or assisted suicide) is expressly stated in the Quran[11] and comports with the religion's general emphasis on the sanctity of human life.

E. Organ Donation and Transplantation

As in other areas of life, the views of Islamic scholarship on organ donations have evolved over time and are far from unanimous. While many reputable organizations and leaders within the Muslim faith have come to accept and even encourage organ donation as a form of charity on the part of both living and posthumous donors, others withhold or otherwise qualify their approval of harvesting from the dead, primarily out of concern over desecration of the human corpse. This confusion surrounding the propriety of organ donations has resulted in a shortage of ethnic donors in countries such as the UK, where Muslims from India, Pakistan, and Bangladesh wait an average of a year longer than their non-Muslim counterparts for organ transplants.[12]

Complicating matters in this area is the ongoing debate regarding the Islamic definition of death. As previously mentioned, a minority of

10. Padela & Qureshi, *supra* note 5, at 555.

11. *The Qur'an: English Translation and Parallel Arabic Text* 4:29 (M.A.S. Abdel Haleem trans., 2005) ("O you who have believed . . . do not kill yourselves [or one another]. Indeed, Allah is to you ever Merciful."); *id.* at 2:195 ("[D]o not contribute to your destruction with your own hands.").

12. John McManus, *Hospitals Urge Muslims to Donate Organs*, BBC (June 17, 2015), http://www.bbc.com/news/uk-33155326.

Muslim scholars continues to view cardiopulmonary activity as the sole standard for assessing whether a person has passed. According to this perspective, it would be impermissible to harvest organs from an individual based on brain death alone.

Because of the lack of consistency among experts, Muslim clients may take varying positions on whether they wish to donate their organs upon death. In addition, it may be advisable for the client's living will to stipulate his or her desired definition of death for organ donation. Alternatively, a client may wish to express his or her deference to an attendant Muslim physician(s) in making this decision.

Islamic scholars differ regarding the receipt of organ donations as well. Specifically, there is a lack of consensus surrounding the suitability of certain sources of organs (and tissue) for transplantation into a Muslim.

With respect to human sources, most scholars agree that transplantation from a non-Muslim to a Muslim is permissible. Some also approve of animal sources, including pigs, whose consumption the Quran explicitly forbids. The justification cited by those who condone this apparently sacrilegious act—and by those in favor of organ donations in general—is the Islamic principle of *idtirar*, or the affirmation that necessity renders the forbidden permissible. Due to lack of consensus in this area, the estate-planning attorney should advise his or her Muslim clients to consult their own religious advisors to determine how to address questions surrounding organ transplantation in their living wills.

Lastly, consistent with U.S. law,[13] Islam forbids Muslims from financially benefiting from organ donations.

F. Funeral and Burial Arrangements

Islamic law requires that a decedent be washed, shrouded, and prayed upon by a group of Muslims as soon as practicable after death in a ritual prayer known as a *janazah*. Cremation is not an acceptable form of disposing of the human body. Rather, the deceased should be buried directly into the earth immediately after the *janazah* prayer, preferably in a nearby Muslim cemetery or a cemetery that has a designated area for members of the Muslim community.

13. 42 U.S.C. § 274e (2018).

Beyond that, specific customs vary from community to community. Some clients may prefer to provide specific burial instructions,[14] while others may omit them altogether. The latter case is particularly likely for those with Muslim families, since their community may already have an established system for burial. However, clients whose families are not Muslim and those living outside well-established Muslim communities will likely need to specify their wishes to ensure compliance with their faith and avoid potential disputes among surviving family members with respect to the disposition of their bodies. Sample clauses have been included in Appendix B.

G. Cadavers and Public Display of Corpses

Many Muslim scholars who hold organ donations to be permissible have taken the position that human remains must be buried and that cadaver donation is *haram*, or impermissible. On the other hand, the Islamic Medical Association of North America has held that Muslims may donate their bodies to science to be used as cadavers through a testamentary document and eschew traditional burial.[15] This disparity among the experts means that Muslim estate-planning clients will likely differ in their views as well, and the attorney should act to implement those views accordingly.

While it is unlikely Muslim clients will wish to donate their bodies to science, it is probably even less likely they will desire to have them displayed in museums, as with the traveling Body Worlds exhibit that makes its way across the United States. Nonetheless, we note that such practices are almost unanimously denounced by Muslim scholars as an abasement of the human form, and therefore Muslim clients may wish to expressly prohibit such use of their remains in their estate-planning documents.

14. For example, a client may request that family members not wail over his or her body and instead recite certain prayers.

15. *The Position of Islamic Medical Association of North America on Issues of Medical Ethics*, HHLF,http://hhlf.org/the-position-of-islamic-medical-association-of-north-america-on-issues-of-medical-ethics/ (last accessed Oct. 3, 2018).

CHAPTER

5

Disposition of Property at Death

Preparing for death and the afterlife is a fundamental tenet of Islam. In a famous narration, the Prophet Muhammad exhorted his followers to prepare an estate plan, stating that any believer who has something of value should not allow two nights to pass without preparing a written will governing its disposition.[1]

The obligation to distribute one's assets in accordance with Islamic law—particularly in a country where the default intestacy laws are markedly different—is laid out in the Quran itself.[2] Moreover, whereas all other religious injunctions described in the Quran—ranging from daily prayers, fasting in the month of Ramadan, and mandatory almsgiving to the pilgrimage to Mecca—are only mentioned in general terms,[3] the instructions relating to inheritance are described in remarkable detail. The fourth chapter of the Quran, titled "*Surah Al-Nisaa*" ("The Women"), addresses laws relating to domestic relations and emphasizes the protection and

1. Sahih Muslim, Book 13, no. 3987, *available at* https://sunnah.com/muslim/25 (last accessed Oct. 4, 2018).

2. *The Qur'an: English Translation and Parallel Arabic Text* 2:180 (M.A.S. Abdel Haleem trans., 2005) ("Prescribed for you when death approaches [any] one of you if he leaves wealth [is that he should make] a bequest for the parents and near relatives according to what is acceptable—a duty upon the righteous.").

3. The details of how to specifically fulfill those obligations are found in the *Sunnah* (prophetic tradition) and in the books of *Fiqh* (Islamic jurisprudence).

preservation of the rights of orphans and women and contains a complex intestacy scheme describing how a Muslim's estate must be distributed upon his or her death. The Prophet Muhammad encouraged his followers to study the subject, known in Arabic as *'ilm al-Fara'id*, or the knowledge of predetermined shares, emphatically stating, "Learn and teach the laws of inheritance for verily it is half of all knowledge."[4]

Upon a Muslim's death, his or her estate—defined as all of the person's wealth, possessions, property, and liabilities on the date of death—should be administered in the following order:

1. Payment of burial and funeral expenses
2. Settlement of obligations
3. Discretionary distribution (*wasiyah* share)
4. Distribution of residuary estate (*faraid* share)

Practice Pointer: Clarifying Ownership in Advance
One of the most important components of Islamic estate planning is to define the client's estate at the initial planning stage. For married couples, it should be clear who owns what. This can be accomplished through a property agreement or, in the case of a joint Revocable Living Trust (RLT), within the trust schedules. In community property states, for instance, a deceased spouse's gross estate will typically consist of half of all community property as well as all the deceased spouse's separate property.

A. Burial and Funeral Expenses

When a Muslim dies, his or her body must be washed, prayed over, and buried in a manner prescribed by the *Sharia* as soon as possible, usually within 24 hours. Burial and funeral expenses are typically deducted from the estate, unless other family members step forward and cover the costs, which is consistent with state laws in the United States. If the decedent is a woman survived by her husband, however, the widower would be responsible for covering all burial and funeral costs. Additional details on burial and funeral counseling are discussed in Chapter 4.

4. Sunan Ibn Maajah, Vol. 4, Book 23, Hadith 2719, *available at* https://sunnah.com/urn/1271870 (last accessed Oct. 4, 2018).

B. Settlement of Obligations

After deducting burial and funeral expenses, but before making any distributions to heirs, Islamic law requires that an estate pay the decedent's debts. The practice of paying such debts is derived from a *Hadith*: "The soul of the deceased believer remains pending on account of the debt till it (the debt) is repayed."[5]

Islamically, debts can be divided into three categories: (a) debts owed to third parties, (b) unfulfilled religious obligations owed to God, and (c) claims of judgment creditors, which are not traditionally considered debts but are included here as a religious obligation that must be repaid.

1. Debts Owed to Third Parties

Islamic financial ethics views lending as a charitable activity and unequivocally discourages the voluntary assumption of debt.[6] The Prophet Muhammad famously stated, "Whoever dies free from three things—arrogance, cheating, and debt—will enter Paradise,"[7] and it is reported that he would not lead the funeral prayer of an individual until his or her debts had been paid off. Accordingly, when creating an estate plan for Muslim clients, it is important to establish a client's outstanding liabilities. The drafting attorney should include provisions reciting the client's intent to comply with the Islamic mandate that any debts that are not forgiven upon death—either automatically or through negotiation with the lender—must be repaid before any distributions are made to the residuary heirs. It is also advisable to include a schedule of debts alongside a schedule of assets that explains to the successor trustees which debts should be paid from the estate first.

For married couples, an oft-neglected debt that must be considered during the planning phase is a woman's *mahr*, or unpaid dower, if applicable. Recall that a *mahr* is part of a marital contract between a husband and

5. Jami` at-Tirmidhi, Book 7, Hadith 943, *available at* https://sunnah.com/riyadussaliheen/7/49 (last accessed Oct. 4, 2018).

6. Debts that involve the taking or payment of *riba*, which include most conventional debt-based contracts, are further emphatically condemned in several verses in the Quran. *See, e.g., The Qur'an, supra* note 2, at 2:275–276 ("[B]ut God has allowed trade and forbidden usury. Whoever, on receiving God's warning, stops taking usury may keep his past gains—God will be his judge—but whoever goes back to usury will be an inhabitant of the Fire, there to remain. God blights usury, but blesses charitable deeds with multiple increase: He does not love the ungrateful sinner.").

7. Jami` at-Tirmidhi, Vol. 3, Book 19, Hadith 1572, *available at* https://sunnah.com/tirmidhi/21/33 (last accessed Oct. 4, 2018).

wife and is considered a gift from the groom to the bride.[8] *Mahr* provisions are designed to protect women in the event of marital dissolution or their husband's death and to compensate them for their contribution to the marriage.[9] The *mahr* may range from a token cash gift to expensive jewelry or real estate, depending on the couple's desires and economic status. In many Muslim cultures, the *mahr* is often divided into two parts: an initial portion given at the wedding and a deferred portion paid upon a summary divorce or the death of the husband.[10] A deferred *mahr* is considered a legal debt on the husband and must be paid in full to a surviving widow before any distributions are made from the husband's estate.[11] For this reason we recommend including a copy of the couple's *mahr* agreement alongside a schedule of assets and liabilities.

In the case of mortgaged properties, those assets do not need to be liquidated. Rather, beneficiaries may inherit assets subject to a mortgage so long as they assume the obligation on the note.

2. Debts Owed to God (Unfulfilled Religious Obligations)

This category refers to religious obligations that a Muslim failed to perform during his or her lifetime. This includes unfulfilled prayers, missed fasts, unpaid *zakat* obligations, or an unperformed *Hajj*. Such debts should be deducted from the decedent's estate only if the decedent left instructions regarding their payment and must be taken out of the *wasiyah* share, which is capped at one-third of the decedent's estate.

These debts are most commonly relevant in the estate-planning context with respect to *zakat* and *Hajj*. In the case of retirement accounts, for instance, clients often do not have liquidity outside their 401(k) or IRA plans and thus may not be paying *zakat* annually on those assets. In such cases, a schedule may be attached to a revocable trust stating how much unpaid *zakat* should be distributed upon death from a client's *wasiyah* share.

Similarly, clients who have not performed the mandatory *Hajj* pilgrimage, despite having the physical and financial means to do so, may

8. Asifa Qureshi, *Rumors of the Sharia Threat Are Greatly Exaggerated: What American Judges Really Do with Islamic Family Law in Their Courtrooms*, 57 N.Y.L. Sch. L. Rev. 245, 249 (2012–13).

9. James Sonne, *Domestic Applications of* Sharia *and the Exercise of Ordered Liberty*, 45 Seton Hall L. Rev. 725, 734 (2015).

10. *Id.*

11. Note that U.S. courts would review the validity of *mahr* agreements under neutral principles whereby the presumption of freedom of contract is balanced against any public policy limits. *Id.* at 733.

want to include a provision in their estate plan to pay for another Muslim to go in their place should they pass away before performing the obligation. An ill client may be especially likely to request such a provision.

3. Claims from Judgment Creditors

Claims of judgment creditors for lawsuits arising from torts are not regarded as debts in the traditional Islamic sense. Accordingly, there are no religious restrictions on creating asset protection trusts to shield individual assets from future potential creditor claims. On the other hand, there remains a religious obligation to repay liabilities that the decedent voluntarily incurred, even if there is no such obligation under the law.

Example:
After a botched operation that left him incapacitated, Kyle sued his neurosurgeon, Dr. Firdaus, and was awarded a verdict of $75 million. Dr. Firdaus's malpractice coverage had a limit of $10 million per incident. Dr. Firdaus also had an outstanding bill to a contractor who had done some remodeling on her home for $300,000. After the verdict, Dr. Firdaus filed for bankruptcy and was able to pay the contractor only $100,000. She lost the building that housed her practice and some other assets but came nowhere close to paying for the verdict in full.

Fortunately for Dr. Firdaus, several years before the lawsuit, she had created an offshore Asset Protection Trust valued at $20 million in which she named herself the beneficiary. The trustee of the Asset Protection Trust does not owe anything to the judgment creditor, and under the terms of the trust, the trustee would not be obligated to pay the contractor either. However, under the Islamic Law of Inheritance, the debt to the contractor should be paid.

C. *Wasiyah*—Discretionary Share

A Muslim may dispose of only up to one-third of his or her estate through a *wasiyah*, or discretionary bequest upon his or her death. That is, rather than allowing the entire net estate (i.e., assets remaining after payment of funeral expenses and settlement of debts) to pass to his or her Islamic heirs according to Islam's mandatory succession rules, known as the *faraid*, a Muslim may dispose of up to one-third of his or her estate through a discretionary bequest to an individual who is not entitled to inherit as an Islamic heir, a charitable institution(s), or any combination thereof.

1. Basis of the *Wasiyah*

The Quran exhorts Muslims to leave a bequest to relatives: "[I]t is prescribed that he should make a proper bequest to parents and close relatives—a duty incumbent on those who are mindful of God."[12] The majority of Muslim jurists hold that the obligatory nature of the *wasiyah* in this verse was abrogated by subsequently revealed verses that state that the residuary shares are to be distributed only "after payment of any bequests or debts."[13]

Under Sunni law, this discretionary bequest is capped at one-third of the decedent's estate. When one of the Prophet's companions, Saad Bin Abi Waqqas, sought to bequeath the bulk of his estate to charity, the Prophet prevented him from doing so and limited the discretionary bequest to one-third, informing him that it was better to leave his heirs wealthy than to leave them as a burden on others:

> I was stricken by an ailment that led me to the verge of death. The Prophet came to pay me a visit. I said, "O God's Apostle! I have much property and no heir except my single daughter. Shall I give two-thirds of my property in charity?" He said, "No." I said, "Half of it?" He said, "No." I said, "One-third of it?" He said, "You may do so, though one-third is also too much, for it is better for you to leave your offspring wealthy than to leave them poor, asking others for help.[14]

2. Rules Relating to the *Wasiyah*

As described previously, a *wasiyah* must not exceed one-third of the decedent's estate. The bequests may be drafted in the form of a pecuniary gift, a percentage of the estate, or a specific item of property and should be

12. *The Qur'an, supra* note 2, at 2:180.

13. *The Qur'an, supra* note 2, at 4:11.

14. Sahih al-Bukhari, Vol. 8, Book 80, Hadith 725, *available at* https://sunnah.com/bukhari/85/10 (last accessed Oct. 4, 2018).

designated to allow the gift(s) to fail if the cumulative value of the *wasiyah* share exceeds one-third of the decedent's net estate.

When planning for a married couple, or where liquidity of the estate is an issue, a bequest may be made payable upon the death of the first spouse, upon the death of the second spouse, or in both circumstances.

A *wasiyah* may be directed to a particular individual (e.g., to my grandson), class of individuals (e.g., to all my grandchildren, in equal shares), a charitable beneficiary (e.g., to my local mosque), a group of charitable beneficiaries (e.g., to be distributed equally between the following three charitable organizations), or any combination thereof. When leaving a *wasiyah*, clients are not restricted by the rule that males receive double the share of similarly situated females and may distribute to all in equal shares.

According to classical Sunni tradition, a client may not use a *wasiyah* to disproportionately enhance the share of an Islamic heir. The rule is derived from an explicit tradition of the Prophet stating, "God has already given to each entitled relative his proper entitlement. Therefore, no bequest in favor of a legal [Islamic] heir."[15] While such a bequest is permitted according to some Shia jurists and is also codified into law in certain Muslim-majority countries, it is permitted according to Sunni scholars only where all beneficiaries consent to the enhanced legacy following the decedent's death.

3. Purposes of the *Wasiyah*

The *wasiyah* can serve a variety of estate-planning purposes for Muslim clients, including payment of unfulfilled religious obligations, distributions to non-Islamic heirs, distributions to non-Muslims, and charitable bequests.

a. *Payment of Unfulfilled Religious Obligations*

Unfulfilled religious obligations, also known as debts owed to God, are actions that a Muslim failed to complete properly during his or her lifetime. These may include unfulfilled prayers, missed fasts during the month of Ramadan, unpaid *zakat*, or an unperformed *Hajj* (assuming the person had the physical and financial means to complete the journey).

If a client wishes to ensure that these obligations are performed on his or her behalf or to instruct the trustee to pay a *fidyah*, or penalty, for each missed obligation, he or she would need to provide clear instructions to do

15. Sunan Abi Dawud, Book 17, Hadith 2864, *available at* https://sunnah.com/abudawud/18/9 (last accessed Oct. 4, 2018).

so as part of the *wasiyah* share, as such debts are capped at one-third of the decedent's gross estate.

Example:
Hamza is a 33-year-old executive at a technology startup in San Francisco. He and his wife Alia have two young children but do not have any other family in California. Although Hamza has ample financial means as well as the physical strength to perform the *Hajj*, he and Alia have been delaying their journey until the kids grow up and are no longer dependent on them.

While hiking through the mountains one day, Hamza has a heart attack and suddenly passes away. Pursuant to Hamza's *wasiyah*, which stipulated that Hamza had not yet performed *Hajj*, his trustee was able to identify someone who could perform the journey on Hamza's behalf using funds from Hamza's *wasiyah* share.

If Hamza lives longer and had already performed the sacred pilgrimage, he could easily edit the RLT schedule to reflect that this obligation is no longer outstanding.

b. Distributions to Non-Muslim Heirs

A *wasiyah* is a particularly useful tool for Muslim clients who wish to benefit an individual who would not ordinarily be entitled to inherit under Islamic law. Such individuals may include adopted children, stepchildren, and certain distant relatives.

In certain Muslim-majority countries, orphaned grandchildren—who would not be entitled to inherit from a decedent's *faraid* share if the decedent were survived by at least one son—receive an obligatory bequest from the decedent's *wasiyah* share, while others have sought to resolve this issue by establishing inheritance rights for orphaned grandchildren based upon the right of representation.[16]

---

16. Egypt, Syria, Tunisia, and Morocco have enacted such reforms. Pakistan, meanwhile, adopted the right of representation for lineal descendants, thereby providing the children of a predeceased child (male or female) a share of their grandparent's estate. *See* Lucy Carroll, *Orphaned Grandchildren in Islamic Law of Succession: Reform and Islamization in Pakistan*, 5(3) ISLAMIC L. & SOC'Y 409–47 (1998).

Example:
Sarah, a widow, is survived by two adopted children, Bilal and Nadia, and four biological grandchildren from her two sons, Ali and Hassan, both of whom predeceased her.

Sarah seeks counsel to help her draft an Islamic estate plan. Her attorney incorrectly treated Bilal and Nadia the same as Sarah's biological children and drafted Sarah's RLT to state that she was leaving one-third of her estate to Nadia and the remaining two-thirds to Bilal.

Under Islamic inheritance law, adopted children only inherit from their biological parents. Since Bilal and Nadia are not Sarah's biological children, they are only entitled to receive bequests from Sarah's *wasiyah* share, which would be collectively capped at one-third of Sarah's estate.[17] The remaining two-thirds should be distributed among Sarah's four biological grandchildren.

c. *Distributions to Non-Muslims*

Under Islamic inheritance law, a difference in religion between a decedent and a potential heir disqualifies that potential heir from inheriting from a Muslim decedent's *faraid* share. As such, if a client has non-Muslim relatives who would be entitled to inherit as Islamic heirs but for the difference in religion, the client may want to bequeath a share to them as part of the *wasiyah* share.

Note here that such bequests are not governed by the rule that males should receive double the share of similarly situated females, nor is an individual restricted by the share that he or she would otherwise receive as an Islamic heir, absent the difference in religion.

Example:
Brian, a Muslim man from Florida with three children from a previous marriage, intends to marry Katelyn, who is a Christian. Brian knows that Katelyn will not be eligible to inherit as an Islamic heir due to the difference in their religions. Brian and Katelyn execute a legally enforceable prenuptial agreement with

17. Note that the rule that a male heir receives double the share of a similarly situated female does not apply to bequests, so Sarah can leave Bilal and Nadia one-sixth each if she so chooses.

Katelyn waiving all rights to exercise an elective share in Brian's property. Brian does want Katelyn to receive a share of his wealth upon his death, however, and accordingly decides to leave a *wasiyah* bequest of one-fourth of his estate to Katelyn.

This bequest is permissible, even though it exceeds the share Katelyn would have received if she were Muslim, because she is not receiving Brian's mandatory share but rather a bequest in the form of a *wasiyah*. If Katelyn later converted to Islam, she would be entitled to inherit as an Islamic heir. Brian's *wasiyah* bequest would then fail, and Katelyn would receive her mandatory entitlement of one-eighth of Brian's estate.

d. *Charitable Bequests*

Finally, and perhaps most commonly, a major function of the *wasiyah* is the bequeathing of assets to charity.

In a famous *Hadith*, the Prophet Muhammad is reported to have said, "When a person dies, their good deeds come to an end, except three: ongoing charity, beneficial knowledge, and a righteous child who will pray for them."[18] Ongoing charity, or *sadaqah jariyah*, refers to a special type of charity that continues to benefit others, even after the donor's death. One of the most effective ways of leaving a *sadaqah jariyah* is through a charitable bequest in one's estate plan.

Such gifts may be in the form of an outright charitable bequest or, alternatively, a charitable trust for the benefit of a specific charity.

4. Incorporating the *Wasiyah* into an RLT or Last Will and Statements

The process of incorporating a *wasiyah* into a last will or RLT is fairly straightforward. The specific bequests should be stipulated in the will or RLT itself and should be paid after funeral expenses and outstanding debts and before any mandatory *faraid* distributions. If the *wasiyah* share is likely to change, for instance, when dealing with unfulfilled religious obligations, the drafting attorney may choose to incorporate the specific bequests as an attachment to a living trust or will.

---

18. Sunan an-Nisai, Vol. 4, Book 30, Hadith 3681, *available at* https://sunnah.com/nasai/30/41 (last accessed Oct. 4, 2018).

D. *Faraid*—Islamic Law's Mandatory System of Succession

After funeral expenses, debts, and *wasiyah* distributions have been satisfied, the balance of a decedent's estate is to be distributed to his or her Islamic heirs, based on their relationship to the decedent, in predetermined shares known as the *faraid*.[19] In many ways, these rules are analogous to various states' intestacy statutes in that they lay out in express detail how a decedent's assets are to be distributed to his or her heirs.

Unlike a statutory intestacy scheme, however, the Islamic Law of Inheritance is not simply a set of default rules. Historically, in most Muslim societies they were treated as nondiscretionary mandates that operated as a matter of law without the directive of the decedent or his or her heirs.[20] Of course, if a client wishes to comply with the Islamic Law of Inheritance in the United States, he or she must prepare an estate plan that memorializes those wishes.

The Quran ordains a set of fixed shares for each beneficiary based on gender, class, degree, and strength of blood relationship, as described in three verses of "*Surah Al-Nisaa*" ("The Women").[21]

1. Rights of Parents and Children

In Chapter 4, Verse 11, the Quran stipulates the shares for a decedent's parents and children:

> Concerning your children, God commands you that a son should have the equivalent share of two daughters. If there are only daughters, two or more should share two-thirds of the inheritance, if one, she should have half. Parents inherit a sixth each if the deceased leaves children; if he leaves no children and his parents are his sole heirs, his mother has a third, unless he has brothers, in which case she has a sixth. [In all cases, the distribution

19. *The Qur'an, supra* note 2, at 4:7 ("Men shall have a share in what their parents and closest relatives leave, and women shall have a share in what their parents and closest relatives leave, whether the legacy be small or large: this is ordained by God.").

20. Under classical Islamic law, an heir could disclaim his or her share of inheritance only after the death of the decedent.

21. Noel Coulson, *A Comparison of the Law of Succession in the Islamic and British Legal Systems*, 26(2) Am. J. Comp. L. 227, 227 (1978).

> comes] after payment of any bequests or debts. You cannot know which of your parents or your children is more beneficial to you: this is a law from God, and He is all knowing, all wise.[22]

Rules Derived from This Verse

1. If a decedent is survived by male and female offspring, males will inherit double the share of similarly situated females.
2. If a decedent is survived by two or more daughters and no sons, the daughters shall inherit two-thirds of the estate.
3. If a decedent is survived by only one daughter and no sons, the daughter shall inherit one-half of the estate.
4. If a decedent is survived by one or more parents and one or more children, the parents' share of the estate shall be one-sixth each. Note that in certain cases, the father's share will exceed one-sixth, as some of the residue—after all shares have been distributed—may revert back to him.
5. If the decedent is survived by his or her mother and is not survived by any offspring, the mother shall inherit one-third of the estate, subject to rule six below.
6. If the decedent is survived by his or her mother, two or more siblings, and no offspring, the mother shall only inherit one-sixth of the estate.

2. Rights of Spouses

In the first half of Chapter 4, Verse 12, the Quran describes the shares for surviving spouses:

> And for you is half of what your wives leave if they have no child. But if they have a child, for you is one fourth of what they leave, after any bequest they [may have] made or debt. And for the wives is one fourth if you leave no child. But if you leave a child, then for them is an eighth of what you leave, after any bequest you [may have] made or debt.[23]

22. *The Qur'an*, *supra* note 2, at 4:11.
23. *The Qur'an*, *supra* note 2, at 4:12.

Rules Derived from This Verse

1. If a female decedent is not survived by any offspring, her widower shall inherit one-half of her estate.
2. If a female decedent is survived by one or more offspring, her widower shall inherit one-fourth of her estate.
3. If a male decedent is not survived by any offspring, his widow shall inherit one-fourth of his estate.
4. If a male decedent is survived by one or more children, his widow shall inherit one-eighth of his estate.

3. Rights of a *Kalalah* Individual

A decedent who is survived by neither ascendants nor descendants is known in Islamic inheritance law as a *Kalalah*. The rules pertaining to a *Kalalah* are described in the Quran in two verses of Chapter 4:

Verse 12

> And if a man or woman leaves neither ascendants nor descendants but has a brother or a sister, then for each one of them is a sixth. But if they are more than two, they share a third, after any bequest which was made or debt, as long as there is no detriment [caused]. [This is] an ordinance from Allah, and Allah is Knowing and Forbearing.[24]

Verse 176

> They ask you [Prophet] for a ruling. Say, "God gives you a ruling about inheritance from someone who dies childless with no surviving parents. If a man leaves a sister, she is entitled to half of the inheritance; if she has no child her brother is her sole heir; if there are two sisters, they are entitled to two-thirds of the inheritance between them, but if there are surviving brothers and sisters, the male is entitled to twice the share of the female." God makes this clear to you so that you do not make mistakes: He has full knowledge of everything.[25]

---

24. *Id.*
25. *The Qur'an, supra* note 2, at 4:165.

Rules Derived from These Verses

1. If a decedent is survived by neither ascendants nor descendants but is survived by one maternal half-sibling, the maternal half-sibling will inherit one-sixth of the estate. If there are multiple maternal half-siblings, they shall split one-third of the estate.[26]
2. If the decedent is survived by neither ascendants nor descendants but is survived by one or more full or paternal siblings, the following possibilities apply:
   a. If there is only one sister, she will inherit one-half of her brother's estate.
   b. If there is only one brother, he receives the remainder of the estate.[27]
   c. If there are two or more sisters, they will share in two-thirds of their brother's estate.
   d. If there is at least one brother and one sister, they shall share in the remainder of the estate, with male siblings inheriting double the share of the female siblings.

4. A Systematic Approach to Understanding the *Faraid* Shares

Remarkable precision and care have gone into the development of the Islamic law of inheritance. Although the Quranic injunctions described previously are relatively straightforward, there are significant differences in the application of these principles between Sunni and Shia jurists. Thus, a lawyer who is counseling Muslim clients in developing an estate plan must apply a significantly different analysis than they may be accustomed to when explaining a state's default rules of intestacy.

As a primary matter, clients who seek out the services of an estate-planning attorney will almost always have close family members, which is often the primary motivation behind seeking counsel in the first place. As a result, we provide more attention here to categories of heirs that are close in relation to the client and thus more likely to inherit under Islamic law.

Further, when describing the Sunni rules of inheritance, we have selected the Hanafi juristic school, which is one of the four main schools

26. Note that the rule that males shall inherit double the share of similarly situated females does not apply here.

27. Note that if there are two or more brothers and no sisters, the brothers shall split the estate evenly.

of law, as the primary method for describing the apportionment of inheritance under Sunni law. The Hanafis have, for a variety of historical reasons, played a disproportionate role in the development of law in the Islamic tradition. Moreover, on matters of inheritance law, the other three Sunni schools are largely aligned with the Hanafi school.

In addressing the Shia rules of inheritance, we have chosen to explain the Ithna Ashari tradition, which is substantially different in several essential respects from the Hanafi positions. The Ismaili Shia sect is similar in its inheritance rules to the Ithna Ashari system.

In discussing diverse juristic traditions when it comes to inheritance, it is not our intent to extensively compare and contrast. Instead, we hope to provide a framework for practitioners to counsel and serve clients who wish to draft estate plans consistent with their values.

This chapter also does not address every rule relating to Islamic inheritance law, many of which we discuss in other parts of this book. In this chapter, we focus on how to calculate mandatory shares of inheritance under Islamic law. Understanding who is entitled to inherit—which is not always intuitive—will enable the practitioner to ask the client the right questions and determine the rightful Islamic heirs.

E. Sunni Inheritance Law

Hanafi jurists have divided Islamic heirs into four categories: (a) Quranic heirs; (b) residuary heirs, also referred to as agnatic heirs; (c) distant kindred; and (d) public treasury. Discussion of the distant kindred and public treasury will be brief, as they are of limited value to practitioners.

Heirs within each of the first three categories have priorities. An heir's right to inherit in Islam depends on the presence or absence of other heirs. For instance, while daughters normally inherit one-half of what a son inherits, women do not always inherit less than men. In some instances, they may inherit just as much or more, depending on who the other surviving relatives of the deceased may be.

1. Quranic Heirs

There are twelve heirs that are explicitly or implicitly mentioned in the Quran. Four of them are male: the father, the paternal grandfather, the widower, and the maternal half-brother. The remaining eight are female:

the widow, the daughter, the granddaughter,[28] the mother, the grandmother (both paternal and maternal), the full sisters, the paternal half-sister, and the maternal half-sister. However, merely being a Quranic heir does not denote a right to inherit unless the individual is a primary Quranic heir.

a. *Primary Quranic Heirs*

It is often not necessary for the practitioner to ask about all Quranic heirs, since many Quranic heirs will not actually be entitled to inherit due to the presence of other relatives.

The primary Quranic heirs are the surviving spouse (widow or widower), sons, daughters, and parents. If there are no children, then grandchildren take their place. If a father predeceases the decedent, he is replaced by his father, if living, who is known as a "true grandfather." If a mother predeceases the decedent, she is replaced by her mother, if living, who is known as a "true grandmother."

Assuming no other applicable rule bars them from inheriting, primary Quranic heirs will always inherit from the decedent. If the list of potential heirs includes a combination of these individuals, plus any other Quranic heirs or agnatic heirs, as described below, we need to look no further and will distribute the estate among the heirs.

Example:

Kim is survived by her husband, Zulfiqar; her mother, Lisa; and her father, Bilal. She also has three full sisters—Karen, Tess, and Zahra—and a maternal half-sister, Bilquis. Because Bilal is the highest male agnate, a concept discussed below, his presence prevents Kim's siblings from inheriting, even though they are all Quranic heirs. Kim's only heirs in this situation are Zulfiqar, Lisa, and Bilal.

---

b. *Specific Quranic Heirs*

Quranic heirs are the most frequent beneficiaries. The determination of whether they are Islamic heirs and, if so, what shares they shall inherit differs by context.

28. Only a son's daughter qualifies as a Quranic heir.

i. Father

The father's Quranic share of inheritance is one-sixth. However, the father may also receive a share as a residuary heir if he is the highest male agnate. He will be outranked as the agnate if the decedent is survived by a son or a grandson from a son, however low, in which case he would only receive his Quranic share of one-sixth. If the decedent is not survived by any offspring or a mother but has a father, the father will be a residuary beneficiary regardless of how many other Quranic heirs exist.

Example:
Yusuf is survived by his father, Shahrukh, and full brothers Amir and Salman. Shahrukh takes 100 percent as the highest male agnate, excluding Amir and Salman completely.

---

ii. Paternal Grandfather

Sunni jurisprudence distinguishes between the "true" grandfather and "false" grandfather. The father's father is a true grandfather and would take the father's share of inheritance (one-sixth or more depending on the situation) if the father predeceases the grandfather. On the other hand, a mother's father or a father's mother's father is considered a "false" grandfather and would not stand in the place of a father.

iii. Widower

The widower is a primary Quranic heir who is always entitled to inherit. He receives one-half of his late wife's estate if she is not survived by any offspring or one-fourth if she is survived by offspring.

iv. Widow

A surviving Muslim widow is likewise always entitled to inherit. She receives one-fourth of her late husband's estate if he is not survived by any offspring. Her share is reduced to one-eighth if the decedent is survived by children. Under Islamic law, it is possible for a man to have up to four wives. In such cases, the multiple wives would split the one-eighth or one-fourth share.

Note that while Muslim men are permitted to marry non-Muslim women, such women would not be entitled to inherit from the decedent's *faraid* share. To account for this, however, a husband could plan in advance and leave up to one-third of his estate to his non-Muslim wife, as a *wasiyah*.

Example:
Farhan passes away and is survived by his son, Latif, who is Muslim, and his wife, Nadia, who is Muslim, and another wife, Rida, who is also Muslim. He has two additional wives, Melissa and Kathy, who are not Muslim. The one-eighth share for a widow must be split equally between Nadia and Rida, who get one-sixteenth each, and the remaining seven-eighths goes to Latif.

The wife has a special status among heirs because the relationship is contractual. As a Quranic heir, her share may not be augmented through the *wasiyah* in Sunni jurisprudence. However, the marriage contract may include a *mahr*, or specifically *mahr mu'akhar*—that is, a payment upon the end of marriage, either death or divorce. A woman can negotiate the *mahr* in advance of the wedding, and although it is technically considered a debt rather than inheritance, it may be used as a tool to protect the surviving widow after the death of her husband.

v. Daughter

A daughter is a primary Quranic heir who always inherits, assuming no other rule excludes her. The daughter's share varies depending on if there is one daughter or two or more daughters and if there is also at least one son. If she is the only daughter, her share is one-half. If she is one of two or more daughters and there are no sons, she shares two-thirds of the decedent's estate equally with the other daughter or daughters. If there are multiple children and at least one of them is male, she becomes a residuary heir and receives half the share of what her brother or brothers inherit.

Example 1:
Sahira is the only daughter of Ahmed, who has passed away. Ahmed is also survived by his widow, Sasha, and a brother, Hamid. Sahira would receive one-half of Ahmed's estate, Sasha would receive one-eighth, and three-eighths would go to Hamid.

Example 2:
Malik passes away, leaving behind three daughters, Salma, Zayna, and Malika. Malik also leaves a father, Rahim. Salma, Zayna, and Malika would share two-thirds between them, or two-ninths each. The balance, one-third, would go to Rahim.

Example 3:
Safiah passes away, leaving daughters Hind and Maha, son Jordan, and widower Jonathan. Jonathan takes one-fourth, while the balance, three-fourths, will be divided between Hind, Maha, and Jordan. Jordan takes 5/12 while Hind and Maha take 5/24 each.

vi. Granddaughter from a Son

The granddaughter is a Quranic heir but inherits only in the absence of any living children. Under these circumstances, she is treated the same way as a daughter. If there is no grandson from a son, she gets one-half of the estate. If she is one of two or more granddaughters from the son, she shares equally among them in two-thirds of the estate. If there is at least one grandson from the son along with a granddaughter from the son, then the grandson takes twice the inheritance she does.

If the decedent is survived by one daughter and one granddaughter from the son but no son and no grandson from a son, the granddaughter of the son inherits one-sixth. As previously described, the granddaughter becomes a residuary heir if the grandson of the son is the highest agnate.

Example:
Tariq passes away and is survived by his father, Zulfiqar; his mother, Betty; and three grandchildren from a deceased son: a grandson, Mobeen, and two granddaughters, Nathania and Radia. Zulfiqar and Betty take one-sixth each. The highest agnate here is Mobeen, who takes one-third, while Nathania and Radia take one-sixth each.

vii. Mother

The mother receives a one-third share if the decedent is not survived by any offspring or by two or more siblings. The mother takes a one-sixth share if the decedent is survived by any offspring or by one or more siblings.

Note that where the only surviving heirs are spouse, mother, and father, a special rule applies. A surviving widow would inherit one-fourth, the mother one-fourth, and the father one-half. If the wife passes away first, the surviving widower inherits one-half, the mother one-sixth, and the father one-third.

viii. "True" Maternal Grandmother

Unlike a "true" paternal grandfather, there can be more than one "true" maternal grandmother, since a father's mother and a mother's mother fall under this category. The maternal grandmother takes the place of the mother and inherits her share in her absence. The share is one-sixth if a mother does not survive the decedent. If there is more than one true grandmother, they divide the one-sixth equally between them.

Example:
Amirah passed away, leaving behind a son, Shafiq; his deceased mother's mom, Sameena; and his father's mother, Kinza. Shafiq would inherit five-sixths, and the two grandmothers would take 1/12 each.

---

ix. Full Sisters

Full sisters are excluded from inheritance entirely by the presence of sons or grandsons, however low, or parents and paternal grandparents, however high. If there are no surviving brothers, a sister inherits one-half of the estate. If there are two or more sisters and no brothers, the sisters split two-thirds. However, if there are any surviving brothers, the brothers shall receive double the share of the sisters.

x. Paternal Half-Sister

A paternal half-sister takes the same share as a full sister in her absence. If a paternal half-sister survives the decedent but there is no offspring, male paternal ancestors, or full brothers and sisters, the paternal half-sister inherits one-half. If there are two or more paternal half-sisters and the decedent left no offspring, male paternal ancestors, or full brothers and sisters, the paternal half-sisters divide two-thirds between them. If the decedent is survived by one or more paternal half-sisters and one full sister but no offspring, male paternal ancestors, or full brothers, the paternal half-sisters split one-sixth of the estate equally.

xi. Maternal Half-Brothers

Maternal half-siblings are excluded by the presence of children or grandchildren of a son, however low, or a father or paternal grandfather, however high. One distinguishing feature of maternal half-siblings is that they inherit equally regardless of gender. If there is only one maternal half-sibling, the share is one-sixth. If there is more than one, they share one-third between them equally.

Example:
Bilquis passes away. She leaves behind a full sister Muna, full brother Shadman, paternal half-brother Fahad, and paternal half-sister Fariha. The distribution of inheritance is as follows: Shadman takes five-ninths, Muna takes 5/18, Fariha takes one-sixth, and Fahad gets nothing. In this instance, the paternal half-brother does not inherit because the higher agnate is the full brother, who shares with his sister, taking twice as much as her. The paternal brother is not a Quranic heir but could be a residuary heir if he were the higher agnate. As it happens in this example, he is not.

---

xii. Maternal Half-Sisters

As described previously, a maternal half-sister and half-brother shall inherit in equal shares.

2. Residuary Heirs (Agnates)

As explained above, a father's presence can be consequential when calculating inheritance. This is because the concept of *Asabah*, or male agnates, as well as the female agnate, is essential in Sunni inheritance law. Agnates fill the role of residuary heirs and prevent inheritance from being distributed to further levels of heirs. The Prophet Muhammad instructed his companions, "Give the portion of the inheritance to the Quranic heirs, and whatever is left should go to the closest male relative of the deceased."[29]

Residuary heirs can be classified in the following groups, the presence of any member of which shall exclude all members of any groups below:

29. Sahih al-Bukhari, Vol. 8, Book 80, Hadith 724, *available at* https://sunnah.com/bukhari/85/9 (last accessed Oct. 4, 2018).

Groups	**Members of Group**
Group 1—Descendants	Son Son's male descendants, however low
Group 2—Ascendants	Father Father's male ascendants, however high
Group 3—Brother and Male Issue	Full Brother Paternal Half-Brother Full Brother's Son Paternal Half-Brother's Son Descendants of Group 3, however low
Group 4—Paternal Uncle and Male Issue	Full Paternal Uncle Paternal Half-Uncle Full Paternal Uncle's Son Paternal Half-Uncle's Son Descendants of Group 4, however low

Certain female heirs are converted from Quranic heirs to residuary heirs due to presence of certain similarly situated male heirs. For instance, daughters become residuary heirs if the decedent was also survived by sons. A son's daughters become residuary heirs if they have any brothers or cousins of the same rank. Full sisters become residuary heirs when they have one or more full brothers.

A paternal full or half-sister may also inherit as an agnatic heir without the presence of a paternal full or half-brother. The presence of this sister can act to completely cut off all agnatic heirs in group 4 when the deceased is not survived by brothers but is survived by a daughter or son's daughter. If higher agnates are present, the sister may not inherit at all, as would be the case if a father or son were present, or she may share in the inheritance, in the case of a brother.

Example 1:
Sarah is survived by a daughter, Hana; a sister, Sehrish; and the son of a deceased brother, Bilal. Hana's share is identified in the Quran as one-half. The other Quranic heir in this example, Sehrish, shall serve as a female agnate. She would inherit the residuary, as her presence serves to exclude any other potential heirs, including Bilal.

Example 2:
Faisal dies and leaves behind a father, Abdul Aziz; a son, Ibrahim; and a daughter, Maryam. Abdul Aziz would receive his Quranic share (one-sixth) while the balance, five-sixths, is divided between Ibrahim and Maryam, who would both be considered agnates, with Ibrahim taking twice the share of Maryam (five-ninths for Ibrahim and 5/18 for Maryam).

3. Relationship between Fixed Shares and Residuary

Quranic heirs take either a fixed share or the residuary. For example, a widow takes one-fourth if the decedent does not leave behind any children or one-eighth if there are any living children. A father takes one-sixth, as does the mother, though this can vary depending on who the other heirs are. A mother may also take one-third and a father may become a residuary heir. An only daughter takes one-half but shares in two-thirds if there is more than one daughter. However, if there is a son, the daughter(s) and son(s) do not get a fixed share but instead take from the residuary, with a son inheriting twice the share of a daughter.

Example:
Salma passes away and is survived by her father, Elyas; her mother, Didi; her husband, Yahya; three daughters, Kulsum, Aisha, and Khalida; and a son, Faisal. Yahya would inherit one-fourth, one-sixth would go to Elyas, one-sixth would go to Didi, and the balance would go to the children, with Faisal inheriting twice the share of his sisters. So Faisal would get one-sixth while Kulsum, Aisha, and Khalida would take 1/12 each.

In this example, the presence of the son meant that the three daughters were no longer entitled to two-thirds as stated in the Quran. However, if Faisal did not survive Salma, it would be mathematically impossible for daughters Kulsum, Aisha, and Khalida to share two-thirds of their mother's estate, as the total shares would exceed 100 percent. In such cases, it is necessary to proportionally decrease everyone's shares to achieve unity, as explained below.

a. The Doctrine of Awl

The doctrine of *Awl* is a proportional decrease of shares to achieve unity when the fixed shares total more than 100 percent.

Example:
Salman dies and is survived by his widow, Wahida; two daughters, Rizwana and Jameela; his father, Musa; and his mother, Jihan. Under the fixed shares of the Quran, his widow Wahida is entitled to one-eighth because Salman was survived by children, the daughters Rizwana and Jameela would split two-thirds, while the parents, Musa and Jihan, take one-sixth each. These shares combine to equal 112.5 percent. Applying the doctrine of *Awl*, each heir's share is proportionally decreased resulting in a distribution to Wahida of one-ninth, to Rizwana and Jameela of 16/27 (16/54 each), and to Musa and Jihan of 4/27 each.

b. Doctrine of Radd

In some instances, if you combine all of a decedent's Quranic heirs and residuary heirs, the total of the shares equals less than 100 percent. The doctrine of *Radd* is employed in these scenarios and is conceptually the mirror image of *Awl*—instead of a decrease, the beneficiaries would receive a proportional increase in their shares. Not all beneficiaries share in the increase, however. As the doctrine is based on a Quranic verse that references blood relatives,[30] a surviving spouse's share may not be enhanced through the doctrine of *Radd*.

Example:
Felicia passes away and is survived by her husband, Idrees, and four daughters, Sasha, Anisa, Hameeda, and Vildana. The four daughters share two-thirds while Idrees takes one-fourth. As a result, 1/12 of the estate remains unassigned. Instead of distributing this to more distant relatives or allowing the remainder to escheat to the public treasury, as the Shafi and Maliki juristic schools require, the Hanafi juristic school increases the shares of

30. *The Qur'an, supra* note 2, at 33:6 ("In God's Scripture, blood-relatives have a stronger claim than other believers and emigrants, though you may still bestow gifts on your protegees.").

the daughters. So instead of splitting two-thirds, the daughters divide three-fourths among themselves, taking 3/16 each.

---

4. Distant Kindred

For individuals with Muslim family members who are more distant than the group previously discussed, there is another set of relatives in Hanafi jurisprudence known as "distant kindred." As members of this group are typically too remote to be relevant to the practice of an American estate-planning attorney, we have not included that discussion here. A full table of all the heirs under Islamic law including distant kindred is provided as a reference in Appendix A.

5. The Public Treasury

In even more remote scenarios, under classical Islamic law, if there were no identifiable or eligible beneficiaries of an estate, something similar to the common law doctrine of escheating would occur in which the public treasury would receive the residuary. In such circumstances today a client may leave his or her residuary estate to a charitable organization that serves the poor or needy.

Example:
Zeyn, 61, marries Cathy, 58, who is a recent convert to Islam. Zeyn has three adult children from a prior marriage, all of whom are Muslim. Cathy has three children from a prior marriage, none of whom are Muslim. Because Cathy's children are not Muslim, they are not entitled to inherit from Cathy's *faraid* share. She can, however, provide a discretionary bequest for them through her *wasiyah* share, which is limited to one-third of her estate.

Assuming Cathy leaves one-third of her estate to her three children, the remaining two-thirds must be distributed according to the Islamic Law of Inheritance. Cathy's only Muslim heir is her husband, Zeyn, who is entitled to one-fourth of her estate as a Quranic heir. Under classical Islamic law, spouses are not entitled to a reversion interest, and thus the remainder would pass automatically to the public treasury. Instead, today, Zeyn would receive the entire estate.

However, if Zeyn predeceases Cathy, up to one-third of Cathy's estate may still pass to her children at her death through the *wasiyah* share. The remaining two-thirds should be assigned to a charity or charities of Cathy's choosing since she has no Muslim heirs.

F. Shia Inheritance Law

Most Muslims who identify as Shia, including much of the large Shia community in the United States, follow the Ithna Ashari (Twelver) branch. Our approach to explaining Ithna Ashari inheritance law is again to focus on scenarios a practitioner in the United States is most likely to see and to deemphasize less common scenarios that may only be of theoretical value. As will be seen, this is easier to do in the Ithna Ashari system of inheritance than in the Sunni system, discussed previously.

1. Philosophical Underpinnings

The principal textual source of both Sunni and Ithna Ashari traditions is the Quran. Thus, in many instances, the residuary distribution provisions will be the same. Nonetheless, there is a significant philosophical difference between Sunni and Ithna Ashari traditions when it comes to inheritance. In the Sunni tradition, the Quran did not completely replace the pre-Islamic system of inheritance that existed in Arabia but instead served to reform it. In the Ithna Ashari view, the old Arabian tribal system was upended entirely and replaced with something different. In describing the Ithna Ashari inheritance rules, we rely on the works of N.J. Coulson,[31] Lucy Carroll,[32] and Al-Sayyid Ali Al-Husseini Al-Sistani.[33]

In the Ithna Ashari inheritance system, the doctrine of *Qaraba* tends to favor nuclear families and direct lineal descendants, whereas in the Sunni system, male relatives and the link to males are given some level of priority, mainly when the estate is undersubscribed among close relatives.

31. *See generally* Noel Coulson, *A Comparison of the Law of Succession in the Islamic and British Legal Systems*, 26(2) Am. J. Comp. L. 227, 230 (1978).

32. *See generally* Lucy Carroll, *The Ithna Ashari Law of Intestate Succession: An Introduction to Shia Law Applicable in South Asia*, 19(1) Modern Asian Studies, 85–124 (1985).

33. Sistani, *Islamic Laws*, *available at* https://www.sistani.org/english/book/48/ (last accessed Oct. 8, 2018).

The Ithna Ashari system of inheritance is also sometimes considered to be more favorable to female family members. However, female family members will not necessarily come out with more inheritance as compared to the Sunni distribution scheme. The real effect of the Ithna Ashari inheritance regime is that close female relatives will exclude more distant relatives that the Sunni system would not eliminate.

Another feature of Ithna Ashari rules is that there is more flexibility to utilize the *wasiyah* share to enhance the share of a beneficiary than in the Sunni tradition. So to the extent a client wishes to use up to one-third of the estate to increase the share of a specific beneficiary, the Ithna Ashari tradition allows for that.

Finally, unlike the Sunni system, the Ithna Ashari system of inheritance distinguishes between different types of property. There is a distinction between personal (movable) property and realty (immovable) property when considering the shares for various heirs. For instance, an eldest son has the right to the personal property of his father (e.g., sword, Quran, etc.) in addition to his share. A surviving wife without living children from the deceased is disfavored as she is not entitled to real property of her late husband but only cash, inventory, and other equivalents.[34] A childless widower, meanwhile, is not subject to an analogous rule.[35]

2. Classes of Heirs

The Ithna Ashari system includes three broad classes of heirs. For purposes of this book, they are defined as Class A, B, and C. Members of the classes are as follows:

Class A	(1) Parents, (2) children, and (3) descendants of children, however low
Class B	(1) Grandparents, (2) ancestors of grandparents, however high, (3) siblings (including half- and full-blood), and (4) descendants of siblings, however low
Class C	(1) Paternal and maternal uncles and aunts, (2) descendants of paternal and maternal uncles and aunts, however low, (3) paternal and maternal great-uncles and great-aunts, and (4) descendants of paternal and maternal great-uncles and great-aunts, however low

34. Carroll, *supra* note 32, at 101.

35. *Id.* at 100.

The classes of heirs are vital in this system, as the presence of even one heir in a higher level will exclude all heirs in subsequent levels. The beneficiaries of the class take what remains, regardless of the gender makeup of the class members.

3. Requirement That a Beneficiary Be Muslim

In the Ithna Ashari rules, only Muslims may inherit from Muslims. However, Muslims may inherit from non-Muslims.[36] Religion is a prerequisite for all shares that will be described, including the spouse and class A beneficiaries.

4. Quranic Heirs

Ithna Ashari jurisprudence has a shorter list of Quranic heirs than Hanafi jurisprudence. It excludes the paternal grandfather (however high), the paternal grandmother (however high), and the granddaughter from the son as Quranic heirs. The Quranic heirs entitled to inherit fixed shares include the husband, wife, mother, father, daughter, full sister, and paternal half-sister; the maternal half-brother and maternal half-sister get specific shares under specific circumstances, while other beneficiaries such as the sons and paternal half-brothers are residual heirs.

Unlike in the Sunni tradition, the paternal grandfather does not take the place of the father in his absence. While the daughter of a son may be a beneficiary under Ithna Ashari law when there are no children, she is not considered to be one of the heirs that are specifically accounted for in the Quran.

5. Undersubscription and the Doctrine of *Radd*

Because of the class cutoff in the Ithna Ashari system of inheritance, undersubscription of the estate will happen frequently. While undersubscription of Quranic heirs happens regularly in the Sunni inheritance system, the gap will be filled either through *Radd* or by adding beneficiaries from another class, depending on the presence of male blood relatives in the class. The Ithna Ashari system will rely exclusively on *Radd* within the class regardless of its gender makeup.

36. Sistani Fatwa 2791, *available at* https://www.sistani.org/english/book/48/2388/ (last accessed Oct. 8, 2018).

There are exceptions for which beneficiaries inherit through the process of *Radd*. While a mother's share may generally be enhanced through *Radd*, a spouse's share may not. Likewise, maternal half-siblings do not participate in *Radd* if any full-blood siblings survive the decedent.

Example:
Haris leaves behind a mother, Bilquis; a daughter, Serina; and a full brother, Ali. Because Ali is a class B relative, he gets nothing. The Quranic share of Serina is one-half, and the share for Bilquis is one-sixth. This leaves one-third remaining, which will be proportionally increased by *Radd* to one-fourth for Bilquis and three-fourths for Serina.[37]

---

6. Oversubscription

Ithna Ashari law, in the event of an oversubscription, does not recognize the Sunni doctrine of *Awl*, which is a proportional reduction. Instead, the shares of a daughter or sister would be reduced in the event of an oversubscription.

Example:
Cathy is survived by a husband, David; a mother, Cindy; and three daughters, Erica, Patricia, and Khadija. David's one-fourth share, Cindy's one-sixth share, and the daughters' two-thirds share are all specified in the Quran. However, since these shares add up to 108.33 percent, a reduction is necessary to reach unity. Only the shares of the daughters will be reduced, so the portions for David and Cindy stay as is. And instead of the daughters splitting two-thirds, they would accept 7/12 split equally between them, getting 7/36 each.

---

37. Carroll, *supra* note 32, at 94.

7. Surviving Spouse

The spouse takes a fixed portion of inheritance and does not become a beneficiary of any residual inheritance, so long as relatives from other classes exist. The spouse is treated separate and apart from various blood relatives, who may either receive the fixed portion or be the beneficiary of any remaining portion. As specified in the Quran, a widower is entitled to one-half if there are no children or one-fourth if there are children. The widow is entitled to one-fourth if there are no children or one-eighth if there are children. The spouse will not be a remainder beneficiary so long as other beneficiaries remain and will be limited to the Quranic portion.

8. Children and Parents

Class A beneficiaries include children and parents. Most American estate-planning attorneys planning for families in the Ithna Ashari tradition will not need to look further than class A beneficiaries and the spouse. The father and the mother inherit equally, at one-sixth for each, and the sons will take twice the share of the daughters.

If only one daughter is present, the share of the daughter will be one-half, but the share may be increased by *Radd* as described in the preceding example. If there is more than one daughter and no son, the daughters would share two-thirds of the decedent's estate and would be eligible for *Radd* as described previously.

Under no circumstances would a class B beneficiary inherit if even one class A beneficiary is alive. The gender of the beneficiary does not matter. The class (A, B, or C) is controlling.

Example:
Hamza dies and is survived by two daughters, Naba and Khalida; a brother, Wahid; and a wife, Precious. Precious will receive one-eighth since Hamza was survived by children. Wahid will not inherit at all because he is a class B relative. The two daughters, Naba and Khalida, will split two-thirds between them. However, since the shares combined do not equal a whole, the daughters will also take the residuary through the process of *Radd*. Thus, the daughters split seven-eighths and Precious will receive one-eighth.

---

9. Children of the Decedent, However Low

Grandchildren inherit in the absence of any children. As is the case with Sunni distributions, it is possible for grandchildren from a predeceased child to be beneficiaries under the *wasiyah*. However, if a decedent is survived by grandchildren and no children, the presence of grandchildren (or lower if all grandchildren are deceased) will serve to exclude lower-tiered relatives, such as siblings.

Grandsons inherit twice the share of granddaughters on a per stirpes basis. This means that the parent-child link will be resurrected for determining the shares of grandchildren. The shares will then be allotted for the grandchildren as if the inheritance passed from child to grandchild, with twice the share for grandsons as granddaughters. Childless predeceased children do not enter into the calculation.

Example:
Bilal is survived by his wife, Maimoona. He also has three deceased children, sons Abdullah, Amir, and Haroon. Abdullah was survived by three children, Bilal's grandsons Salman and Dawud and granddaughter Sultana. From Amir, there was only one granddaughter, Isra. Haroon was childless. Maimoona gets one-eighth. The share for the deceased sons with descendants (we ignore Haroon's inheritance), Abdullah and Amir, 7/16 each, would be divided up among their respective offspring. So Salman and Dawud would take 7/40 each while Sultana would take 7/80. Isra would take 7/16.

If all children and grandchildren are deceased but grandchildren left issue, the same procedure is used in determining heirship.

---

10. Class B Heirs

Ithna Ashari inheritance will exclude siblings, grandparents, and other class B heirs more frequently than Sunni law. The presence of any class A beneficiary regardless of gender will serve to exclude this group.

The presence of any grandparent does not act to exclude siblings. There is no preference for maternal over paternal grandparents. Relative closeness to the decedent is what matters. So, for example, a maternal grandmother will exclude a paternal great-grandfather. This would not happen in the Sunni system of inheritance.

Siblings can of course be either full-blood or half-blood on the maternal or paternal side. The presence of full-blood siblings will serve to exclude all paternal half-brothers and -sisters but not maternal half-brothers and -sisters. In the presence of full-blood siblings, maternal half-brothers and -sisters will either take one-sixth if there is only one or share one-third. While male siblings generally inherit at twice the ratio of female siblings, maternal siblings, in the presence of either paternal half-siblings or full siblings, share their one-third allotment equally, regardless of gender.

Children of siblings inherit in the absence of siblings. As is the case with grandchildren among class A beneficiaries, the line between decedent and sibling is reconstructed for determining shares.

Example:
Salah is survived by a full sister, Sarah. He also has a maternal half-sister, Khadija. The full sister will take five-sixths, and the half-sister will take one-sixth.

---

11. Class C Heirs

In the absence of class A or class B heirs, we then move to more remote relatives. That includes aunts and uncles, then issue of the same. Full-blood uncles and aunts will exclude any half-blood uncles and aunts. There is no priority for maternal or paternal relatives. The presence of any close relatives will act to exclude relatives further out, with female relatives taking half of what male relatives take.

After descendants of uncles and aunts, however low, the next priority falls to great uncles and aunts. The presence of any of these would act to exclude the next group, their decedents, however low.

12. Polygamy and *Mut'a*

Muslims in the Ithna Ashari tradition can marry up to four wives, which is the same as the Sunni tradition. The share for wives must be divided by the number of wives to whom the decedent was married. If a decedent left two wives who had offspring, each wife would inherit 1/16.

An additional feature of Ithna Ashari traditions is *mut'a*, or a temporary marriage contract. Such wives are distinguished from "*nikah*" wives, which do not have a fixed term. Men in Ithna Ashari traditions may marry an unlimited number of *mut'a* wives, who have no right to inherit unless specified in a contract. The children from *mut'a* wives are considered legitimate and entitled to inherit under Ithna Ashari inheritance law.

13. Lifetime Charitable Obligations

Muslims who follow the Ithna Ashari tradition generally have charitable obligations that substantially exceed those of Muslims in the Sunni tradition. While all Muslims are encouraged to give charity voluntarily, known as *sadaqa*, and all Muslims with means must pay *zakat* for the poor, the Ithna Ashari tradition includes an additional financial obligation known as *khums*.

While *zakat* and *khums* (discussed below) are vast subjects, they are largely outside the scope of this volume. We include only information relevant to estate planning attorneys.

a. Zakat

Shia Muslims are obligated to pay *zakat* annually when wealth reaches a particular level. Unlike Sunni Muslims, who have a 2.5 percent rate of *zakat* with various exclusions and methods of calculation for different assets, the Ithna Ashari rules of *zakat* include different rates. So, for example, there is a 2.5 percent rate on gold while various rates are applied to crops.

As is the case in the Sunni tradition, *zakat* is calculated and paid for specific charitable purposes annually. *Zakat* is a "debt to God" and should be paid by the estate or the heirs if the decedent did not pay *zakat* during his or her lifetime.

b. Khums

Muslims in the Ithna Ashari tradition are also obligated to pay *khums*, which is a 20 percent tax on profits and "excess earnings." *Khums*, which means one-fifth, is paid to an authorized "*Syed*" (a religious leader) on the value of the following:

- Profits and earnings that exceed living expenses
- Minerals
- Found treasure

- Mixed property (prohibited or "*haram*" property mixed with permissible or "*halal*" property)
- Precious stones acquired from underwater diving
- Value of land a Christian or Jewish person purchases from a Muslim

Gifts are generally liable for *khums*, except property exchanged as a result of marriage. This includes *mahr* and the returned funds from a *khul*; the returned *mahr* is sometimes paid when a wife initiates a divorce.

i. *Khums* and Inheritance

While, as a general rule, inheritance is not subject to *khums*, there are important exceptions. The first can appear in mixed Sunni/Ithna Ashari families, where inheritance is distributed in a manner that is not valid under Ithna Ashari law but mandated in the Sunni system. The term for this in Ithna Ashari jurisprudence is *ta'sib*. The second is in situations where an individual receives an unexpected inheritance from a distant relative.

Example 1:
Reza's sister, Fatima, passed away. In addition to her brother Reza, Fatima left behind a daughter, Noor, and her mother, Zahra. Reza is Ithna Ashari, but his sister, Fatima, was Sunni and planned her estate such that Reza would receive one-third, while his mother would receive one-sixth and Noor would receive one-half. Reza's share is subject to *khums* since this distribution is wrong from the Ithna Ashari perspective.

Example 2:
Ali receives an inheritance from Sultana, his brother's daughter, who died of cancer only three months after her parents and brother died in a car accident. Ali would be expected to pay *khums* on the inheritance.

A related possibility is that a Sunni heir may receive a share based on Ithna Ashari rules that does not comport with Sunni law. In such cases it is the responsibility of the heir in Sunni tradition to return inheritance that he or she does not have the right to receive. There is no analogous rule concerning *khums*.

Example:
Maryam has a father, Abdullah, who planned his estate under Ithna Ashari rules, so despite his having a brother, Abdul-Rahman, he left all his inheritance to her, the only daughter. As Maryam is Sunni, she has a moral obligation to disclaim a portion of her inheritance so that her uncle can claim funds she did not have a right to.

ii. *Khums* and *Zakat* in Estate Plans

Both *khums* and *zakat* are continuing obligations after death and are obligations for heirs as well. If an individual was not paying *khums* during his or her lifetime, the estate should pay the *khums*. Accordingly, the client's estate plan should expressly authorize the successor trustee to pay unpaid *khums* before distributing the residuary estate to the heirs. This is also the case with *zakat*.

G. General Applicability Rules

1. Individuals Who Do Not Inherit by Right

There are two categories of would-be Islamic heirs who are disqualified from inheriting: (1) murderers, or persons who caused the decedent's death, and (2) non-Muslims.

a. Murderers/Killers

Much like the slayer statutes found in common law and incorporated into most states' probate codes, Islamic law prohibits a murderer from inheriting from his or her victim. While all Muslim jurists agree that intentional or unjustifiable killing constitutes a bar to inheritance, they differ as to whether an unintentional killing or manslaughter should similarly serve as a bar.

b. Non-Muslim Relatives

Islamic inheritance law contains a rule of exclusion prohibiting a Muslim from inheriting from a non-Muslim and vice versa. This rule raises several important questions relating to the definition of a Muslim and who gets to make that determination.[38] While it is impossible to prevent all future family disputes, we recommend leaving a specific distribution to non-Muslim relatives in the *wasiyah* share, coupled with a contest clause stating that if the relative challenges a provision of the decedent's will or trust and loses, he or she will also lose the *wasiyah* share.

c. *Extramarital Children*

A child born out of wedlock does not inherit from his or her father. If a father would like to leave an inheritance to an extramarital child, he may leave the child a discretionary bequest of up to one-third of the estate through his *wasiyah* share.

Note that historical rulings by jurists on gestation periods have largely been eclipsed by the available science concerning paternity. Nonetheless, there is a continuing presumption of paternity for any child born to a married couple.

d. *Stepchildren*

Stepchildren inherit from only their biological parents under Islamic law. If a client would like to leave bequests to his or her stepchildren, he or she may leave a discretionary bequest of up to one-third of the estate through the *wasiyah* share.

e. *Adopted Children*

In the United States, an adopted child is treated by law as if he or she had been born to the adopting parents. Among the rights an adoption decree confers on an adopted child is the right to inherit from his or her adoptive parents. In some jurisdictions, adoption extinguishes the right of the adopted child to inherit from the child's biological parents.

By contrast, under Islamic law, adopted children do not automatically inherit from their adoptive parents. Rather, they retain the right to inherit from their biological parents. As with extramarital and stepchildren, if an adoptive parent would like to leave an inheritance to his or her adopted child, he or she may leave a discretionary bequest of up to one-third of the estate through the *wasiyah* share.

38. For a discussion of the public policy issues raised by this rule, see Chapter 3(C)(1).

f. Same-Sex Couples

As described in more detail in Chapter 3, Islamic law only recognizes marriage between a man and a woman. Thus, because same-sex marriages are not recognized in Islam, a homosexual couple would not be eligible to inherit from each other's *faraid* shares but could choose to leave a *wasiyah* for one another.[39]

g. Transgender Individuals

Inheritance rights in Islam are based on an individual's biology rather than gender. If an individual has male reproductive organs, he will be treated as a male, regardless of how the individual identifies, for the purposes of calculating his share. Likewise, if an individual has female reproductive organs, she will be treated as a woman irrespective of her professed gender and assigned her share accordingly.

If an individual has both male and female reproductive organs, this individual receives a share that is halfway between that of similarly situated male and female heirs.

h. Missing Persons

A missing person's estate cannot be distributed to the heirs until a court of competent jurisdiction declares the person deceased. On the other hand, if the missing person is an heir, he or she will not inherit from the estate of a decedent until the person's whereabouts are known.

2. Simultaneous Death Rules

The Islamic rule concerning simultaneous death is different from the Uniform Simultaneous Death Act and similar state statutes, which state that deaths that take place within 120 hours of each other are to be considered simultaneous.[40] A majority of jurists hold that if the sequence of death of two mutual heirs cannot be ascertained, they will be treated as predeceasing each other. If it is certain that one died before the other, the heirs of the second to die shall be entitled to inherit his or her share of the first decedent's estate.

39. For more information regarding the requirements of a valid marriage under Islamic law, see Chapter 3, Section B, pages 22–25.

40. *See, e.g.,* Tex. Estates Code § 121.052 (2018).

Example:
While test driving Ahmed's new car, Ahmed and his father Talha were hit by a drunk driver. Ahmed was declared dead on the scene. Despite paramedics' best efforts, Talha passed away during the ambulance ride to the hospital. Since Talha survived Ahmed by a few moments, his heirs—in this case, Ahmed's two brothers, Asim and Abdullah—are entitled to inherit the share that Talha would have received from Ahmed.

3. *Munasakha*—When a Beneficiary Dies before Receiving His or Her Distribution

The distribution of an Islamic estate, like any other, can be a lengthy process. As such, it's possible that a beneficiary could pass away before receiving his or her share. In such scenarios, the beneficiary's share must pass to his or her Islamic heirs as well.

4. Chemical Dependencies and Other Addictions

Muslim parents, just like other parents, may be concerned about distributions to children with addictions, including drug or alcohol abuse. Naturally, such parents may worry that their children might exploit an inheritance for self-destructive purposes.

The use of recreational drugs and alcohol is prohibited in Islam. While parents may feel it is their religious obligation to deny inheritance if their children are involved in these forbidden activities, the mere fact that a beneficiary is engaging, even openly and unabashedly, in activities that are prohibited by Islam does not preclude that person from receiving his or her inheritance.

That said, if an activity reaches the point of becoming destructive to an individual, there is precedent for protective actions by judges to prevent further harm to that individual. In the absence of such a system, the trustee may take on this role. The structure of such an arrangement should not appear to be punitive or to single out an individual beneficiary, at least not at the planning stage. The goal of any such plan should be to prevent harm to the beneficiary. For example, the trustee of a discretionary trust may be able to prevent the beneficiary from obtaining assets that would harm him or her but also provide income for the beneficiary's sustenance and treatment.

Example:
Fatima and Ali have a son named Elyas, who has been in and out of drug treatment for the past seven years and is unable to hold a job. Fatima and Ali want to make sure that Elyas does not use his inheritance to feed his drug habit. Instead of developing a trust that singles out Elyas for his poor choices, they create a trust that states that assets are to be distributed to beneficiaries as part of a Discretionary Dynasty Trust. Should Elyas be in need of protection from himself, the trustee will deny requests for funds from the trust but may use funds for the legitimate needs of the beneficiary.

5. Trustee Compensation

It is customary for grantors to compensate trustees for their services. In many instances, the trustee is an institution, such as a bank, trust company, or another professional fiduciary. Alternatively, the trustee may be a beneficiary of the trust itself. This latter situation raises concerns relating to the Islamic Law of Inheritance.

In general, trustee compensation is based on either a percentage of the value of assets being managed or the amount of time spent by the trustee. For a nonbeneficiary trustee, either form of compensation is acceptable. Certainly, excessive compensation could occur in either hourly or percentage-based calculations and would violate the rights of the heirs.

Preventing this type of abuse at the planning stage is difficult but may be mitigated by incorporating a few planning considerations. First, trustee succession is paramount. Trustee selection can lead to disputes among beneficiaries, particularly where the trustee is also a beneficiary and has discretion as to valuing and distributing property. The Quran states that a trustee may not favor him- or herself with superior assets while distributing inferior assets to others.[41] Further, if the successor trustee is a beneficiary of the trust, compensation should not be based on a percentage of the estate as it could have the appearance of unduly increasing the individual's share of inheritance.

41. *The Qur'an*, *supra* note 2, at 2:181 ("If anyone alters the bequest after hearing it, the guilt of the alteration will fall on them: God is all hearing and all knowing.").

Example:
Fahad has three children—Sultana, Dawud, and Haaris. He names Haaris the first successor trustee of his RLT. After Fahad's death, Haaris distributes cash to his siblings while taking for himself real property appraised at an amount equal to his share of the inheritance. The value of the property is expected to rise rapidly due to nearby development. Haaris's siblings would have preferred a share of the property and believe it to be worth much more than the appraised value. Haaris acted inappropriately in distributing this property to himself. To avoid such self-dealing, it would have been ideal for Fahad to name an independent trustee rather than one of his heirs as his successor.

CHAPTER

6

Drafting Estate-Planning Documents

A typical estate plan will include the following core planning documents:

- Last will and testament
- Revocable Living Trust (RLT)
- Power of attorney
- Advance healthcare directives
- Deeds, beneficiary designations, and other funding documents

Many of these items will have relevance to Islamic inheritance law, while some will be common for all clients regardless of faith tradition. Given the limited scope of this book in assisting the attorney in drafting a religiously compliant estate plan, we will not address many additional routine tasks and documents that do not present issues relating to Islamic law.

A. Drafting a Last Will and Testament

A will-based estate plan utilizes a last will and testament to direct disposition of a person's property after his or her death. Such a document may be simple or extraordinarily complex and may include provisions for one or more continuing trusts.

Except in rare circumstances, a last will and testament requires probate, the court-supervised process of submitting a decedent's will, proving its validity, appointing a personal representative, and distributing the decedent's assets in accordance with his or her wishes.[1]

A simple will that distributes the testator's estate pursuant to the Islamic Law of Inheritance is fraught with limitations that make it difficult to truly comply with those regulations. Most notably, a will does not control the disposition of any jointly owned assets or assets with existing beneficiary or transfer-on-death designations.

Additionally, a will does not effectively account for the fact that heirs under Islamic law and their shares may change due to the birth or death of other individuals. Under Islamic inheritance law, the birth of a son, for instance, not only creates a new inheritance right but may also act as an "excluder" for certain individuals previously named in the last will and testament. Furthermore, individuals who might otherwise be entitled to inherit could be excluded based on differences in religion with the decedent. Making such determinations is obviously outside the constitutional power and competence of a state court.

Due to these concerns, we generally discourage Muslim clients from creating a will-based estate plan that relies on probate to transfer assets. We prefer the use of estate plans based on RLTs.

B. Drafting a Revocable Living Trust

In most states, it is customary for attorneys to recommend trust-based estate plans due to the high cost and inefficiency associated with probate.[2] In our view, even when probate is not expensive or time-consuming, an RLT-based plan is superior for several reasons. First, an RLT is an agreement that remains private after a grantor's death. Second, an RLT contains important incapacity provisions not present in a last will and testament. Finally, living trusts afford a degree of flexibility for religious planning that is difficult to achieve in a court-supervised process.

For clients seeking to comply with Islamic inheritance law, eliminating the probate court's involvement and privatizing the administration of the estate enables them to ensure that their estate can be distributed

1. *See, e.g.*, Cal. Prob. Code §§ 13100–13116 (2018).

2. Probate fees vary significantly by jurisdiction. For an example of probate code fees, see Cal. Prob. Code § 10810 (2018).

consistent with the Islamic Law of Inheritance. This is possible because trusts generally do not require judicial supervision absent a dispute. As such, the trust can include customized provisions that may vary from most states' probate codes.

It follows, then, that the most significant portions of an estate plan governing succession of a Muslim client's estate should appear within an RLT. In such cases, the client's last will and testament serves as a "pour-over" will functioning to distribute any remaining probate property consistent with the terms of the trust.

In this chapter we analyze the components and provisions of an RLT in order to assist the practitioner in distinguishing between the planning of an RLT for Muslim clients and that of a conventional RLT, with which most estate-planning attorneys will already be familiar. In an attempt to illustrate the most common planning situations, we have chosen to utilize a married couple in a stable first marriage as hypothetical clients in most instances. While not all provisions will be applicable to every client, they may nonetheless be instructive and assist in the client intake and RLT design process.

1. Separate versus Joint Trusts

In the case of a married couple, the primary question a practitioner must discuss with his or her Muslim clients is how their assets are currently titled, as any conversation regarding Islamic inheritance law is meaningless unless each client's assets are understood and clearly identified.[3]

When preparing living trusts, a practitioner will have to decide between creating a joint trust or separate trusts for each spouse. Joint trusts are typically employed in stable marriage situations, especially in community property jurisdictions, and can be utilized for Muslim clients so long as the assets of each spouse are clearly identified in the property schedules attached to the trust.

If the spouses own some assets jointly and others separately, we recommend the creation of three trusts—a His, Hers, and Ours design—so that 50 percent of the assets in the joint trust automatically flow to the deceased spouse's separate trust upon his or her death to be distributed to his or her Islamic heirs with the other 50 percent flowing to the survivor's separate trust.

3. For a discussion of the various modes of property ownership and their analysis under Islamic law, see Chapter 3(C).

2. Identification of the Trust

An RLT may include the name of the grantors or someone or something else, depending on the client's wishes. In general, it is not necessary to specify within the name of the trust that it follows Islamic inheritance law. The fact that the provisions are consistent with such rules is a private matter for many clients.[4]

3. Intent to Comply with Islamic Inheritance Law

It is important to clarify within the trust instrument itself, however, that the grantors intend to comply with Islamic inheritance law. This is not for the futile purpose of attempting to direct judicial interpretation of Islamic law[5] but rather to ensure that the grantors' estate is distributed according to their wishes.

Although some Muslim clients may be wary of specifically mentioning Islam or Islamic law in their estate plans for political reasons, it is nonetheless vital to provide guidance to fiduciaries, including trustees and trust protectors, regarding the grantors' intent. Attorneys should also assure their clients that the Free Exercise Clause of the U.S. Constitution permits individuals to decide how their estates will be distributed upon death.[6]

In expressing their intent, the grantors may wish to clarify whether they follow Sunni or Shia inheritance law, as there are notable differences between the two sects with respect to the priority of beneficiaries.[7] This may be particularly relevant where a family has both Shia and Sunni members, since there may be some confusion as to which law is to be followed. If a family is entirely Sunni or entirely Shia, this clarification may not be necessary.

A standard clause in a joint RLT articulating a married couple's intent might read as follows:

---

4. *See* Frances H. Foster, *Trust Privacy*, 93 Cornell L. Rev. 555 (2008).

5. Such would not comport with the Supreme Court's Establishment Clause jurisprudence. *See* Eugene Volokh, *Religious Law (Especially Islamic Law) in American Courts*, 66 Okla. L. Rev. 431, 437 (2014).

6. Furthermore, the Tenth Circuit Court of Appeals has specifically upheld a Muslim citizen's right to plan his or her estate in accordance with Islamic law. Awad v. Ziriax, 670 F.3d 1111 (2012).

7. For a detailed analysis of the dispositive distribution provisions under Sunni and Shia inheritance law, see Chapter 5 of this text.

> We are creating this RLT and any separate trusts established under this instrument with the intent that assets transferred to the trust be held for our benefit while we are living and be distributed upon our death in accordance with [Sunni/Shia] Islamic inheritance law as defined in [section defining Islamic inheritance law]. I fully understand that distributions based upon Islamic inheritance law may result in (a) distributions to individuals who are not our heirs under State law, (b) unequal distributions to my children on the basis of gender, (c) no inheritance for stepchildren, (d) loss of the Unlimited Marital Deduction, the spousal rollover, or other potential tax benefits from a different distribution, and/or (e) liquidation and distribution of assets that may otherwise benefit a surviving grantor, causing [him or her] to receive a smaller share than [he or she] may be entitled to under a state's statutory elective share.
>
> We specifically disclaim any right to receive a spousal elective share under state law and direct our successor trustees and beneficiaries to honor our wishes as stated.
>
> To accomplish the intent set forth in this Section, we have given our Trustee broad discretion with respect to the management and investment of assets in our trust. We have further included provisions for a Trust Protector with the ability to recalculate shares of inheritance in accordance with Islamic law in the event our family circumstances have materially changed after the date of execution of this trust instrument.

This section would not be the only reference to the Islamic Law of Inheritance within the trust. Its scope would be limited to expressing the grantors' intent rather than setting forth specific inheritance rules. Thus, the previous section would serve as an introductory mission statement that would guide the reader for the remainder of the document.

4. Family Information

As with any RLT, it is necessary to ascertain the clients' desired beneficiaries for providing notice of the trust under the controlling state law. For Muslims, this section of the RLT may include a set of family members not typically represented within conventional RLTs.

When listing beneficiaries, it is important to be comprehensive. Often, identifying beneficiaries under Islamic law may not be intuitive. Sometimes siblings are beneficiaries, and sometimes they are not. Grandparents, great-grandparents, uncles, and aunts may be beneficiaries as well. The Islamic Law of Inheritance distinguishes between half- and full-blood relatives as well as between maternal and paternal relatives, in terms of both their right to inherit and their proportion of inheritance, should it exist.

In general, we recommend naming three classes of relatives when identifying family members:

1. Relatives entitled to inherit under the Islamic Law of Inheritance
2. Relatives who *may* be entitled to inherit under the state's intestacy statute
3. Relatives not entitled to inherit by right under the Islamic Law of Inheritance but who, nonetheless, are included in the grantors' discretionary *wasiyah* share

In many instances, these three categories will overlap. For example, some relatives otherwise entitled to inherit under both Islamic and state law may ultimately take nothing because they are not Muslim.

Example:

A sample family provision is printed below:

Article Two

Family Information

We were married on January 25, 1996. All references to "husband" within this agreement are references to Faisal Ali. All references to "wife" within this agreement are references to Laila Ali.

We have three children. Their names and dates of birth are:

Bilal Ali, born on May 13, 2002
Amina Ali, born on January 22, 2006
Fatima Ali, born on February 19, 2012

All references in this agreement to "our children" are to these children, as well as any children subsequently born to us.

Though not part of our immediate family, we have also named the following heirs under Islamic inheritance law as beneficiaries of this trust:

> Abdullah Ali—Faisal Ali's father
> Khadija Rahman—Faisal Ali's mother
> Shahid Iqbal—Laila Ali's father
> Bilquis Iqbal—Laila Ali's mother
>
> References to our "heirs" are to those persons who are entitled to inherit under the Islamic Law of Inheritance.

5. Use of "Beneficiary" and "Heir" Nomenclature

When creating a trust for a Muslim client, we recommend avoiding use of the term "descendants," as beneficiaries under Islamic law often include more than just descendants. In Islam, inheritance rights flow both "downstream" (i.e., to children, grandchildren, etc.) as well as "upstream" (i.e., to parents, grandparents, etc.) and may also include siblings, uncles, and aunts.

When referring to those beneficiaries who are entitled to mandatory shares under the Islamic Law of Inheritance, we use the term "Islamic heirs," which should be defined in the trust as follows:

> The term "Islamic heirs" shall refer to those individuals who have the right to inherit under the Islamic Law of Inheritance. This group may include, but is not limited to, my lineal descendants of all generations; ancestors, including parents and grandparents; and other, more distant relatives.

Individuals who will be receiving discretionary distributions through the decedent's *wasiyah* share should simply be referred to as "beneficiaries."

The drafting attorney should ensure that the definition of the term "heir" used within the RLT expressly supersedes any alternative definition of the term present in a state's probate code.

6. Disinheritance

Under Islamic inheritance law, a non-Muslim cannot inherit from a Muslim's estate by right. He or she may, however, be a beneficiary under the *wasiyah*. Some clients may also express a desire to disinherit a specific Muslim beneficiary for some other reason, besides a difference in faith. Under Islamic inheritance law, however, no such discretion exists. So long as an heir is a Muslim, he or she is entitled to his or her mandatory portion of the decedent's estate.

Many estate planners advise clients to leave some devise to a disfavored heir, combined with a no-contest clause to discourage the recipient from challenging the limited nature of the legacy in court.[8] If the purpose is to completely disinherit a non-Muslim relative, however, this carrot-and-stick tactic is unavailing.

The attorney should draft a living trust in a way that affords some flexibility to modify beneficiaries after death. The appointment of a trust protector who is empowered to amend distribution provisions and disinherit heirs who may have left the Islamic faith in accordance with the grantors' intent can readily achieve this goal.

In assessing whether an individual qualifies as an heir, the trust protector, or grantors themselves, should accept at face value the person's assertion that he or she is Muslim. There should be no inquiries into religious practices or whether the beneficiary is "sinful." Such inquiries are irrelevant, as it is purely the nature of the individual's faith that matters for the purposes of Islamic inheritance law. Thus, if a beneficiary states he or she is not Muslim, or claims to be Muslim but is so doctrinally opposed to the perspectives of mainstream Sunni or Shia theologians that he or she is no longer within "the fold of Islam," only then would such a person be subject to disinheritance under Islamic law. It is not appropriate for any family member, though, to quiz a beneficiary on theological matters.

Finally, if the client is not in contact with a person who would be a rightful heir under Islamic law and has no way of knowing whether the individual is Muslim, there are two potential courses of action to assess the person's eligibility to inherit. First, if the potential beneficiary was born into a Muslim family, the trustee should assume the beneficiary is a Muslim and provide him or her with his or her rightful share. Alternatively, if the potential beneficiary was not born into a Muslim family, he or she will be entitled to inherit only if the trustee has basis to believe that he or she has converted to Islam.

8. *See* Ralph C. Brashier, *Disinheritance and the Modern Family*, 45 Case W. Res. L. Rev. 84 (1994). Note, however, that some states will not enforce a no-contest clause. T. Jack Challis & Howard M. Zaritsky, *State Laws: No-Contest Clauses*, http://www.actec.org/assets/1/6/State_Laws_No_Contest_Clauses_-_Chart.pdf (last accessed Sept. 6, 2018).

7. Trust Protector Provisions

The appointment of a trust protector is a powerful tool to ensure that the grantors' wishes are reflected within their estate-planning documents and to account for subsequent changes that would impact the distribution of their estate. Trust protectors are essential in both maintaining flexibility and ensuring compliance with the grantors' wishes.[9] Thus, an important feature of any RLT for Muslim clients is a provision nominating such a person. This person could be either the drafting attorney him- or herself or someone whom the beneficiaries may appoint at a later date, if necessary.

Trust protector provisions are generally reserved for making administrative modifications to the trust, such as scrivener's errors, but may also be used to remove a trustee or to grant a power of appointment for the purposes of estate inclusion and basis planning. As suggested previously, however, the trust protector solves another issue by serving to modify distribution provisions to ensure they reflect changes in the eligible heirs. Thus, the trust protector can potentially add or remove beneficiaries from an RLT not only where there is a question of a recipient's Islamic faith but also where a named beneficiary predeceases the grantor or where other beneficiaries are born between the time of document-drafting and a grantor's death.

Under Islamic inheritance law, the birth of a child or death of a beneficiary can fundamentally alter inheritance rights. For example, if Salman's family consists of a wife, a daughter, and eight siblings, all of them would have the right to inherit from Salman upon his death under Sunni jurisprudence. If Salman were to have a son, however, his wife and daughter would continue to enjoy inheritance rights, but his eight siblings would no longer be Islamic heirs. An RLT must have the flexibility to address the concept of these "includers" and "excluders." While including a lengthy schedule of all present and contingent beneficiaries under Islamic law may aid the trustee in determining who is entitled to inherit, it is likely not essential, as there are Islamic inheritance calculators available online that would suffice for this purpose.

The trust protector may also be called upon to determine whether a beneficiary qualifies as a Muslim. In the event a child was previously disinherited by his or her parents because he or she left Islam but rejoined the

9. Richard C. Ausness, *Sherlock Holmes and the Problem of the Dead Hand: The Modification and Termination of "Irrevocable" Trusts*, 28 Quinnipiac Prob. L.J. 237 (2015).

faith before the parents' deaths, the trust protector may similarly be able to modify the trust postmortem and include the child as a beneficiary.

A trustee would not be able to make such determinations since they involve a substantive amendment to the trust. Furthermore, as alluded to earlier, a judge will not modify the distribution of trust assets for the purpose of excluding non-Muslims from inheriting.

Accordingly, we recommend not only including a trust protector in the RLT but also providing instructions and authorization for that individual to amend the trust consistent with Islamic inheritance law to exclude certain individuals who may not be entitled to inherit. This power must be final and unreviewable by any court, and the trust protector must be released of any liability and indemnified by the trust for making such decisions.

Example:
Ilyas creates an RLT that names his father, Yacoob; his wife, Hannan; and his daughter, Sultana, as beneficiaries. The trust states that upon his death, his inheritance should be distributed as follows:

Yacoob (father)—three-eighths
Hannan (widow)—one-eighth
Sultana (daughter)—one-half

Yacoob predeceases Ilyas, but Ilyas fails to update his trust accordingly. Upon his own death, Ilyas is survived by two siblings: a sister, Habiba, and a brother, Salah. Ilyas's trust protector determines that these siblings have the right to inherit under Islamic law, even though this was not the case when he originally drafted the trust. The trust protector can create a postmortem amendment to the trust pursuant to instructions left by Ilyas to modify the trust as necessary to comply with Islamic inheritance law. The resulting shares would be as follows:

Salah (brother)—one-fourth
Habiba (sister)—one-eighth
Hannan (widow)—one-eighth
Sultana (daughter)—one-half

A similar result may be obtained through an independent trustee with decanting authority who may also have similar authority. Decanting is more likely to be used by older trusts, however, where no trust protectors are appointed.

8. Incapacity Planning

Unlike a will, a living trust can provide for management of a grantor's assets if he or she becomes incapacitated. Though not directly related to the Islamic Law of Inheritance, incapacity powers often raise social and cultural issues that affect Muslim families. These provisions are relevant to both the RLT and a durable power of attorney, which is typically drafted to cover incapacity planning for assets not funded into the trust.[10]

An important issue to discuss with clients is the method of determining incapacity; this determination is typically made by (a) a court, (b) one or more physicians, or (c) a disability panel. Because the incapacity determination impacts the clients' personal freedom, the attorney should advise clients to consider their options thoroughly before assigning such authority.

As privacy is one of the reasons clients create an estate plan in the first place, requiring a court determination would be self-defeating and is generally disfavored. While the second option of relying on a physician determination is comparatively favorable, clients may be ambivalent about delegating this authority to individuals they do not know.

For many clients, the third option of engaging a disability panel is often the best choice. This arrangement affords the client a level of privacy while allowing for the involvement of persons he or she knows, such as close family or friends, in the determination. Admittedly, a relative's assessment of another's capacity can cause controversy within a family. But the incorporation of multiple family members or close family friends in the decision-making process can enhance inclusiveness and reassure the client that his or her best interest is at heart. Furthermore, the client is probably less likely to challenge the decision of a panel composed of family members he or she chose precisely for this purpose than that of a judge or unfamiliar physicians.

For Muslim clients, the disability panel can be considered a form of *shura*, or mutual consultation regarding one's affairs, a trait that is encouraged in the Quran. While there are no Islamic restrictions as to who may serve on this panel, clients may select trusted family members and friends

10. *See generally* John C. Craft, *Preventing Exploitation and Preserving Autonomy: Making Springing Powers of Attorney the Standard*, 44 U. Balt. L. Rev. 407 (2015).

who may reside in other states or countries. In such cases, clients should be advised that a geographically distant relative might not be able to make an independent determination of incapacity and must rely on friends and relatives who are closer geographically.

Additionally, incapacity planning often incorporates a gifting program for implementing a preexisting estate plan. In other instances, gifting powers may be included for elder planning for Medicaid qualification. Both because the cost of nursing home care is prohibitively expensive for many middle-class families and because health insurance often does not pay for long-term care, utilizing gifting powers in a living trust or power of attorney may be critical. In each of these cases, incapacity planning should be in accordance with Islamic inheritance law and Islamic financial ethics.

9. Distribution Provisions

The Islamic Law of Inheritance is similar to state intestacy statutes in that both provide fixed shares for specific beneficiaries. To convey these rules, many practitioners choose to attach to their trusts charts and schedules, known as the *Mawarith* schedules, and instruct the successor trustee to refer to the charts to determine the rightful beneficiaries under Islamic law. Since a state court judge will not interpret Islamic inheritance law unless the document defines the distribution provisions with particularity, many practitioners feel this is an effective method of ensuring compliance with the Islamic Law of Inheritance.

Given the complicated series of relationships that determine the beneficiaries and their shares, one cannot easily reduce the Islamic Law of Inheritance to charts. The *Mawarith* schedules are often difficult to navigate—even for attorneys who are trained in classical Islamic law. Moreover, they often fail to take into account cases where beneficiaries may be excluded.

For example, if a decedent outlives his son, the decedent's brother would qualify as an Islamic heir. If the brother were not Muslim, however, he would be ineligible to inherit.

The decedent may also have an extramarital son, something the Islamic Law of Inheritance treats differently than do U.S. state laws. Relying on charts, therefore, cannot substitute for human judgment. As explained previously, we believe a trust protector is best equipped to decide many of the important issues relating to the distribution of shares.

Finally, the attachment of lengthy Islamic inheritance charts may expand the notice requirements under certain state notice statutes.

Accordingly, we do not recommend simply attaching a *Mawarith* schedule to a client's estate-planning documents as the method for determining the shares of inheritance. Rather, we recommend calculating and assigning inheritance shares to the grantors' then-living Islamic heirs while providing guidelines for how the trust protector may amend the distribution provisions to comply with Islamic law in the event of changed circumstances.

10. Tangible Personal Property

Many clients have specific items of property they want to distribute to a particular beneficiary. Personal property is often distributed by a memorandum, which provides the grantors with a measure of flexibility as they would not need to modify the RLT itself to change which tangible personal property goes to whom.

From an Islamic perspective, if the beneficiary of a specific gift is not an Islamic heir, the distributions must flow from the discretionary *wasiyah* share. On the other hand, if the beneficiary is an Islamic heir, the distribution must count toward the beneficiary's total share. To avoid inadvertently conveying property to an heir in excess of his or her rightful share, the attorney should draft an RLT to allow such gifts to fail. The same applies to drafting for gifts of personal property that could exceed the amount allowed in a *wasiyah* share, which is one-third of the aggregate for all such property, including any other *wasiyah*, such as bequests to charitable organizations. The trust should also allow these gifts to fail if they exceed one-third of the decedent's estate.

11. Estate-Tax Planning

Estate-tax planning used to constitute a much more significant part of an estate-planning attorney's job than it does today.

For many years, estate-planning attorneys advised their clients to create A-B or A-B-C trusts. In a typical A-B trust, upon the death of the first spouse, an amount equal to the federal estate-tax exemption would be funded into the B trust, and anything over this amount would be funded into the A trust, otherwise known as the survivor's trust. Assets in the B trust, often known as a bypass trust, or Credit Shelter Trust, utilize the decedent's estate-tax exemption and pass outside of the surviving spouse's estate on his or her death. If necessary, clients could also utilize a C trust, often known as a Qualified Terminable Interest Property (QTIP) or marital trust, in second-marriage situations or in states with estate taxes below the federal exemption level. We will discuss QTIPs in greater detail below.

The federal estate-tax exemption has increased significantly since 2001. The amount used to be $675,000. In 2011, the Unified Gift and Estate Tax Exemption was set at $5 million per person, indexed for inflation. As of 2019, the amount has increased to $11.4 million, with each spouse's exemption now permanently portable, meaning that any amount of the decedent spouse's unused exemption can be carried over to the surviving spouse.

Given the higher federal estate-tax exemption, many components of these A-B-C trusts are no longer necessary for most clients.[11] Nonetheless, these tools still have non-estate-tax planning benefits such as asset protection, and thus many practitioners use them for both estate-tax and non-estate-tax planning purposes. For Muslim clients, the use of these techniques is subject to applicable Islamic restrictions. To clarify the implications of these restrictions, we analyze a number of techniques below and examine their permissibility under Islamic law. Of course, because much of the discussion involves marital-trust planning, some of the sections will be inapplicable to unmarried clients.

12. Estate-Tax Apportionment

In taxable estates, estate-tax apportionment clauses can become an unexpected source of contention and even litigation.[12] These disputes often arise when there are instructions for apportionment of assets designated to one or more beneficiaries while other beneficiaries can obtain an asset free of the federal estate tax. This presents concerns for heirs who may be responsible for paying taxes unevenly if apportionment is attributable differently based on different instruments.[13]

An RLT should include provisions for the protection of the Federal Estate Tax Marital Deduction. Under such a provision, the surviving spouse's share would be tax-favored and not subject to the estate tax. For assets in a QTIP trust, the estate tax is delayed until the death of the surviving spouse. Since inheritance shares under the Islamic Law of

11. Currently, 12 states and the District of Columbia still have their own estate tax systems, and six states have inheritance taxes, so practitioners in those jurisdictions may still need to consider such planning tools.

12. *See In re* Estate of Kuralt, 68 P.3d 662 (Mont. 2003).

13. *Id.*

Inheritance are predetermined, however, these types of estate-tax apportionment clauses have the potential to skew those distributions unfairly in favor of certain beneficiaries. The following example illustrates this potential pitfall.

Example:
Idrees is a widower with a net worth of $40 million who remarries. After he passes away, he leaves one-third of his assets to charity, with the balance going to his family, comprised of his three sons and his widow.

Applying Islamic inheritance law, one-third of Idrees's estate is distributed first to charity; of the remainder, one-eighth is distributed to Idrees's widow and 7/24 to each of his sons.

The distributions to charity and Idrees's widow would be protected from the estate tax, while his children's shares would be taxed before the children received them.

While the Islamic Law of Inheritance treats the estate tax as a debt, the payment of this debt is subject to rules that favor some beneficiaries over others. It is thus especially vital to attempt to eliminate any estate-tax liability whenever possible. If eliminating the tax is not possible, the tax should be apportioned equally among all beneficiaries.

C. Distribution Options

One of the most important decisions for a grantor—and a critical counseling opportunity for the drafting attorney—is to decide how a beneficiary should receive his or her inheritance.

1. Outright Distributions

The simplest distribution option is to distribute a decedent's assets outright to specific beneficiaries. In the case of married couples, this can be done through separate or joint trusts that contain provisions for distributions at the death of each spouse. As with any RLT, a property agreement and trust schedules would be necessary to clarify each spouse's ownership rights. This plan is optimal for clients who do not need to maintain a family residence upon the death of the first spouse.

Example:

Aisha and Sulayman, a married couple living in Arizona, wish to create an estate plan consistent with Islamic inheritance law. Their parents are deceased, and they have three adult children together—Adam, Khalid, and Sarah—all of whom are married with children and are in good health. They own all their property as community property. This couple is retired and lives off a pension that includes a joint-and-survivor annuity. The pension income is sufficient to meet the couple's living requirements.

Aisha and Sulayman's assets consist of the following:

- One personal residence worth $400,000
- Five rental properties valued at a combined $2.9 million
- Cash and other liquid assets valued at $1 million

The couple does not have an estate-tax concern, as their gross estate is well below the federal exemption level and Arizona does not have a state estate tax. Additionally, Aisha and Sulayman have no need to keep all assets in a bypass trust after the death of the first spouse and want their children to receive their rightful shares of the deceased spouse's inheritance immediately for their needs.

Such a scenario is the simplest from the perspective of Islamic inheritance law. Assuming Sulayman passes away first, Aisha would retain her 50 percent ownership interest in all the community assets, and the remaining 50 percent would be distributed as follows:

- Aisha: one-eighth
- Adam: 7/20
- Khalid: 7/20
- Sarah: 7/40

If Aisha chooses, she may buy out the other beneficiaries' shares in the personal residence. The liquid assets can be divided and distributed outright or in trust to each beneficiary. Aisha and Sulayman would also be well advised to place the rental properties in one or several limited liability companies, which could be centrally managed, sold, or distributed to each beneficiary in the appropriate shares.

2. Distribution at Ages or Based on Milestones

Many clients may be uncomfortable with the idea of leaving a large inheritance to a young adult. They fear their children will spend their money irresponsibly if it is given to them at too young of an age. To account for these concerns, clients often seek to restrict withdrawal rights based on age or certain life milestones. For instance, an RLT may state that a child can withdraw the balance of trust principal at the following ages: one-third at age 25, one-third at age 30, and one-third at age 35. Or perhaps the trustee may state that a beneficiary may withdraw fixed amounts upon achieving certain milestones. For instance, $50,000 upon graduating college, $50,000 for a child's first wedding, and $50,000 for a down payment on his or her first house.

Making withdrawal rights contingent upon meeting certain life goals is not permissible under Islamic inheritance law, as it exerts too much "dead hand" control over a beneficiary's wealth. Implementing reasonable age-based restrictions is permissible, however, based on a concept of *rushd*, or intellectual maturity, that exists under classical Islamic law.

Assets need not be liquidated and distributed to beneficiaries outright after death. Rather, it is possible to provide inheritances in trusts, including discretionary dynasty trusts, or as interests in a limited liability company or limited partnership. These restrictions are based on the nature of the asset, however, and do not stem from a desire to unreasonably deny inheritance or control beneficiaries from the grave.

3. Continuing or Cascading Trusts

Many estate planners advise against distributing assets outright to a beneficiary. Rather, they suggest that assets should be distributed to a trust for the benefit of the beneficiary. The trustee of the continuing trust can make distributions pursuant to an ascertainable standard, such as the popular Health, Education, Maintenance, and Support (HEMS) standard, also known as the ascertainable standard, as referenced in Internal Revenue Code section 2041(b)(1)(A), or on a discretionary basis.

The HEMS standard strikes a balance between the prevention of distributions for spendthrift purposes and providing for the beneficiary's needs. This standard of distribution is common when there is no independent trustee. Asset protection under a trust governed by the HEMS standard will be weaker than under a discretionary standard, however, because creditors for items related to health, education, maintenance, and support may be able to collect against such a trust.

A discretionary standard option provides enhanced asset protection when paired with an independent trustee. Uninhibited by distribution requirements, the independent trustee may choose to grant or deny requests for payment by any beneficiary. In general, the intent is for denials to apply in a nonarbitrary way, as arbitrary denials of an heir's rightful claim to trust property would violate Islamic law. Thus, an independent trustee empowered with distributive discretion can protect trust assets by using such discretion to more readily deny requests by beneficiary creditors than those by beneficiaries themselves.

4. Multigenerational Dynasty Trusts

The Rule Against Perpetuities (RAP) is rapidly becoming the minority rule in the United States. While some states continue to terminate trusts after a few generations to prevent endless dead-hand control, this policy goal is increasingly viewed as anachronistic. Trusts in non-RAP states may last hundreds or even thousands of years. For example, South Dakota abolished the common-law rule against perpetuities by statute, allowing for a trust to exist in perpetuity.[14] Such trusts are primarily designed to preserve the funds in perpetuity. The trustee, typically a professional fiduciary, will manage available funds per the needs of current and future beneficiaries.

There is no inherent prohibition against multigenerational trusts in Islam. However, the drafting attorney must ensure that considerations of future beneficiaries do not interfere with the rights of current heirs to receive their Islamic shares. The grantor should, however, include trust protector provisions, which can be effective in determining beneficiary eligibility or exclusion under Islamic inheritance law.

Since a multigenerational trust may last hundreds of years and provide for future, unknown beneficiaries—including possibly non-Muslims who would be ineligible to inherit under Islamic law—the drafting attorney should be sure to clarify the following points:

1. The purpose of the trust
2. The method for identifying beneficiaries
3. The method for resolving disputes

14. S.D. Codified Laws § 43-5-8 (2018).

A sample exclusionary clause in a joint RLT may look like this:

> We direct that no part of our estate shall be distributable to any non-Muslim relative of ours, whether this relative is kin, spouse, parent, or child. For the purposes of calculating shares of inheritance under Islamic inheritance law, any non-Muslim relatives shall be treated as predeceasing us.
>
> Should a grantor or beneficiary of this trust be murdered by an individual who would otherwise be entitled to inherit a share under Islamic law, we direct that the adjudged murderer, principal, or accessory to the murder be disqualified from receiving any part or share of the trust estate.

5. Testamentary Special-Needs Trust

At times, receiving an inheritance can be harmful to the interests of a beneficiary. An outright inheritance to beneficiaries receiving needs-based government assistance may disqualify them from continuing to receive this assistance. Since it is often hard to predict whether a beneficiary will need government assistance, a Testamentary Special-Needs Trust is an effective and flexible tool the attorney ought to consider for such situations. Because these trusts allow the trustee to distribute assets to a subtrust instead of outright to the beneficiary, they can preserve the beneficiary's ongoing receipt of government assistance.

Such a trust is inherently restrictive in that its purpose is to ensure that the beneficiary's inheritance avoids classification as an available resource for public benefits purposes. To accomplish this, a trustee actively manages the trust per the needs of the beneficiary while being sensitive to public benefits law. If the cause for a special-needs trust has passed or never occurred in the first place, the trustee can disregard the special-needs provisions and make an outright distribution to the beneficiary.

Despite its restrictiveness, a Testamentary Special-Needs Trust is permissible under Islamic law because the restrictions serve to benefit the beneficiary.

6. Testamentary Power of Appointment

A Testamentary Power of Appointment is a tool that allows a person who holds it to decide how to dispose of assets inside the trust. Absent a Testamentary Power of Appointment, assets must pass pursuant to the particular formula preselected by the grantor (e.g., per stirpes, by right of representation, or—in the case of most Muslim clients—pursuant to the Islamic Law of Inheritance).

Granting beneficiaries Testamentary Powers of Appointment over assets in their subtrusts is acceptable in Islam. Islamic inheritance law requires every Muslim to develop his or her own estate plan for distributing assets pursuant to the Islamic Law of Inheritance. It does not and cannot, however, force a beneficiary to distribute assets he or she earns or inherits according to Islamic law. If a beneficiary, or any Muslim for that matter, decides not to comply with the law, that is a matter of personal choice and nobody can force him or her to do so.[15]

7. Testamentary Charitable Remainder Trusts

A Charitable Remainder Trust (CRT) is an irrevocable trust in which the grantor makes a gift of appreciated property or other assets to the trust and designates at least one noncharitable beneficiary as the income beneficiary and at least one qualifying charity as the remainder beneficiary.[16] A CRT can be created during the grantor's life (inter vivos trust) or upon the grantor's death (testamentary trust). In both cases, the trust pays the noncharitable beneficiary or beneficiaries either a fixed dollar amount or a percentage of trust assets for a stipulated number of years. At the end of the term, the assets remaining in the trust will pass to the charity.

When created during a donor's lifetime, a CRT is a great vehicle for providing a charitably inclined donor or his or her beneficiaries with an immediate income stream while reducing future estate taxes, obtaining an immediate income-tax deduction, and benefiting a charity of the donor's choice. Similarly, a testamentary CRT provides an income stream to named beneficiaries upon the testator's death, with the remainder interest going to charity. Although a testamentary CRT does not offer a charitable income-tax deduction, it does have significant benefits, including a possible estate-tax deduction and avoidance of capital-gains or income taxes on the sale of trust assets.

A grantor can fund a testamentary CRT with a qualified retirement plan. There are no tax advantages to creating testamentary CRTs for other types of assets. The tax-advantaged nature of the CRT allows a grantor, over a period of years, to give the same amount to named beneficiaries

15. Quran 2:256.
16. 26 U.S.C. § 664 (2018).

that they would have received without a CRT while donating an often-equivalent remainder interest to charity.

Since a testamentary CRT is part of either a last will and testament or an RLT, it is governed by the Islamic Law of Inheritance and restrictions on the discretionary *wasiyah* share.

Example:
Mahmood is married to Sumayah and has three children. He owns an IRA that is currently worth $2 million and constitutes approximately 50 percent of his estate. Mahmood's attorney shows him an illustration of the way testamentary CRTs work with IRAs. If his investments perform as expected, Mahmood hopes to be able to give his estate away "twice": once to his beneficiaries in an amount equal to about $2 million over 20 years, and another $2 million 20 years after his death for the charitable purpose of building a mosque.

From a religious standpoint, Mahmood must develop this plan with the trust beneficiaries being his Islamic heirs. If, on the other hand, Mahmood's retirement-plan assets are expected to be worth less at his death than one-third of his overall estate, he can name beneficiaries other than his Islamic heirs and treat the CRT as his *wasiyah* share. Note, however, that if the CRT names any family member entitled to inheritance as a beneficiary, it must name all such family members, and their corresponding percentages would need to be consistent with the Islamic Law of Inheritance.

8. Testamentary Charitable Lead Trust

A Charitable Lead Trust (CLT) is often described as the inverse of a CRT. Both are split-interest trusts with an income interest and a remainder interest. However, in a CRT, the income interest—which may be a unitrust interest or an annuity interest—goes to named beneficiaries while the remainder interest goes to a charity. In a CLT, the income interest goes to a charity for a fixed number of years while the remainder interest goes to the named beneficiaries.

The purpose behind a testamentary CLT is to prevent the imposition of the federal estate tax after death. However, the downside is that family members may not see their inheritance for decades. One possible mechanism to allow for distributions over time is a five-layered testamentary CLT. In such an arrangement, beneficiaries receive the residual interest in five-year installments over 20 years. Even in this scenario, however, a substantial delay in distribution remains.

The law treats CLTs as having been created after the death of the testator. The trust administrator may fund the CLT after settlement, allowing for a "reasonable time" between death and funding. The obligation to pay the annuity or unitrust starts at the date of death of the decedent. However, the payments may be deferred until the end of the tax year.

Under the Islamic Law of Inheritance, such an arrangement would be acceptable only if combined with comprehensive estate planning designed to eliminate the estate tax through some other means. The testamentary CLT is thus merely a "poison pill" used in the event of postmortem disputes over estate-tax-planning techniques. Many practitioners believe the existence of such a provision as a backup estate-tax-elimination strategy would be a helpful supplement to other estate-planning techniques and as a defensive measure in the event of a tax controversy. Because of the long-term denial of inheritance, the technique should not be used by itself without the use of other estate-tax techniques.

When the charitable payments under a CLT end, distribution should be consistent with the Islamic Law of Inheritance. If the beneficiaries are no longer alive, their heirs should inherit the allocated shares through the principle of *munasakha* described previously.

Example:

Waleed has three children and an estate worth $40 million, much of which he holds in illiquid real estate. Waleed's attorney informs him that his estate faces a multimillion-dollar federal estate-tax liability upon death. At the advice of his lawyer, Waleed develops an aggressive estate-tax plan involving discounting through business entities and sales to grantor trusts. He is concerned that his estate plan may result in an audit or litigation from the IRS after death, causing needless hardship and a potentially catastrophic loss. This is because Waleed's real estate is illiquid and particularly difficult to sell.

Because the IRS expects payment of estate taxes within nine months,[17] Waleed creates a testamentary CLT to be funded with

17. 26 U.S.C. § 6075 (2018).

the assets from his estate necessary to avoid imposition of the federal estate tax. This plan utilizes Waleed's unlimited estate-tax charitable exemption.[18] The result is that most of his fortune would be unavailable to his beneficiaries for 20 years, while 5 percent of his estate is directed to charity each year. At the end of the 20-year term, assets would pass per Islamic law.

D. Planning Options for a Married Couple

One of the most important issues to consider when planning for a Muslim couple is the treatment of the surviving spouse. Many married couples will privilege the marital relationship over other relationships since they often live as a single economic unit, file joint taxes, co-own the marital home, share joint bank accounts, and, very commonly, rely on each other's savings for their retirement. Meanwhile, Islamic law limits the widower's share of his late wife's estate to one-half or one-fourth and limits the widow's share of her late husband's estate to one-fourth or one-eighth. Thus, many Muslim clients will want to find a way to protect the surviving spouse while still adhering to the sacred law.

The most notable issue that arises in this context is the management and ownership of the couple's primary residence. Family homes are typically one of the largest investments made by married couples, and a surviving spouse often would like to continue living in the house upon the first spouse's death. Under the Islamic Law of Inheritance, this would not be permissible if the decedent's interest in the home was worth more than the surviving spouse's share of the total estate.

To resolve this problem, the surviving spouse could simply receive his or her pro rata share of the home along with the other beneficiaries and buy out the other beneficiaries' shares if he or she has sufficient liquidity. Alternatively, if all the co-owners consent, they may allow him or her to remain in the home.

Such an arrangement is fraught with obvious peril. The more owners of the house, the less secure the surviving spouse will be in ensuring he or she can continue to live there. Beyond the negative tax implications of joint ownership of a family home, family members may have disagreements about what to do with the property, grow estranged, or face creditor

18. 26 U.S.C. § 2055 (2018).

problems in the form of a lawsuit, divorce, or bankruptcy. All these circumstances present the surviving spouse with significant risk.

Another option that would ensure that the surviving spouse can live in the marital home after the first spouse's death, while preserving the right to inheritance for nonspouse family members, is the use of a Credit Shelter Trust (also known as a bypass trust).

1. Credit Shelter Trusts

Prior to portability becoming a permanent part of the federal estate-tax system, married couples typically established a Credit Shelter Trust on the death of the first spouse in the amount of the estate-tax exclusion, which effectively sheltered the assets in the trust from the surviving spouse's estate. With the advent of portability and the higher estate-tax exemption, these trusts are now less common.

Nonetheless, the Credit Shelter Trust still maintains popularity among estate-planning attorneys for a few reasons. First, relying on portability requires the surviving spouse to file a timely estate-tax return, which may or may not happen. Second, assets inside a Credit Shelter Trust avoid estate taxes not only on the initial value of the assets but also on the appreciation and accumulated income between the deaths of the two spouses. Third, portability does not apply to the decedent's generation-skipping tax exemption.

In addition, there are potential asset-protection benefits to a Credit Shelter Trust that would prevent future creditors of the surviving spouse from reaching trust assets. The trust also provides inherent design flexibility, including "remarriage protection," which could stipulate that the surviving spouse lose any trustee powers to a replacement trustee in the event of remarriage. Such a provision may also be drafted to mandate that the surviving spouse create a binding prenuptial agreement as a condition for continuing to act as trustee.

The Credit Shelter Trust has two significant drawbacks. First, because assets inside the Credit Shelter Trust are excluded from the surviving spouse's estate, they fail to receive a second step-up in basis on the death of the second spouse or, in non-community-property states, any step-up in basis. This issue can be resolved by authorizing the trust protector to grant the surviving spouse a general power of appointment under section 2041, which would cause the assets to be includible in the second spouse's gross estate for the purpose of obtaining a step-up in basis.

Second, Credit Shelter Trust assets are subject to trust taxation at a significantly higher rate than nontrust assets. Given that trusts containing as little as $12,400 in taxable income are taxed at the top bracket, and that long-term capital gains (and qualified dividends) are taxed at a 23.8 percent (20 percent + 3.8 percent) rate (along with any applicable state taxes), this tax burden can be a significant one.

While the tax code allows trusts that distribute their income to beneficiaries to also allocate applicable taxes to the beneficiaries, thereby mitigating some of the aforesaid concerns, the drafting attorney should be sure to fully understand the tax implications of utilizing a Credit Shelter Trust before deciding to employ this tool.

A Credit Shelter Trust normally includes a funding formula that instructs the trustee to transfer assets to the trust on a pecuniary or fractional basis. While the specific language of the clauses may be complex, the basic ideas behind the clauses are similarly intended to maximize the federal unified credit. The pecuniary formula does this by including language that a pecuniary amount be used based on the credit, while the fractional marital deduction formula involves the use of a fractional formula to accomplish essentially the same thing.

The formula may have the effect of transferring wealth from one spouse to another, so, to the extent it changes the shares of inheritance, it would not be permissible under Islamic law.

The pecuniary marital deduction formula could result in unfavorable tax liability during trust administration. Accordingly, many estate planners prefer to use a fractional marital deduction formula, which avoids imposition of the estate tax and can easily be supplemented with a property agreement.

Example:
Bilal and Rukhsana are married. Bilal has assets of $10 million while Rukhsana has $300,000. They create an estate plan with a fractional marital deduction formula. The result of the formula clause could be to transfer several million dollars to Rukhsana's estate or, alternately, to a QTIP Trust. Neither of these results would be acceptable under the Islamic Law of Inheritance.

A Credit Shelter Trust is an acceptable tool for Muslim clients under Islamic law, provided a few conditions are met:

1. The surviving spouse must not be the sole beneficiary except in the rare case that the surviving spouse is the only Islamic heir. The trust must treat all Islamic heirs as beneficiaries.

2. There must be "sprinkling power" that permits the trustee to distribute assets to the various beneficiaries.
3. If any sprinkling power is used to make distributions to a beneficiary, the distribution amount should count as part of the total share to which the beneficiary is entitled upon final distribution of the trust.

The Credit Shelter Trust's inclusion of a sprinkling power does not mean beneficiaries possess a "demand right" to forcibly withdraw funds during the life of the surviving grantor. Such a plan recognizes that there are limitations to beneficial ownership of property. The mere fact that a person is a beneficiary does not mean that a trustee must make a distribution if it is impractical or harmful to do so. Under ordinary circumstances, however, Islamic law mandates that the trustee comply with a beneficiary's wishes to withdraw part or all of his or her rightful share of the trust assets.

Example:
Reshma is the successor trustee and widow of Ibrahim. Their daughter, Firdaus, requests and receives $150,000 for a down payment on a new home she is purchasing with her husband. This represents 50 percent of Firdaus's inheritance. Several years later, upon final distribution of the estate, Firdaus would be entitled to the remaining 50 percent of her inheritance, regardless of the size of the estate at that time; the estate may have either increased or decreased in the meantime.

A good way to describe the trust and sprinkling power provisions to clients is to use the analogy of a corporation. Ownership in shares of a corporation entails certain shareholder rights, which may include the right to dividends, if declared, as well as certain voting rights, limited or not. But shareholders in a corporation do not have unlimited rights. For example, there may be restrictions on share liquidity. Some shareholders may not even have the right to park in the corporate parking lot. Similarly, various rules apply to the beneficiaries of the Credit Shelter Trust.

2. Remarriage Protection While the Surviving Spouse Is the Trustee

The Credit Shelter Trust arrangement exists to provide a continuing benefit to the decedent's estate and, more specifically, to the surviving spouse, who is often appointed as trustee. Many clients are concerned, however, about the possibility that a surviving spouse may remarry and, in doing so, inadvertently disinherit the couple's children or otherwise inappropriately exercise his or her discretion as trustee.

Accordingly, the trust can be structured such that remarriage would cause the bypass trust to terminate and the assets therein to pass to beneficiaries in accordance with their allotted shares. This strategy may achieve the grantors' desire to keep assets in trust to minimize disruption to the family after the death of the first spouse. Where a new spouse replaces the decedent, that objective no longer remains.

Alternatively, the trust can include a provision requiring the surviving spouse to resign as trustee in the event of remarriage or to enter into a prenuptial agreement with his or her new spouse that protects the rights of all the decedent spouse's beneficiaries.

This may have the effect, however, of discouraging remarriage, which some courts have voided as against public policy. The key difference in this case is that the surviving spouse would still receive everything he or she is entitled to inherit when the Credit Shelter Trust terminates, so the surviving spouse is not actually losing any assets. A potential risk, however, would be the use of property partially owned by other beneficiaries.

Example:

Haaris and Bilqis are married. They execute an estate plan that allows for a Credit Shelter Trust after the first spouse's death. The trustee of the Credit Shelter Trust is the surviving spouse.

Haaris passes away first. Under the terms of the trust, Haaris's Islamic heirs would be the beneficiaries of the Credit Shelter Trust. Bilqis, as trustee, may during trust administration sell the home at fair-market value to the survivor's trust in exchange for a note to be held by the bypass trust. This note would have no interest in order to comply with the Islamic prohibition on *riba,* and the principal would be the value of the home, less the surviving spouse's own share. If Bilqis gets remarried, she may no longer serve as trustee of the Credit Shelter Trust. The new trustee may then sell the home and distribute the trust's assets consistent with the grantors' instructions for the benefit of the Islamic heirs.

This plan is useful in a blended family situation. While it may appear to discourage remarriage, the continued use of the home under Islamic law is an accommodation to the survivor, not a legal right. The paramount interests to be protected, rather, are the inheritance rights of the beneficiaries.

3. QTIP Trusts

The QTIP Trust is a versatile trust that allows a grantor to exercise the unlimited marital deduction, provide the surviving spouse with continuing income and the use of the trust principal for the duration of his or her life, and ensure that assets pass to the original grantor's beneficiaries upon the death of the second spouse.

QTIP Trusts are particularly useful in second-marriage scenarios where the grantor would like to provide for the surviving spouse for life while ensuring that the property ultimately passes to the grantor's children from a prior marriage.

To qualify for the unlimited marital deduction, the terminable interest must be "qualified,"[19] meaning that it must meet a number of requirements under IRC section 2056 and related regulations. Most notably, all income from the trust must be distributed to the surviving spouse annually. Failure to qualify for the unlimited marital deduction will subject the assets to estate tax on the first grantor's death.

Since Credit Shelter Trusts are becoming less useful in the current tax environment, many practitioners recommend that clients with legacy Credit Shelter Trusts replace their plans with QTIP Trusts.

While lifetime QTIP Trusts are permissible under Islamic law, testamentary QTIP Trusts are generally not, because they contain a requirement that all trust income be distributed at least annually to the surviving spouse. The income requirement is problematic because the surviving spouse's portion is fixed under the Islamic Law of Inheritance. In other words, it is conceivable that the income generated from the QTIP Trust could far exceed the inheritance entitlement over a lifetime.

A QTIP Trust may appear to be an adequate solution in cases where there are few assets outside the family home, since the home can be placed in the QTIP Trust, and the right to use the home free of rent will qualify as an income interest without actually changing the surviving spouse's share of the decedent's inheritance.[20] However, if a requirement to use the trust for productive property results in a sale of nonproductive assets and use

19. I.R.C. § 2056 (2018).
20. 26 C.F.R. § 20.2056(b)–.2057(h) (2018).

of the proceeds to purchase income-producing property, the effect could be to modify the shares of inheritance in an Islamically impermissible way.

4. General Power of Appointment Trusts

Another way to utilize the unused estate-tax exemption of the surviving spouse while not invoking the "terminable interest" rule is a General Power of Appointment Trust.[21] In a General Power of Appointment Trust, the surviving spouse is typically entitled to all income for life and is allowed to determine the disposition of the assets upon his or her death.

In addition to the income requirement, which could alter the distribution provisions in a manner that violates the Islamic Law of Inheritance for the same reason the QTIP trust would, the general power of appointment further disqualifies the technique and renders this trust impermissible for most Muslim families.

5. Disclaimer Trusts

Disclaimer Trusts provide a "wait-and-see" approach to Credit Shelter Trust planning and are frequently utilized when the combined assets of the spouses are less than one applicable exclusion amount.[22] A disclaimer allows the surviving spouse the ability during the postmortem trust administration to transfer some or all assets to a Credit Shelter Trust to prevent imposition of the estate tax. Given the current estate-tax environment and the portability of a decedent spouse's exemption, a Disclaimer Trust is less appealing.

In any event, Disclaimer Trusts are also not consistent with Islamic inheritance law because they automatically pass all assets to the surviving spouse on the decedent's death and rely on the spouse to fund the Credit Shelter Trust. Since the Islamic Law of Inheritance mandates distribution of assets to beneficiaries in addition to the surviving spouse, it would not be permissible to leave all the assets to the surviving spouse.

A similar device to the Disclaimer Trust is the Clayton Election.[23] This tool provides the surviving spouse with the option of keeping assets in a traditional bypass trust, which provides estate-tax protection but does not provide a second step-up in basis, or treating the trust as a QTIP Trust so assets can be included in the surviving spouse's estate and thereby enable

21. 26 U.S.C. § 2056(b)(5) (2018).
22. 26 U.S.C. § 2518 (2018).
23. *See* Estate of Clayton v. Comm'r, 976 F.2d 1486 (1992).

assets to obtain a second step-up in basis. While the Clayton Election is advantageous for tax-planning purposes, it also suffers from the same issues as Disclaimer Trusts.

E. Common Trusts

A Common Trust, also known as a family pot trust, is an estate-planning tool that addresses the concern of disparate treatment of differently aged children because of the death of one or more parents.

Example:
Sulaiyman and Rania have five children—Intisar, Yacoob, Bilal, Zaynab, and Adam. Intisar and Yacoob are 25-year-old twins who graduated from medical school, and their parents covered both of their expenses throughout their education. In addition, Intisar married last year, and her parents spent $100,000 on her wedding festivities. The parents have assisted these two adult children in other ways as well, including buying cars, paying for rent, and taking them on ski trips. The three younger children are all under the age of ten. The parents believe it would be unfair to provide equal distributions to all the children of the same gender given the disparate lifetime spending and would like to address the college, graduate school, and wedding costs of the three younger children separately from their eventual inheritance.

Under Islamic inheritance law, a Common Trust is impermissible. Unequal expenditures during life are not taken into consideration when calculating shares of inheritance.

Rather, an alternative solution to such client concerns would be to implement lifetime gifting strategies for the minor children to assist with education or other support. For example, a parent may wish to create an irrevocable trust and act as the trustee. Funds from the trust may be used for a wedding, down payment on the child's first home, and even education. Tax-advantaged devices, such as a 529 plan for educational expenses, may also be useful for these purposes.

CHAPTER 7

Planning for Individuals and Assets Abroad

Counseling Muslim clients may involve some degree of international estate planning. According to a 2012 survey by the Pew Research Center, nearly 65 percent of American Muslims are first-generation immigrants, and Muslims account for nearly 10 percent of all legal immigration to this country.[1] Many Muslims are married to immigrants and often maintain family, property, and business relationships overseas. In addition, some international clients—who may or may not hold U.S. citizenship—own property in the United States.

Planning around international succession systems can be challenging, as they vary widely in substance. First, not all jurisdictions recognize trusts, and some impose forced heirship via statute. In addition, Muslims in certain Western countries may face discrimination due to stigmas surrounding Islam and *Sharia*. Thus, a client who seeks to plan his or her estate according to Islamic inheritance law may not be able to legally do so in such jurisdictions. This is in stark contrast to planning within the borders of some Islamic countries, which would automatically implement some version of Islamic inheritance law upon the client's death.

1. *The Religious Affiliation of U.S. Immigrants: Majority Christian, Rising Share of Other Faiths: Muslim Immigrants*, Pew Research Ctr. (May 17, 2013), http://www.pewforum.org/2013/05/17/the-religious-affiliation-of-us-immigrants/#muslim.

Each scenario requires an attorney to provide special care when advising clients on structuring U.S. investments and maximizing federal and state tax advantages on the transfer of those investments to future generations.

While the subject of international estate planning, like so many other topics in this book, is far more complex than we can possibly cover, our purpose here is to enable the drafting attorney to identify the important issues affecting his or her client. Given the assortment of international rules involved, we recommend coordinating with local counsel in the applicable foreign jurisdiction or seeking out further tax counsel whenever necessary.

A. Who Is Subject to U.S. Tax Laws?

The IRC treats "U.S. persons" differently from "foreign persons" (or "nonresident aliens"). Citizens and permanent residents (green-card holders), as well as domestic business entities and trusts, are categorized as U.S. persons and are subject to the full scope of the U.S. transfer-tax and income-tax systems, including a range of reporting requirements, on all income earned and assets held worldwide. U.S. persons are entitled to an estate-tax exemption, or applicable exclusion amount, of $11.4 million in 2019, indexed for inflation.

Foreign persons, on the other hand, pay income tax only on their U.S.-sourced income. While that may initially seem advantageous, the U.S. estate- and gift-tax system is significantly more onerous for foreign persons than for their American counterparts and thus requires a high degree of caution and awareness. Unlike U.S. persons, who are entitled to an applicable exclusion amount of $11.4 million, nonresident aliens are entitled to an applicable exclusion amount of only $60,000 on U.S.-based assets.

Example:
Sharifa is a U.S. citizen and resident of Georgia. Her father, Abdullah, is a wealthy landowner in Morocco. He only visits his daughter in Georgia for two weeks at a time every two years and neither earns income nor conducts any business in the United States. Abdullah gives Sharifa a gift of ranch land in Morocco valued at $10 million. There are no U.S. gift-tax implications for this gift.[2]

Similarly, if Sharifa were to receive this property after Abdullah's death, there would be no estate- or gift-tax implications.

2. IRC sections 2501 and 2511 cover the rules on gift taxes for nonresident aliens.

The Generation-Skipping Transfer (GST) tax mostly comes into play for assets where the gift tax and the estate tax already apply. Specifically, it would apply to a transfer to a trust if the transfer were subject to other transfer taxes.[3]

Despite their comparative disadvantages on paper, foreign persons can often escape U.S. taxation completely if they properly manage their assets in the United States. There are several classes of assets, for instance, that are free of any withholding or federal income tax. Most of these sources, however, include forms of interest income as well as nonbusiness gambling earnings and are typically of no interest to religious Muslim clients.

In general, foreign persons should not directly own property in the United States, as such property would be subject to both federal gift and income taxation. Rather, foreign clients should own their American property through a foreign business entity to avoid such taxation. Accordingly, it is vital for non-U.S. persons with at least part of their assets in the United States to plan their estates in a way that minimizes exposure to these systems of taxation.

B. Defining Residency

The IRC treats U.S. residents differently from nonresidents for the purposes of transfer taxes (i.e., estate and gift taxes) and income taxes.

With regard to estate and gift taxes, a person may be considered a U.S. resident if he or she is living in the United States at the time of his or her death or at the time of making a gift. The test is based on domicile, defined as living in the United States with no present intent of leaving. Courts will consider a wide range of criteria to determine domicile, including the decedent's statements, length of time in the country, green-card status, living habits, ties to a former country, local affiliations, and whether any bilateral estate-tax treaties exist between the United States and the client's country of origin.[4]

For income-tax purposes, section 7701(b) of the Tax Code provides a more concrete definition of "resident." Specifically, a person can qualify as a resident for income-tax purposes by either (a) becoming a lawful permanent resident or a green-card holder, or (b) meeting the "substantial presence" test—presence in the United States for at least 31 days during the current year and a total of 183 days during the three-year period containing the

3. 26 C.F.R. § 26.2662-2 (2018).

4. A list of estate-tax treaties can be found at https://www.irs.gov/businesses/small-businesses-self-employed/estate-gift-tax-treaties-international (last updated Apr. 3, 2018).

current year and the two years immediately prior. All the days of presence in the current year are counted, as well as one-third of the days of presence in the immediately preceding year and one-sixth of the days of presence in the year immediately preceding that one.

Example:
Hafsa, a German citizen, was physically present in the United States for 120 days in each of the years 2016, 2017, and 2018, totaling 360 days overall. She has not, however, qualified as a resident under the substantial presence test because, while all of her 120 days in 2018 are included in the calculation, only 40 (or one-third) of her days in 2016 are counted, and only 20 (or one-sixth) of her days in 2015 are counted. Therefore, only 180 days are included in the calculation—three shy of the requirement—even though she has actually spent 360 days in the country.[5]

Notably, under the substantial presence test, a person who may be considered undocumented from the perspective of immigration authorities may still qualify as a U.S. resident where the IRS is concerned.

Notwithstanding the preceding, there are several exceptions that permit an individual to override the substantial presence or green-card tests. These include the "first-year choice" rule, electing residency along with a resident spouse, claiming a closer connection to a foreign country, or invoking bilateral treaties that the United States may have in place with the person's home country.

C. U.S. Citizenship and Transfers to Noncitizen Spouses

American citizenship is determined according to the Immigration and Nationality Act of 1965 (INA). Under the act, a person is a U.S. citizen if he or she is (a) born in the United States or certain U.S. territories, (b) born outside the United States to one or more U.S.-citizen parents, or (c) naturalized by fulfilling the requirements established by Congress in the INA.

---

5. Example derived from IRS Publication 519, *U.S. Tax Guide for Aliens*, at 4 (Feb. 28, 2018), https://www.irs.gov/pub/irs-pdf/p519.pdf.

U.S. citizenship comes with various privileges. But acquiring citizenship in the United States may mean giving up citizenship somewhere else. While the United States does permit dual citizenship with caveats noted below, many other countries do not. Acquiring U.S. citizenship may mean that a client loses significant rights in his or her home country, including the ability to visit freely, the right to own property or operate a business, the right to vote or run for public office, and in some cases the right to inherit.

In rare instances, American citizens who have left the United States or are contemplating doing so may opt to relinquish their citizenship to reduce or eliminate the burdens of compliance with the U.S. tax code. Section 877A(g)(4) describes the requirements for relinquishing citizenship for U.S. tax purposes. Because the consequences of expatriating are significant and often irreversible, the client should be careful not to perform any of the following actions without obtaining proper counsel, as they may result in immediate loss of U.S. citizenship:[6]

- Voluntarily obtaining citizenship in another country
- Swearing an oath of allegiance to a foreign country
- Entering the armed forces of another country whose armed forces are engaged in hostilities against the United States
- Formally renouncing citizenship before a U.S. foreign service officer abroad
- Committing treason

D. Non-U.S.-Citizen Spouse

One of the most fundamental tools in the estate planner's toolbox is IRC section 2056(a), also known as the "unlimited marital deduction." Perhaps the most important estate-tax-saving device available, assets left to a U.S.-citizen spouse upon the decedent's death—irrespective of their value—are exempt from estate tax.

One common challenge for an estate-planning attorney in advising Muslim clients is that spouses are frequently non-U.S. citizens. Under section 2056(d), assets transferred to a non-U.S.-citizen spouse through a gift or inheritance do not qualify for the unlimited marital deduction. The two exceptions to this rule are when

6. I.N.A. § 101(a) (2018).

1. the surviving spouse becomes a U.S. citizen, or
2. assets are left for the surviving spouse inside a Qualified Domestic Trust (QDOT).

A QDOT is a statutorily created trust designed to allow a noncitizen surviving spouse to benefit from the unlimited marital deduction. For estates that may be subject to the federal estate tax, a QDOT can serve as a valuable tool by enabling the surviving spouse to benefit from the unlimited marital deduction while ensuring that he or she subsequently leaves the country without paying applicable estate taxes. A QDOT contains numerous requirements, including a timely election, a U.S.-citizen or domestic-corporation trustee authorized to retain estate tax from the trust assets, and various additional criteria contained in the Treasury regulations under IRC section 2056(a).

E. Annual Gift Exclusion

All gifts to a citizen-spouse qualify for the unlimited marital deduction. The citizenship status of the donor spouse is irrelevant. So long as the donee-spouse is a U.S. citizen and the requirements of IRC section 2523 are met, the marital deduction will apply.

A gift from a U.S. citizen to a noncitizen spouse, however, does not benefit from the unlimited marital deduction. Instead, the donor is entitled to a large annual exclusion. IRC section 2523(i)(2) provides that, where the donee-spouse is not a U.S. citizen, a donor is eligible for an inflation-adjusted, modified annual exclusion that, for 2018, was set at $152,000.

For gifts above this amount, the U.S. citizen making the gift either will use up some of his or her unified credit of $5.49 million or, if that is already exhausted, will need to pay applicable gift taxes.

Example 1:
Aisha is a non-U.S. citizen residing in France. She gives her husband, Daniel, a U.S. citizen, shares of stock valued at $1 million. There are no U.S. transfer-tax implications for this gift.

Example 2:
Daniel, a U.S. citizen, gives his wife, Aisha, a citizen of France and not the United States, a diamond ring valued at $500,000. This exceeds the annual exclusion amount. Daniel would be required to file a Form 709, the gift-tax return, evidencing a gift of $347,000, or $500,000 minus the $152,000 of the annual exclusion. If he has not yet used his entire applicable exclusion amount of $11.2 million (in 2018), no gift tax would be due.

The lack of an unlimited exclusion is important to note when advising clients with noncitizen spouses. For example, it is common for taxpayers to add a noncitizen spouse as a joint owner of a marital home, bank account, or investment account upon marriage. If the amount of the gift exceeds the exclusion amount allowable for gifts to noncitizen spouses, a gift-tax return will need to be filed with applicable gift-tax payments due if necessary.

Comparatively, under IRC section 2523(i), the creation of a joint tenancy for real property will not constitute a gift unless an election is made to treat it as such or the property is sold. There may also be estate-tax consequences upon the death of a U.S.-citizen spouse. Unlike real property, however, the creation of a joint interest for personal property, such as brokerage accounts or bank accounts, will be deemed a gift, and the interest of each spouse will be treated as one-half the value of the jointly held personal property.[7]

F. Interspousal Loans

As a general rule, the IRS presumes that intrafamily loans are actually disguised gifts. For this reason, IRC section 7872 treats the economic benefit of a low-interest or interest-free loan as a gift for gift- and estate-tax

7. Recall that owning property as joint tenants with a right of survivorship is typically not a religiously compliant method of property ownership under Islamic inheritance law. Because the decedent will almost always have more Islamic heirs than just the surviving spouse, Islamic inheritance law provides mandatory shares to multiple beneficiaries.

purposes. This is somewhat problematic for Muslims, who, under the *Sharia*, are not allowed to lend or borrow with interest.

Even so, the caveat to these rules is that spouses are treated as one individual, even if one spouse is not a U.S. citizen. As such, there is no imputed interest on interspousal loans under section 7872. Transfers to other family members must be properly documented, however, to avoid treatment of the loan as a taxable gift. Such documentation should preferably include a promissory note, collateral or other security that supports the loan, a fixed maturity date, and a consistent recording of repayment.

G. Preimmigration Planning

Wealthy individuals hoping to immigrate to the United States must understand that, after immigration, all worldwide assets and income will be subject to U.S. taxes. Thus, clients should take reasonable steps prior to immigration to allow for assets to pass to entities and individuals not subject to U.S. taxation.

Example:
Ahmed is a wealthy asylum-seeker fleeing war in the Middle East. Most of his holdings are in various countries in the Middle East and Europe. Ahmed moves to the United States, where he hopes to establish himself and embark on future business ventures. In time, Ahmed obtains a green card, which renders him a permanent U.S. resident. As a resident, all of Ahmed's income from his varied business holdings abroad is subject to the federal income tax, and his entire worldwide estate is subject to estate tax. If Ahmed becomes a U.S. citizen and subsequently elects to live overseas, all his assets will continue to be subject to all forms of U.S. income and transfer taxation, unless exempted by a treaty.

Ahmed could have avoided the negative tax consequences associated with U.S. residency through preimmigration estate planning. Prior to relocating to the United States, he should have sold or gifted his assets to various irrevocable trusts to develop the tax, income, and ownership structure he would prefer upon arrival.

For example, Ahmed could have taken the following steps:

1. Created a foreign corporation to hold his business assets
2. Gifted the bulk of his assets to a foreign grantor trust with distribution provisions consistent with the Islamic Law of Inheritance
3. Created a dynasty trust and gift his assets to it to shield his wealth from future creditors for generations
4. Accelerated income and deferred expenses to minimize the impact of income taxation as he makes his transition to the United States

Because Ahmed is not subject to U.S. taxation on his foreign assets as a nonresident and noncitizen, the limited scope of the U.S. gift tax means he can establish a foreign grantor trust or even, under some circumstances, a U.S.-based dynasty trust and transfer a variety of assets into it for the benefit of U.S. beneficiaries. There is no gift-tax or GST liability on the foreign assets and potentially no GST liability for the gift if it falls within GST limits. There is, however, a reporting requirement if the gift exceeds $100,000.

H. Holding Foreign Assets

U.S. citizens are required to pay income taxes on all their assets here and abroad. As such, Muslims with U.S. citizenship must include all assets owned overseas in their estate plans.

Clients with international financial accounts, including bank and brokerage accounts—or anyone taking responsibility for such an account—will be subject to certain disclosure rules and must electronically file a Report of Foreign Bank and Financial Accounts, or FBAR.

There is a series of special reporting requirements for property overseas. It is common for individuals with property overseas to not report foreign assets. In many instances, clients may be hesitant to disclose overseas property, as they may regard it as irrelevant for American taxation purposes, or the ownership structure may be uncertain. Oftentimes clients must clarify their overseas ownership of property to ensure their own heirs are the beneficiaries.

Many clients will also be required to file Form 8938 for specified foreign assets if those assets attain a certain value. The assets specified include stocks issued by a non-U.S. person, financial accounts maintained by a foreign financial institution, financial instruments or contracts with a non-U.S. counterparty, and any interests in foreign entities. A beneficial interest in a trust may require reporting if the beneficiary is aware of such an interest. With respect to a discretionary trust, the interest in the trust amounts to the distribution received by the trust in a given year.

In 2018, single filers and married couples filing separately were required to file Form 8938 if the total value of their qualifying foreign financial assets exceeded $50,000 on the last day of the tax year or more than $75,000 at any time during the tax year. Conversely, married couples filing jointly were required to file Form 8938 if such assets were valued at more than $100,000 on the last day of the tax year or more than $150,000 at any time during the tax year.

Example:

Hamza's father established an offshore discretionary dynasty trust valued at $80 million for the benefit of Hamza and his three siblings. Within a year, the trustee made a distribution to Hamza, a U.S. citizen, in the amount of $300,000. As a result, Hamza reports the $300,000 on Form 8938. The following year, Hamza receives no distribution from the trust. He therefore does not file Form 8938.

I. Domestic and Foreign Corporations

Shares in a corporation owned by a U.S. resident are deemed to be situated in the United States, regardless of where the certificates are physically located. The opposite is true of shares in foreign corporations, which are always deemed to be located outside the United States.

The IRS regards foreign corporations as Controlled Foreign Corporations (CFCs) if ownership of shares is controlled by a U.S. person through vote or value. Control is defined somewhat expansively under IRC section 958. A "person" can be a corporation, domestic partnership, estate, or trust.[8]

8. 26 U.S.C. § 7701(a)(30) (2018).

This control can be exerted through foreign entities, and there is a series of constructive ownership rules that may apply in such circumstances.[9]

If a person holds shares in a CFC, that individual will be taxed at ordinary income-tax rates on the corporation's pro rata income, regardless of whether any income was distributed. Liquidation of the interest will subject the seller to ordinary income-tax rates on the unrealized income as well as any gain in excess of basis.

A Passive Foreign Investment Company (PFIC) is a company that meets either of the following two criteria: (1) 50 percent or more of the company's assets consist of investments that generate income in the form of earned interest, dividends, or capital gains, or (2) 75 percent or more of the entity's gross income is "passive"—income derived from investments rather than active trade or business or gains on the sale of property. It can include rents, interests, royalties, and other investment income. This income is subject to ordinary income tax. There is also a penalty on "excess distribution," which is a distribution that exceeds 125 percent of what was received in previous years.

U.S. persons who have an indirect or direct interest in a PFIC or a Qualified Electing Fund should file a Form 8621 annually. Beneficiaries through a discretionary trust or foreign nongrantor trust will need to report these interests.

J. International Succession to Property

Muslims who prefer to have their estate distributed in accordance with the Islamic Law of Inheritance may find that holding assets outside the United States will complicate their efforts. A number of civil law countries across continental Europe impose a system of "forced heirship" that would prevent Muslims from distributing their assets consistent with *Sharia*. In contrast, U.S. jurisdictions generally refrain from interfering with testamentary transfers of property, with the exception of state statutes designed to protect a surviving spouse. Holding assets inside a U.S.-based trust provides additional flexibility for planning and distributing assets pursuant to the client's own desires.

In most Muslim-majority countries, meanwhile, the default system of inheritance is typically Islamic inheritance law. Though there may be some

9. 26 U.S.C. § 958(b) (2018).

slight variations between jurisdictions, such details are beyond the scope of this book.

Example:
Muhammad is a French citizen with substantial business interests in France. He also owns a vacation home in California valued at $4 million. He would like to ensure that his assets are distributed in accordance with the Islamic Law of Inheritance. Furthermore, he wants to minimize the impact of any transfer taxes in the United States.

Muhammad's estate-planning attorney advises that he hold his vacation home in an offshore corporation. This will minimize the impact of transfer taxes upon death, since his estate-tax exemption as a nonresident alien is only $60,000. If he owns his property through the foreign corporation, the property would be deemed to be owned outside the United States.

Even if Muhammad follows this advice, he would still face the problem of owning property in France, a country that may not permit Islamic succession to assets because of statutory forced heirship. The best move for Muhammad would be to own his property through entities in an offshore trust in a jurisdiction that allows free alienation of property. This jurisdiction would not be the United States, of course, since he does not want to create U.S.-based assets and thereby be subject to U.S. transfer taxes.

In light of the above, Muhammad creates a trust in the island of Nevus. The trust holds shares to all of his business entities. While French law mandates stringent reporting requirements for all trusts due to money laundering regulations, it does not limit this form of planning.

By taking the foregoing steps, Muhammad is able to accomplish his goals of minimizing taxation in the United States while implementing a succession plan consistent with his faith tradition.

APPENDIX

A

Detailed Order of Heirs under Sunni Inheritance Law

This section provides a detailed explanation of Sunni inheritance law, based on the Hanafi school of jurisprudence. Note that there are several online tools a practitioner can use to perform these calculations.

A. Categories of Heirs

Hanafi jurists have divided a decedent's Islamic heirs into three categories: (A) Quranic heirs (*Dhawil Furood*), (B) residuary heirs (*Asabah*), and (C) distant kindred (*Dhawil Arham*).

Quranic heirs inherit first and receive fixed portions from the estate. If any assets remain in the estate, residuary heirs receive their share next. If there are no Quranic or residuary heirs, the estate passes to distant kindred.

1. Quranic Heirs (*Dhawil Furood*)

There are twelve *Dhawil Furood*, or Quranic heirs (four male and eight female), entitled to receive predetermined shares as specified in the Quran.

However, not all the heirs may inherit, as some may be excluded by the presence of other heirs. We use the terms "high" and "low" to refer to ascendants and descendants.

1. **Father:** A father inherits in one of three ways:
    a. A father receives a one-sixth share if the decedent is survived by a son or grandson through a son, however low.
    b. A father receives a one-sixth share as a Quranic heir plus the residue of the estate if the decedent is survived by at least one daughter or a daughter from a son, however low.
    c. A father converts to a residuary heir if the decedent is not survived by children or grandchildren, however low.
2. **Paternal Grandfather:** The paternal grandfather or great-grandfather, however high, will take the place of the father if the decedent's father is deceased. According to the Hanafi school of jurisprudence, the presence of a paternal grandfather will cause siblings to be excluded.
    a. A paternal grandfather receives a one-sixth share if the decedent is survived by at least one son or grandson through a son, however low.
    b. A paternal grandfather receives a one-sixth share plus any residue if the deceased is survived by at least one daughter or a daughter from a son, however low.
3. **Husband (Widower):** A widower always inherits.
    a. A widower receives a one-fourth share of his late wife's estate if she is survived by any children or son's children, however low.
    b. A widower receives one-half of his late wife's estate if she is not survived by any children or son's children, however low.
4. **Wife (Widow):** A widow always inherits.
    a. A widow receives a one-eighth share of her late husband's estate if he is survived by any children or son's children, however low.
    b. A widow receives a one-fourth share of her late husband's estate if he is not survived by any children or son's children, however low.
5. **Daughter:** A daughter will always inherit in one of the following three conditions:
    a. If the decedent is survived by one daughter and no sons, the daughter receives one-half of the gross estate.

   b. If the decedent is survived by two or more daughters and no sons, the daughters will split two-thirds of the gross estate equally.
   c. If the decedent is survived by one or more sons and one or more daughters, all the children shall be converted into residuary heirs, and the sons receive twice the daughters' share.
6. **Granddaughter from Son:** In the absence of living children, a son's daughter is treated like a daughter.
   a. If the decedent is not survived by children or a grandson from a son but is survived by one granddaughter from a son, the granddaughter receives one-half of the estate.
   b. If the decedent is not survived by children or a grandson from a son but is survived by more than one granddaughter from a son, the granddaughters will split two-thirds of the estate equally.
   c. If the decedent is survived by one daughter and a granddaughter from a son, but no son and no grandson from a son, the granddaughter receives a one-sixth share.
   d. If the decedent is survived by more than one daughter and no sons and is survived by a granddaughter from a son, the granddaughter would be excluded unless the decedent was also survived by a grandson from a son.
7. **Mother**
   a. If the decedent is not survived by any children or two or more siblings, the mother receives a one-third share.
   b. If the decedent is survived by children or grandchildren or two or more siblings, the mother receives a one-sixth share.
8. **Grandmother** (paternal and maternal)
   a. A paternal grandmother receives a one-sixth share if the decedent is not survived by a mother, father, or maternal grandmother.
   b. A paternal grandmother receives a 1/12 share if the decedent is not survived by a mother or father but is survived by a maternal grandmother.
   c. A maternal grandmother receives a one-sixth share if the decedent is not survived by a mother, father, or paternal grandmother.
   d. A maternal grandmother receives a 1/12 share if the decedent is not survived by a mother or father but is survived by a paternal grandmother.

9. **Full Sisters**
   a. If the decedent is survived by one full sister but not by offspring, male paternal ancestors, or full brothers, the sister receives one-half of the estate.
   b. If the decedent is survived by two or more full sisters but not by offspring, male paternal ancestors, or full brothers, the sisters will split two-thirds of the estate equally.
10. **Agnate Sisters** (Paternal Half-Sisters)
   a. If the decedent is survived by one agnate sister but not by offspring, male paternal ancestors, or full brothers or sisters, the agnate sister receives one-half of the estate.
   b. If the decedent is survived by more than one agnate sister but not by offspring, male paternal ancestors, or full brothers or sisters, the agnate sisters will split two-thirds of the estate equally.
   c. If the decedent is survived by one or more agnate sisters and by one full sister but not by offspring, male paternal ancestors, or full brothers, the agnate sisters will split one-sixth of the estate equally.
11. **Uterine Brother** (Maternal Half-Brother): A uterine brother is excluded if the decedent is survived by a child or a son's child, however low, or a father or paternal grandfather, however high.
12. **Uterine Sister** (Maternal Half-Sister): A uterine sister is excluded if the decedent is survived by a child or a son's child, however low, or a father or paternal grandfather, however high.
   a. If the decedent is survived by one uterine sibling but not by any offspring or male paternal ancestors, the uterine sibling receives a one-sixth share.
   b. If the decedent is survived by two or more uterine siblings but not by any offspring or male paternal ancestors, the uterine siblings will split one-third of the estate equally. (Note that the traditional rule that males receive double the share of females is not applicable in this context.)

Once all the Quranic heirs receive their shares, the remainder of the estate is distributed to the *Asabah*, or residuary heirs. If there are no living *Asabah*, the remainder of the estate is redistributed proportionally to the Quranic heirs (with the exception of the spouse) under the doctrine of return, or *Radd*, before any residuary is distributed to the *Dhawil Arham*, or distant kindred.

2. Residuary Heirs (*Asabah*)

After Quranic heirs receive their shares, the rest of the estate should be distributed to the residuary heirs. Residuary heirs typically are male relatives or are related to the decedent through the paternal lineage and are divided into several groups. Three important rules apply with respect to distribution to residuary heirs:

1. The presence of any member of a higher group (see Table 1) excludes anyone in a lower group from inheriting with two exceptions:
   a. A son can never cause a father to be excluded.
   b. The Shafi, Maliki, and Hanbali schools of jurisprudence hold that a paternal grandfather excludes neither full- nor half-siblings, while the Hanafi school holds that a paternal grandfather excludes agnate siblings.
2. Within a group, an individual who is nearer in degree to the decedent excludes the more remote from inheriting.
3. Full-blood relatives take priority over half-blood relatives of the same degree.

Table 1. Male Residuary Heirs (Asabah)

Groups	Members of Group
Group 1 — Descendants	Son Son's male descendants
Group 2 — Ascendants	Father Father's male ascendants
Group 3 — Brother and Male Issue	Full Brother Agnate Brother Full Brother's Son Agnate Brother's Son Descendants of Group 3
Group 4 — Paternal Uncle and Male Issue	Full Paternal Uncle Agnate Paternal Uncle Full Paternal Uncle's son Agnate Paternal Uncle's Son Descendants of Group 4

Women who would otherwise be categorized as primary heirs become residuary heirs in the presence of a brother, as described in Table 2 below. In such cases, females will receive half the share of their brothers based on the Quranic injunction, "God commands you that a son should have the equivalent share of two daughters."[1] Only the decedent's daughter, son's daughters, full sister, agnate sister, and mother (in only one scenario) can become female residuary heirs through this process. The presence of a female residuary heir does not change any of the distribution rules described previously.

Table 2. Female Residuary Heirs

Relation to Decedent	Converted to Residuary Heirs Only If . . .
Daughters	they have brothers
Son's Daughters	they have brothers or cousins of equal rank
Full Sisters	the decedent is survived by full brothers
Agnate Sisters	the decedent is survived by agnate brothers

There is only one scenario in which a sister can become a residuary heir in the absence of a brother: when the deceased is not survived by brothers but is survived by a daughter or son's daughter. In such a scenario, all the distribution rules stated in the preceding are applicable, and the sister is treated as a male in Table 1.

3. Distant Kindred (*Dhawil Arham*)[2]

If there are any assets in excess of shares distributed to Quranic and residuary heirs, the excess is to be distributed among the distant kindred—all the decedent's remaining relatives who are not categorized as Quranic or residuary heirs. Because the distribution rules pertaining to distant kindred are sufficiently complex and, as a practical matter, they rarely will inherit, we mention them briefly and encourage the practitioner to seek further counsel should such a situation apply.

1. *The Qur'an: English Translation and Parallel Arabic Text* 4:11 (M.A.S. Abdel Haleem trans., 2005).

2. This category exists only under Hanafi jurisprudence. Not all schools of Islamic law recognize *Dhawil Arham* as legitimate beneficiaries.

There are four categories of distant kindred, identified in order in Table 3 below. Two basic rules govern distribution to distant kindred: (1) The presence of any members of a higher category excludes all members of any category below from inheriting, and (2) within each category, the presence of any individuals in a higher class excludes all members of the classes below from inheriting.

Table 3. Distant Kindred

Category 1—Descendants Who Are Not Quranic Heirs or Residuary Heirs	Class 1—Daughter's Children Class 2—Son's Daughter's Children Class 3—Daughter's Children's Children
Category 2—Ascendants Who Are Not Quranic Heirs or Residuary Heirs	Class 1—Maternal Grandfather Class 2—Father's Maternal Grandfather Mother's Paternal Grandfather Mother's Maternal Grandfather Mother's Maternal Grandmother
Category 3—Nieces and Nephews Who Are Not Quranic Heirs or Residuary Heirs	Class 1—Sister's Children Paternal Half-Sister's Children Maternal Half-Sister's Children Brother's Daughters Paternal Half-Brother's Daughters Maternal Half-Brother's Children Class 2—Brother's Son's Daughters Paternal Half-Brother's Son's Daughters Maternal Half-Brother's Son's Children Brother's Daughter's Children Paternal Half-Brother's Daughter's Children Maternal Half-Brother's Daughter's Children Sister's Son's Children Paternal Half-Sister's Son's Children Maternal Half-Sister's Son's Children Sister's Daughter's Children Paternal Half-Sister's Daughter's Children Maternal Half-Sister's Daughter's Children

(continued on next page)

Table 3. Distant Kindred *(continued)*

Category 4—Aunts, Uncles, and Cousins Who Are Not Quranic Heirs or Residuary Heirs	Class 1(a)—Father's Sister Father's Paternal Half-Sister Father's Maternal Half-Sister Father's Maternal Half-Brother Class 1(b)—Mother's Brother Mother's Sister Mother's Paternal Half-Brother Mother's Paternal Half-Sister Mother's Maternal Half-Brother Mother's Maternal Half-Sister Class 2(a)—Paternal Uncle's Daughters Paternal Aunt's Children Father's Paternal Half-Brother's Daughters Father's Paternal Half-Sister's Children Father's Maternal Half-Brother's Children Father's Maternal Half-Sister's Children Class 2(b)—Maternal Uncle's Children Maternal Aunt's Children Mother's Paternal Half-Brother's Children Mother's Paternal Half-Sister's Children Mother's Maternal Half-Brother's Children Mother's Maternal Half-Sister's Children Class 3(a)—Father's Paternal Aunt Father's Father's Paternal Half-Sister Father's Father's Maternal Half-Brother Father's Father's Maternal Half-Sister Class 3(b)—Father's Maternal Uncle Father's Maternal Aunt Father's Mother's Paternal Half-Brother Father's Mother's Paternal Half-Sister Father's Mother's Maternal Half-Brother Father's Mother's Maternal Half-Sister Class 3(c)—Mother's Paternal Aunt Mother's Father's Paternal Half-Sister Mother's Father's Maternal Half-Brother Mother's Father's Maternal Half-Sister Class 3(d)—Mother's Maternal Uncle Mother's Maternal Aunt Mother's Mother's Paternal Half-Brother Mother's Mother's Paternal Half-Sister Mother's Mother's Maternal Half-Brother Mother's Mother's Maternal Half-Sister

The following appendices are sample estate-planning forms. All of the names and entities are common names and do not refer to actual clients.

These materials are adapted from and published with permission from WealthCounsel, LLC's WealthDocx® drafting system and cannot be sold or republished in any medium other than for client use without obtaining express written consent from WealthCounsel, LLC. For permission to utilize the material for commercial use please write to editorial@wealthcounsel.com.

APPENDIX

B

Sample Advance Health Care Directive

Section 1. Appointment of Agent

I, ______________________, appoint ______________________________, as my health care agent to make healthcare decisions for me in accordance with my wishes below. If I have not left any wishes my health care agent shall make decisions for me after consultation with a licensed Muslim physician in accordance with Islamic law and bioethics.

This healthcare power of attorney shall take effect:

_____ immediately, OR

_____ when and if I become unable to make or communicate my own health care decisions, due to physical or mental incapacity, as determined by two licensed physicians, and shall remain effective during the period of incapacity.

In the event _________________ is unable or unwilling to serve as my healthcare agent, I appoint the following individuals, in the order listed below, to serve as my healthcare agents.

____

____

Section 2. Guidance for Agent and Physicians (Optional)

If at any time I should have a terminal condition and am in a permanently unconscious state and two licensed physicians, at least one of which should be specialized in the area of my illness or injury, determine that there is likely no recovery from such condition and my death is likely imminent:

_____ 1. I want to utilize all generally accepted medical treatment standards to attempt to prolong my life.

_____ 2. I do not want life-sustaining treatment, beyond comfort care (treatment given to protect and enhance my quality of life), that would serve only to artificially delay the moment of my death.

_____ 3. I do want the medical treatment necessary to provide care that would keep me comfortable, but I do not want the following:

_________ cardiopulmonary resuscitation, for example, the use of drugs, electric shock and artificial breathing; or

_________ artificially administered nutrition and hydration; or

_________ to be taken to a hospital if at all avoidable.

______4. I have other, more specific wishes, regarding quality of life and reasonable treatments as stated below:

____

____

____

____

____

____

Section 3. Funeral and Burial Preferences

I direct that no autopsy or embalming be performed on my body unless required by law, and that my body be washed and prayed over in accordance with Islamic law and custom, and buried in a nearby cemetery that specifically accommodates Muslims who desire to be buried in accordance with Islamic law, or another cemetery of my healthcare agent's choosing, in any case, without any unjustified delay.

Section 4. Donation of Organs (Optional)

Upon my death:

_____ I give any needed organs, tissues, or parts, OR

_____ I give the following organs, tissues, or parts only:
____
____

_____ My gift is for the following purposes only: (strike out any of the following you do not want:

- Transplant
- Therapy
- Research
- Education

SIGNATURE: Print name: ________________________
Sign name: ________________________
Date: ____________________

STATEMENT OF WITNESSES: I declare under penalty of perjury under the laws of California (1) that the individual who signed or acknowledged this advance health care directive is personally known to me, or that the individual's identity was proven to me by convincing evidence (2) that the individual signed or acknowledged this advance directive in my presence, (3) that the individual appears to be of sound mind and under no duress, fraud, or undue influence, (4) that I am not a person appointed as agent by this advance directive, and (5) that I am not the individual's health care provider, an employee of the individual's health care provider, the operator of a community care facility, an employee of an operator of a community care facility, the operator of a residential care facility for the elderly, nor an employee of an operator of a residential care facility for the elderly.

First witness	Second witness
______________________	______________________
(print name)	(print name)
______________________	______________________
(address)	(address)
______________________	______________________
(city, state zip)	(city, state zip)
______________________	______________________
(signature of witness)	(signature of witness)
______________________	______________________
(date)	(date)

ADDITIONAL STATEMENT OF WITNESSES: At least one of the above witnesses must also sign the following declaration: I further declare under penalty of perjury under the laws of California that I am not related to the individual executing this advance health care directive by blood, marriage, or adoption, and to the best of my knowledge, I am not entitled to any part of the individual's estate upon his or her death under a will now existing or by operation of law.

______________________	______________________
(signature of witness)	(signature of witness)

APPENDIX C

Sample Last Will and Testament

Last Will and Testament of Adam Khan

I, Adam Khan, a resident of Yuma, Arizona, revoke any prior Wills and codicils made by me and declare this to be my Last Will and Testament (*Will*).

Family Information

I am married to Sarah Khan. We were married on August 1, 2006. Any reference in my Will to "wife" is to Sarah Khan.

I have two children:

- Lena Khan, born on October 1, 2014, and
- Muhammad Khan, born on December 1, 2016

Any references to my children refer to these children and any children subsequently born to me.

Funeral Arrangements

My personal representative shall be responsible for my funeral and burial arrangements. I direct that no autopsy or embalming be performed on my body unless required by law, and that my body be washed, and that my body be washed and prayed over in accordance with Islamic law, and buried in a nearby cemetery that specifically accommodates Muslims who desire to be buried in accordance with Islamic law, or another cemetery of my Personal Representative's choosing, in any case, without any unjustified delay.

Designation and Succession of Fiduciaries

Personal Representative

I nominate Sarah Khan as my Personal Representative. If Sarah Khan is unable or unwilling to serve as my Personal Representative, I nominate the following successor personal representatives in the order listed below:

- My brother, Aslam Khan; then
- My sister, Amina Khan.

Guardian

I appoint Sarah Khan as the Guardian of any children of mine who require a guardian. If Sarah Khan is unable or unwilling to serve as guardian, I nominate the following successor guardians in the order listed below:

- My brother, Aslam Khan; then
- My sister, Amina Khan.

I direct that no guardian be required to give any bond in any jurisdiction. But if a guardian's bond is required by law or by court determination, no sureties will be required on the bond.

Conservator

If it becomes necessary to appoint a conservator for the estate of any child of mine, I nominate the child's guardian to serve as conservator of that child's estate.

I direct that no Guardian be required to give any bond in any jurisdiction. But if a Guardian's bond is required by law or by court determination, no sureties will be required on the bond.

Distribution of My Estate

I direct my personal representative to distribute my estate as follows:

Funeral and Burial Expenses

I instruct my personal representative to pay all reasonable funeral and burial expenses from my estate before any other assets are distributed to my beneficiaries.

Outstanding Debts

Next, I instruct my personal representative to pay any legally enforceable debts to my creditors from my estate. Such debts include, but are not limited to, the following:

- Deferred mahr obligation (marital gift) of $20,000 to my wife, Sarah Khan.

Specific Bequests

Next, I direct my personal representative to distribute the following specific bequests from the residuary of my estate:

Bequest to the University of Arizona

I give, devise, and bequeath $10,000 to the University of Arizona Foundation, an Arizona nonprofit corporation, Tucson, Arizona, to be used as determined by the University of Arizona Foundation Board of Directors.

Bequest to my Nieces and Nephews

I give, devise, and bequeath to all my then living nieces and nephews the sum of $1,000 each, outright and free of trust.

Distribution of the Residue of My Estate

I direct my personal representative to distribute the remainder of my estate, outright and free of trust, in accordance with the Islamic Rules of Inheritance as described below.

Name	Relationship	Share
Sarah Khan	Wife	1/8
Naveed Khan	Father	1/6
Asma Khan	Mother	1/6
Lena Khan	Daughter	13/72
Muhammad Khan	Son	13/36

Alternate Disposition

If any of the beneficiaries listed in Section 4.04 above predeceases me, or if the order of our deaths cannot be ascertained, that beneficiary's share shall lapse. In such an event, my personal representative shall recalculate the shares for each of my heirs according to Sunni Islamic Inheritance law as defined in Article Eight and distribute the shares accordingly to my rightful Islamic heirs, outright and free of trust.

Powers of Fiduciaries

Grant of Powers

My Personal Representative may perform every act reasonably necessary to administer my estate and any trust established under my Will. In addition to this general grant of powers, my Personal Representative is specifically authorized to:

> hold, retain, invest, reinvest, sell, and manage any real or personal property, including interests in any form of business entity including limited partnerships and limited liability companies, and life, health, and disability insurance policies, without diversification as to kind, amount, or risk of non-productivity and without limitation by statute or rule of law;

partition, sell, exchange, grant, convey, deliver, assign, transfer, lease, option, mortgage, pledge, abandon, borrow, loan, and contract;

distribute assets of my estate in cash or in kind, or partly in each, at fair market value on the distribution date, without requiring *pro rata* distribution of specific assets and without requiring *pro rata* allocation of the tax bases of those assets;

hold any interest in nominee form, continue businesses, carry out agreements, and deal with itself, other fiduciaries, and business organizations in which my Personal Representative may have an interest;

establish reserves, release powers, and abandon, settle, or contest claims; and

employ attorneys, accountants, custodians for trust assets, and other agents or assistants as my Personal Representative deems advisable to act with or without discretionary powers, and compensate them and pay their expenses from income or principal.

Powers Granted by State Law

In addition to the above powers, Personal Representative may, without prior authority from any court, exercise all powers conferred by my Will by common law, or Arizona law or any other jurisdiction's law that applies to my Will. My fiduciaries have absolute discretion in exercising these powers. Except as specifically limited by my Will these powers extend to all property held by my Personal Representative until the actual distribution of the property.

Distribution Alternatives

My Personal Representative may make any payments under my Will:

directly to a beneficiary;
in any form allowed by applicable state law for gifts or transfers to minors or persons under disability;
to a beneficiary's guardian, conservator, or caregiver for the beneficiary's benefit; or
by direct payment of the beneficiary's expenses.

A receipt by the recipient for any distribution will fully discharge my Personal Representative if the distribution is consistent with the proper exercise of my Personal Representative's duties under my Will.

Administrative Provisions

Bond

To the extent permissible by law, my Personal Representative is not required to give any bond, surety, or security to any court.

Informal Proceedings

I authorize my Personal Representative to initiate an informal probate under Arizona Law.

Compensation and Reimbursement

My Personal Representative is entitled to reasonable compensation commensurate with services actually performed. In addition, my Personal Representative is entitled to reimbursement for reasonable expenses incurred.

Ancillary Personal Representative

If any ancillary administration is required or desired, and my domiciliary Personal Representative is unable or unwilling to act as an Ancillary Personal Representative, my domiciliary Personal Representative may have power to designate, compensate, direct, and remove an Ancillary Personal Representative. The Ancillary Personal Representative may either be a person or a corporation. My domiciliary Personal Representative may delegate to the Ancillary Personal Representative any powers granted to my domiciliary Personal Representative as my domiciliary Personal Representative considers to be proper, including the right to serve without bond or without surety on bond. The net proceeds of the ancillary estate will be paid over to the domiciliary Personal Representative.

Taxes, Claims, and Expenses

I direct that my Personal Representative pay the expenses of my last illness, of my funeral, and of my estate's administration from my residuary estate. My Personal Representative shall pay all estate, inheritance and similar taxes payable with respect to property included in my estate, whether or not passing under my Will, and any interest or penalties, from my residuary estate without apportionment and with no right of reimbursement from any recipient of any estate property.

If payment would decrease the federal estate tax marital deduction available to my estate or violate the provisions of Treasury Regulation Section 20.2056(b)-4(d), my Personal Representative may not pay any administrative expenses from the net income of property qualifying for the federal estate tax marital deduction.

Islamic Rules of Inheritance

The Islamic Law of Inheritance is derived from verses of the Quran and Hadith of the Prophet Muhammad (peace be upon him) and provides a set of rules to determine who is entitled to inherit from a decedent's estate. In the event any of the heirs listed in Section 4.04 predecease me or if we die in a simultaneous death situation, I instruct my personal representative to recalculate the shares of inheritance based upon the following rules which are based upon the Hanafi school of jurisprudence.

Under these rules, Quranic heirs inherit first and receive fixed portions from the estate. If any assets remain in the estate, residuary heirs receive their share next. If there are no Quranic or residuary heirs, the estate passes to distant kindred.

Quranic Heirs (*Dhawil Furood*)

There are twelve *Dhawil Furood*, or Quranic heirs (four male and eight female), entitled to receive predetermined shares as specified in the Quran. However, not all the heirs may inherit, as some may be excluded by the presence of other heirs. The terms "high" and "low" refer to ascendants and descendants.

1. **Father:** A father inherits in one of three ways:
    a. A father receives a 1/6 share of the estate if the decedent is survived by a son or grandson through a son, however low.
    b. A father receives a 1/6 share of the estate as a Quranic heir plus the residue of the estate if the decedent is survived by at least one daughter or a daughter from a son, however low.
    c. A father converts to a residuary heir if the decedent is not survived by children or grandchildren, however low.
2. **Paternal Grandfather:** The paternal grandfather or great-grandfather, however high, will take the place of the father if the decedent's father is deceased. According to the *Hanafi* school of jurisprudence, the presence of a paternal grandfather will cause siblings to be excluded.
    a. A paternal grandfather receives a 1/6 share of the estate if the decedent is survived by at least one son or grandson through a son, however low.
    b. A paternal grandfather receives a 1/6 share of the estate plus any residue if the decedent is survived by at least one daughter or a daughter from a son, however low.
3. **Husband (Widower)**: A widower always inherits from his late wife.
    a. A widower receives a 1/4 share of his late wife's estate if she is survived by any children or son's children, however low.
    b. A widower receives 1/2 his late wife's estate if she is not survived by any children or son's children, however low.
4. **Wife (Widow)**: A widow always inherits from her late husband.
    a. A widow receives a 1/8 share of her late husband's estate if he is survived by any children or son's children, however low.
    b. A widow receives a 1/4 share of her late husband's estate if he is not survived by any children or son's children, however low.
5. **Daughter:** A daughter will always inherit in one of the following three conditions:
    a. If the decedent is survived by one daughter and no sons, the daughter receives 1/2 the [gross] estate.
    b. If the decedent is survived by two or more daughters and no sons, the daughters will split 2/3 of the [gross] estate equally.
    c. If the decedent is survived by one or more sons and one or more daughters, all the children shall be converted into residuary heirs and the sons receive twice the daughters' share.

6. **Granddaughter from Son:** In the absence of living children, a son's daughter is treated like a daughter.
    a. If the decedent is not survived by children or a grandson from a son, but is survived by one granddaughter from a son, the granddaughter receives 1/2 the estate.
    b. If the decedent is not survived by children or a grandson from a son, but is survived by more than one granddaughter from a son, the granddaughters will split 2/3 of the estate equally.
    c. If the decedent is survived by one daughter and a granddaughter from a son, but no son and no grandson from a son, the granddaughter receives a 1/6 share.
    d. If the decedent is survived by more than one daughter and no sons, and is survived by a granddaughter from a son, the granddaughter would be excluded unless the decedent was also survived by a grandson from a son.
7. **Mother**
    a. If the decedent is not survived by any children or two or more siblings, the mother receives a 1/3 share of the estate.
    b. If the decedent is survived by children or grandchildren, or two or more siblings, the mother receives a 1/6 share of the estate.
8. **Grandmother** (paternal and maternal)
    a. A paternal grandmother receives a 1/6 share of the estate if the decedent is not survived by a mother, father, or maternal grandmother.
    b. A paternal grandmother receives a 1/12 share of the estate if the decedent is not survived by a mother or father, but is survived by a maternal grandmother.
    c. A maternal grandmother receives a 1/6 share of the estate if the decedent is not survived by a mother, father, or paternal grandmother.
    d. A maternal grandmother receives a 1/12 share of the estate if the decedent is not survived by a mother or father, but is survived by a paternal grandmother.
9. **Full Sisters**
    a. If the decedent is survived by one full sister, but not by offspring, male paternal ancestors, or full brothers, the sister receives 1/2 the estate.

   b. If the decedent is survived by two or more full sisters, but not by offspring, male paternal ancestors, or full brothers, the sisters will split 2/3 of the estate equally.
10. **Agnate Sisters** (Paternal Half-Sisters)
   a. If the decedent is survived by one agnate sister, but not by offspring, male paternal ancestors, or full brothers or sisters, the agnate sister receives 1/2 the estate.
   b. If the decedent is survived by more than one agnate sister, but not by offspring, male paternal ancestors, or full brothers or sisters, the agnate sisters will split 2/3 of the estate equally.
   c. If the decedent is survived by one or more agnate sisters and by one full sister, but not by offspring, male paternal ancestors, or full brothers, the agnate sisters will split 1/6 of the estate equally.
11. **Uterine Brother** (Maternal Half-Brother): A uterine brother is excluded if the decedent is survived by a child or a son's child, however low, or a father, or paternal grandfather, however high.
12. **Uterine Sister** (Maternal Half-Sister): A uterine sister is excluded if the decedent is survived by a child or a son's child, however low, or a father, or paternal grandfather, however high.
   a. If the decedent is survived by one uterine sibling, but not by an offspring or male paternal ancestors, the uterine sibling receives a 1/6 share of the estate.
   b. If the decedent is survived by two or more uterine siblings, but not by an offspring or male paternal ancestors, the uterine siblings will split 1/3 of the estate equally. (Note that the traditional rule that males receive double the share of females is not applicable in this context.)

Once all the Quranic heirs receive their shares, the remainder of the estate is distributed to the *Asabah*, or residuary heirs. If there are no living *asabah*, the remainder of the estate is redistributed proportionally to the Quranic heirs under the doctrine of return, or *Radd* (with the exception of the spouse) before any residuary is distributed to the *Dhawil Arham*, or distant kindred.

Residuary Heirs (*Asabah*)

After Quranic heirs receive their shares, the rest of the estate should be distributed to the residuary heirs. The Prophet Muhammad instructed his companions, "Give the portion of the inheritance to the Quranic heirs, and whatever is left should go to the closest male relative of the deceased." Residuary heirs typically are male relatives, or are related to the decedent through the paternal lineage, and are divided into several groups. Three important rules apply with respect to distribution to residuary heirs:

1. The presence of any member of a higher group (see Table 1) excludes anyone in a lower group from inheriting with two exceptions:
   a. A son can never cause a father to be excluded.
   b. The *Shafi*, *Maliki*, and *Hanbali* schools of jurisprudence hold that a paternal grandfather excludes neither full nor half-siblings while the *Hanafi* school holds that a paternal grandfather excludes agnate siblings.
2. Within a group, an individual who is nearer in degree to the decedent excludes the more remote from inheriting.
3. Full-blood relatives take priority over half-blood relatives of the same degree.

Women who would otherwise be categorized as primary heirs become residuary heirs in the presence of a brother, as described in Table 2 below. In such cases, females will receive half the share of their brothers based on the Quranic injunction, "For males is twice the share of females." Only the decedent's daughter, son's daughters, full sister, agnate sister, and mother (in only one scenario) can become female residuary heirs through this process. The presence of a female residuary heir does not change any of the distribution rules described above.

There is only one scenario in which a sister can become a residuary heir in the absence of a brother: when the deceased is not survived by brothers but is survived by a daughter or son's daughter. In such a scenario, all the distribution rules stated above are applicable and the sister is treated as a male in Table 1.

Table 1. Male Residuary Heirs (*Asabah*)

Groups	Members of Group
Group 1 — Descendants	Son Son's male descendants
Group 2 — Ascendants	Father Father's male ascendants
Group 3 — Brother and Male Issue	Full Brother Agnate Brother Full Brother's Son Agnate Brother's Son Descendants of Group 3
Group 4 — Paternal Uncle and Male Issue	Full Paternal Uncle Agnate Paternal Uncle Full Paternal Uncle's son Agnate Paternal Uncle's Son Descendants of Group 4

Table 2. Female Residuary Heirs

Relation to Decedent	Converted to Residuary Heirs Only If . . .
Daughters	they have brothers
Son's Daughters	they have brothers or cousins of equal rank
Full Sisters	the decedent is survived by full brothers
Agnate Sisters	the decedent is survived by agnate brothers

If there are no residuary heirs, the remainder will be re-distributed proportionally to the primary heirs under the doctrine of *Radd* – with the exception of the spouse –whose share cannot be increased through *Radd* as she is not related to the decedent by blood but through marriage.

Distant Kindred (*Dhawil Arham*)

If there are any assets in excess of shares distributed to Quranic and residuary heirs, they are to be distributed among the distant kindred—all the decedent's remaining relatives who are not categorized as Quranic or residuary heirs. There are four categories of distant kindred, identified in order below. Two basic rules govern distribution to distant kindred: (1) The presence of any members of a higher category excludes all members of any category below from inheriting, and (2) within each category, the presence of any individuals in a higher class excludes all members of the classes below from inheriting.

Table 3. Distant Kindred

Category 1—Descendants Who Are Not Quranic Heirs or Residuary Heirs	Class 1—Daughter's Children Class 2—Son's Daughter's Children Class 3—Daughter's Children's Children
Category 2—Ascendants Who Are Not Quranic Heirs or Residuary Heirs	Class 1—Maternal Grandfather Class 2—Father's Maternal Grandfather Mother's Paternal Grandfather Mother's Maternal Grandfather Mother's Maternal Grandmother
Category 3—Nieces and Nephews Who Are Not Quranic Heirs or Residuary Heirs	Class 1—Sister's Children Paternal Half-Sister's Children Maternal Half-Sister's Children Brother's Daughters Paternal Half-Brother's Daughters Maternal Half-Brother's Children Class 2—Brother's Son's Daughters Paternal Half-Brother's Son's Daughters Maternal Half-Brother's Son's Children Brother's Daughter's Children Paternal Half-Brother's Daughter's Children Maternal Half-Brother's Daughter's Children Sister's Son's Children Paternal Half-Sister's Son's Children Maternal Half-Sister's Son's Children Sister's Daughter's Children Paternal Half-Sister's Daughter's Children Maternal Half-Sister's Daughter's Children

(continued on next page)

Table 3. Distant Kindred *(continued)*

Category 4—Aunts, Uncles, and Cousins Who Are Not Quranic Heirs or Residuary Heirs	Class 1(a)—Father's Sister Father's Paternal Half-Sister Father's Maternal Half-Sister Father's Maternal Half-Brother Class 1(b)—Mother's Brother Mother's Sister Mother's Paternal Half-Brother Mother's Paternal Half-Sister Mother's Maternal Half-Brother Mother's Maternal Half-Sister Class 2(a)—Paternal Uncle's Daughters Paternal Aunt's Children Father's Paternal Half-Brother's Daughters Father's Paternal Half-Sister's Children Father's Maternal Half-Brother's Children Father's Maternal Half-Sister's Children Class 2(b)—Maternal Uncle's Children Maternal Aunt's Children Mother's Paternal Half-Brother's Children Mother's Paternal Half-Sister's Children Mother's Maternal Half-Brother's Children Mother's Maternal Half-Sister's Children Class 3(a)—Father's Paternal Aunt Father's Father's Paternal Half-Sister Father's Father's Maternal Half-Brother Father's Father's Maternal Half-Sister Class 3(b)—Father's Maternal Uncle Father's Maternal Aunt Father's Mother's Paternal Half-Brother Father's Mother's Paternal Half-Sister Father's Mother's Maternal Half-Brother Father's Mother's Maternal Half-Sister Class 3(c)—Mother's Paternal Aunt Mother's Father's Paternal Half-Sister Mother's Father's Maternal Half-Brother Mother's Father's Maternal Half-Sister Class 3(d)—Mother's Maternal Uncle Mother's Maternal Aunt Mother's Mother's Paternal Half-Brother Mother's Mother's Paternal Half-Sister Mother's Mother's Maternal Half-Brother Mother's Mother's Maternal Half-Sister

General Provisions

Contest Provision

If any person directly or indirectly attempts to contest or oppose the validity of my Will, (including any codicil to my Will), or commences, continues, or prosecutes any legal proceedings to set my Will aside, then that person will forfeit his or her share, cease to have any right or interest in my estate, and will, for purposes of my Will, be deemed to have predeceased me.

Survivorship Presumption

If any of my beneficiaries and I pass away in a manner in which the order of our deaths cannot be readily ascertained, the beneficiary shall be treated as predeceasing me and shall not inherit from my estate. If any beneficiary survives me, even momentarily, that beneficiary shall be entitled to inherit from me.

Applicable Law

The validity and construction of my Will will be determined by the laws of the State of Arizona.

No Contract to Make Will

I have not entered into any contract, actual or implied, to make a Will.

Construction

Unless the context requires otherwise, words denoting the singular may denote the plural, and words indicating the plural may denote the singular. As the context requires, words of one gender may denote another gender.

Internal Revenue Code, IRC, or Code

References to the Internal Revenue Code, the IRC or the Code refer to the Internal Revenue Code of the United States. References to specific sections of the Code apply to any sections of similar import that replace the specific sections due to changes to the Internal Revenue Code made after the date of my Will.

Other Definitions

Except as otherwise provided in my Will, terms will be interpreted as defined by Arizona law after the date of my Will and after my death.

Severability

If any part of this instrument is determined to be void or invalid, the remaining provisions will continue in full force and effect.

Execution of My Last Will and Testament

I, Adam Khan, the Testator, sign my name to this document on January 1, 2019. I have taken an oath, administered by the officer whose signature and seal appear on this document, swearing that the statements in this document are true. I declare to that officer that this document is my will; that I sign it willingly or willingly direct another to sign for me; that I execute it as my voluntary act for the purposes expressed in this will; and that I am 18 years of age or older, of sound mind, and under no constraint or undue influence.

____

Adam Khan, Testator

Witness Attestation

We, ________________________ and ________________________, the witnesses, sign our names to this document and have taken an oath, administered by the officer whose signature and seal appear on this document, to swear that all of the following statements are true: the individual signing this document as the Testator executes the document as his will, signs it willingly or willingly directs another to sign for him, and executes it as his voluntary act for the purposes expressed in this will; each of us, in the Testator's presence, signs this Will as witness to the Testator's signing; and, to the best of our knowledge, the Testator is 18 years of age or older, of sound mind, and under no constraint or undue influence.

________________________ Address: ________________________

____

________________________ Address: ________________________

____

Self-Proving Affidavit

BEFORE ME, the undersigned authority, on this day personally appeared Adam Khan,

__________, and __________, known to me to be the Testator and the witnesses respectively, whose names are subscribed to the annexed or foregoing instrument in their respective capacities, and, all of said persons being by me duly sworn, Testator declared to me and to the witnesses in my presence that said instrument is his last will and testament, and that he had willingly made and executed it as his free act and deed; and the said witnesses, each on his or her oath, stated to me, in the presence and hearing of the Testator that the Testator had declared to them that said instrument is his last will and testament, and that he executed same as such and wanted each of them to sign it as a witness; and upon their oaths each witness stated further that they did sign the same as a witness in the presence of Testator and at his request; that he at that time was eighteen years of age or over and was of sound mind; and that each of said witnesses was then at least eighteen years of age.

____

Adam Khan

______________________ Address: ______________________

Witness 1 ______________________

______________________ Address: ______________________

Witness 2 ______________________

STATE OF ARIZONA)

) ss.

COUNTY OF MARICOPA)

Sworn to and signed in my presence by Adam Khan, the Testator, and sworn to and signed in my presence by __________ and __________ witnesses, on __________ (date).

____

Notary Public

APPENDIX

D

Sample Pour-Over Will

Last Will and Testament of Adam Khan

I, Adam Khan, a resident of Yuma, Arizona, revoke any prior Wills and codicils made by me and declare this to be my Last Will and Testament (*Will*).

Family Information

I am married to Sarah Khan. We were married on August 1, 2006. Any reference in my Will to "wife" is to Sarah Khan.

I have two children:

- Lena Khan, born on October 1, 2014, and
- Muhammad Khan, born on December 1, 2016

Any references to my children refer to these children and any children subsequently born to me.

Funeral Arrangements

My personal representative shall be responsible for my funeral and burial arrangements. I direct that no autopsy or embalming be performed on my body unless required by law, and that my body be washed, and that my body be washed and prayed over in accordance with Islamic law, and buried in a nearby cemetery that specifically accommodates Muslims who desire to be buried in accordance with Islamic law, or another cemetery of my Personal Representative's choosing, in any case, without any unjustified delay.

Designation and Succession of Fiduciaries

Personal Representative

I nominate Sarah Khan as my Personal Representative. If Sarah Khan is unable or unwilling to serve as my Personal Representative, I nominate the following successor personal representatives in the order listed below:

- My brother, Aslam Khan; then
- My sister, Amina Khan.

Guardian

I appoint Sarah Khan as the Guardian of any children of mine who require a guardian. If Sarah Khan is unable or unwilling to serve as guardian, I nominate the following successor guardians in the order listed below:

- My brother, Aslam Khan; then
- My sister, Amina Khan.

I direct that no guardian be required to give any bond in any jurisdiction. But if a guardian's bond is required by law or by court determination, no sureties will be required on the bond.

Conservator

If it becomes necessary to appoint a conservator for the estate of any child of mine, I nominate the child's guardian to serve as conservator of that child's estate.

I direct that no Guardian be required to give any bond in any jurisdiction. But if a Guardian's bond is required by law or by court determination, no sureties will be required on the bond.

Distribution of My Estate

Pour-Over to my Revocable Trust

I give all of my probate estate, excluding any property over which I have a power of appointment, after expenses and taxes are paid under this Will, to the then-acting Trustee of the Khan Family Trust dated January 1, 2019, and executed before this Will, to be added to the property of that trust. I direct that the Trustee administer the property according to the trust and any amendments made prior to my death.

Alternate Disposition

If the trust referred to in Section 4.01 is not in effect at my death, or if for any other reason the pour over fails, I specifically incorporate by reference all the terms of that trust into this Will. I direct my Personal Representative to then establish a new trust under the provisions of that trust and distribute the remainder of my estate, excluding any property over which I have a power of appointment, to that Trustee to administer as provided in the trust:

Powers of Fiduciaries

Grant of Powers

My Personal Representative may perform every act reasonably necessary to administer my estate and any trust established under my Will. In addition to this general grant of powers, my Personal Representative is specifically authorized to:

> hold, retain, invest, reinvest, sell, and manage any real or personal property, including interests in any form of business entity including limited partnerships and limited liability companies,

and life, health, and disability insurance policies, without diversification as to kind, amount, or risk of non-productivity and without limitation by statute or rule of law;

partition, sell, exchange, grant, convey, deliver, assign, transfer, lease, option, mortgage, pledge, abandon, borrow, loan, and contract;

distribute assets of my estate in cash or in kind, or partly in each, at fair market value on the distribution date, without requiring *pro rata* distribution of specific assets and without requiring *pro rata* allocation of the tax bases of those assets;

hold any interest in nominee form, continue businesses, carry out agreements, and deal with itself, other fiduciaries, and business organizations in which my Personal Representative may have an interest;

establish reserves, release powers, and abandon, settle, or contest claims; and

employ attorneys, accountants, custodians for trust assets, and other agents or assistants as my Personal Representative deems advisable to act with or without discretionary powers, and compensate them and pay their expenses from income or principal.

Powers Granted by State Law

In addition to the above powers, Personal Representative may, without prior authority from any court, exercise all powers conferred by my Will by common law, or Arizona law or any other jurisdiction's law that applies to my Will. My fiduciaries have absolute discretion in exercising these powers. Except as specifically limited by my Will these powers extend to all property held by my Personal Representative until the actual distribution of the property.

Distribution Alternatives

My Personal Representative may make any payments under my Will:

directly to a beneficiary;
in any form allowed by applicable state law for gifts or transfers to minors or persons under disability;

to a beneficiary's guardian, conservator, or caregiver for the beneficiary's benefit; or
by direct payment of the beneficiary's expenses.

A receipt by the recipient for any distribution will fully discharge my Personal Representative if the distribution is consistent with the proper exercise of my Personal Representative's duties under my Will.

Administrative Provisions

Bond

To the extent permissible by law, my Personal Representative is not required to give any bond, surety, or security to any court.

Informal Proceedings

I authorize my Personal Representative to initiate an informal probate under Arizona Law.

Compensation and Reimbursement

My Personal Representative is entitled to reasonable compensation commensurate with services actually performed. In addition, my Personal Representative is entitled to reimbursement for reasonable expenses incurred.

Ancillary Personal Representative

If any ancillary administration is required or desired, and my domiciliary Personal Representative is unable or unwilling to act as an Ancillary Personal Representative, my domiciliary Personal Representative may have power to designate, compensate, direct, and remove an Ancillary Personal Representative. The Ancillary Personal Representative may either be a person or a corporation. My domiciliary Personal Representative may delegate to the Ancillary Personal Representative any powers granted to my domiciliary Personal Representative as my domiciliary Personal Representative considers to be proper, including the right to serve without bond or without surety on bond. The net proceeds of the ancillary estate will be paid over to the domiciliary Personal Representative.

Taxes, Claims, and Expenses

I direct that my Personal Representative pay the expenses of my last illness, of my funeral, and of my estate's administration from my residuary estate. My Personal Representative shall pay all estate, inheritance and similar taxes payable with respect to property included in my estate, whether or not passing under my Will, and any interest or penalties, from my residuary estate without apportionment and with no right of reimbursement from any recipient of any estate property.

If payment would decrease the federal estate tax marital deduction available to my estate or violate the provisions of Treasury Regulation Section 20.2056(b)-4(d), my Personal Representative may not pay any administrative expenses from the net income of property qualifying for the federal estate tax marital deduction.

General Provisions

Contest Provision

If any person directly or indirectly attempts to contest or oppose the validity of my Will, (including any codicil to my Will), or commences, continues, or prosecutes any legal proceedings to set my Will aside, then that person will forfeit his or her share, cease to have any right or interest in my estate, and will, for purposes of my Will, be deemed to have predeceased me.

Survivorship Presumption

If any of my beneficiaries and I pass away in a manner in which the order of our deaths cannot be readily ascertained, the beneficiary shall be treated as predeceasing me and shall not inherit from my estate. If any beneficiary survives me, even momentarily, that beneficiary shall be entitled to inherit from me.

Applicable Law

The validity and construction of my Will will be determined by the laws of the State of Arizona.

No Contract to Make Will

I have not entered into any contract, actual or implied, to make a Will.

Construction

Unless the context requires otherwise, words denoting the singular may denote the plural, and words indicating the plural may denote the singular. As the context requires, words of one gender may denote another gender.

Internal Revenue Code, IRC, or Code

References to the Internal Revenue Code, the IRC or the Code refer to the Internal Revenue Code of the United States. References to specific sections of the Code apply to any sections of similar import that replace the specific sections due to changes to the Internal Revenue Code made after the date of my Will.

Other Definitions

Except as otherwise provided in my Will, terms will be interpreted as defined by Arizona law after the date of my Will and after my death.

Severability

If any part of this instrument is determined to be void or invalid, the remaining provisions will continue in full force and effect.

Execution of My Last Will and Testament

I, Adam Khan, the Testator, sign my name to this document on January 1, 2019. I have taken an oath, administered by the officer whose signature and seal appear on this document, swearing that the statements in this document are true. I declare to that officer that this document is my will; that I sign it willingly or willingly direct another to sign for me; that I execute it as my voluntary act for the purposes expressed in this will; and that I am 18 years of age or older, of sound mind, and under no constraint or undue influence.

____

Adam Khan, Testator

WITNESS ATTESTATION

We, ______________________ and ______________________, the witnesses, sign our names to this document and have taken an oath, administered by the officer whose signature and seal appear on this document, to swear that all of the following statements are true: the individual signing this document as the Testator executes the document as his will, signs it willingly or willingly directs another to sign for him, and executes it as his voluntary act for the purposes expressed in this will; each of us, in the Testator's presence, signs this Will as witness to the Testator's signing; and, to the best of our knowledge, the Testator is 18 years of age or older, of sound mind, and under no constraint or undue influence.

______________________ Address: ______________________
____

______________________ Address: ______________________
____

Self-Proving Affidavit

BEFORE ME, the undersigned authority, on this day personally appeared Adam Khan,

___________________, and ___________________, known to me to be the Testator and the witnesses respectively, whose names are subscribed to the annexed or foregoing instrument in their respective capacities, and, all of said persons being by me duly sworn, Testator declared to me and to the witnesses in my presence that said instrument is his last will and testament, and that he had willingly made and executed it as his free act and deed; and the said witnesses, each on his or her oath, stated to me, in the presence and hearing of the Testator that the Testator had declared to them that said instrument is his last will and testament, and that he executed same as such and wanted each of them to sign it as a witness; and upon their oaths each witness stated further that they did sign the same as a witness in the presence of Testator and at his request; that he at that time was eighteen years of age or over and was of sound mind; and that each of said witnesses was then at least eighteen years of age.

____

Adam Khan

______________________ Address: ______________________

Witness 1 ______________________

______________________ Address: ______________________

Witness 2 ______________________

STATE OF ARIZONA)

) ss.

COUNTY OF MARICOPA)

Sworn to and signed in my presence by Adam Khan, the Testator, and sworn to and signed in my presence by ___________ and ___________ witnesses, on ___________ (date).

____

Notary Public

APPENDIX

E

Sample Individual Revocable Living Trust

THE KHAN FAMILY TRUST
January 1, 2019

THE KHAN FAMILY TRUST

Article One Establishing My Trust

I intend to create a valid trust under the laws of Arizona and under the laws of any state in which any trust created under this trust document is administered. The terms of this trust prevail over any provision of Arizona law, except those provisions that are mandatory and may not be waived.

The parties to this trust are Abdullah Khan (the *Grantor*) and Abdullah Khan (my *Trustee*).

Section 1.01 Identifying My Trust

For convenience, my trust may be referred to as:

> "The Khan Family Trust dated January 1, 2019."

To the extent practicable, for the purpose of transferring property to my trust or identifying my trust in any beneficiary or pay-on-death designation, my trust should be identified as:

> "Abdullah Khan, Trustee, or his successors in interest, of the Khan Family Trust dated January 1, 2019, and any amendments thereto."

For all purposes concerning the identity of my trust or any property titled in or payable to my trust, any description referring to my trust will be effective if it reasonably identifies my trust and indicates that the trust property is held in a fiduciary capacity.

Section 1.02 Reliance by Third Parties

Third parties may require documentation to verify the existence of this trust, or particular provisions of it, including the name of my Trustee or the powers held by my Trustee. To protect the confidentiality of this instrument, my Trustee may use an affidavit or a certification of trust that identifies my Trustee and sets forth the authority of my Trustee to transact business on behalf of my trust instead of providing a copy of this instrument. The affidavit or certification may include pertinent pages from this instrument, including title or signature pages.

A third party may rely upon an affidavit or certification of trust that is signed by my Trustee with respect to the representations contained in it. A third party relying upon an affidavit or certification of trust will be exonerated from any liability for actions the third party takes or does not take in reliance upon the representations contained in the affidavit or certification of trust.

A third party dealing with my Trustee will not be required to inquire into this trust's terms or the authority of my Trustee, or to see to the application of funds or other property received by my Trustee. My Trustee's receipt of any money or property paid, transferred, or delivered to my Trustee will be a sufficient discharge to the third party from all liability in connection with its application. A written statement by my Trustee is conclusive evidence of my Trustee's authority. Third parties are not liable for any loss resulting from their reliance on a written statement by my Trustee asserting my Trustee's authority or seeking to effect a transfer of property to or from the trust.

Section 1.03 Intent to Comply with Islamic Law of Inheritance

I am creating this revocable living trust and any separate trusts established under this instrument with the intent that assets transferred to the trust be held for my benefit while I am living, and be distributed upon my death in accordance with my faith of Islam and per [Sunni/Shia] Islamic Inheritance Law as defined in [section determining Islamic Inheritance Law].

I fully understand and recognize that my decision to do so may result in

- (a) distribution to relatives who are not my heirs under State law,
- (b) unequal distribution to my children by gender,
- (c) no inheritance for step-children,
- (d) loss of the Unlimited Marital Deduction, the spousal rollover or other potential tax benefits from a different distribution,
- (e) liquidation and distribution of assets that may otherwise benefit a surviving grantor, causing (him or her) to receive a smaller share than (he or she) may be entitled to under the state's statutory elective share.

Both my spouse and I have expressly disclaimed any right to receive a spousal elective share under state law in a separate property agreement dated ________________________.

I nonetheless instruct my successor trustees and beneficiaries to honor my wishes as stated. In order to accomplish the intent set forth in this Section, I have given my Trustee broad discretion with respect to the management, distribution, and investment of assets in my trust.

Section 1.04 Transferring Property to My Trust

Any person or entity may transfer any property to my trust in any manner authorized by law.

Funding of My Trust

By executing this instrument, I transfer, convey, and assign the property described in the attached Schedule A to my Trustee. I also transfer all my right, title, and interest in and to all of my property that may legally be held in trust and that may be transferred to my trust by this assignment. This assignment includes all of my real, personal, tangible, and intangible property located in the United States, whether separate property or community property, and whether acquired before or after the execution of this instrument, except for these assets that are expressly not transferred by this instrument:

> life insurance policies, unless the ownership of a policy is transferred to my trust by a separate instrument that specifically refers to the policy;
>
> corporate and self-employed (*Keogh*) pension, profit-sharing, and stock bonus plans;
>
> qualified retirement plans;
>
> commercial annuities;
>
> Section 1244 (small business) stock; and
>
> any property, the transfer of which would result in the immediate recognition of income subject to income or other taxes, would result in the loss of a homestead exemption, or would violate a restriction on transfer agreement.

Acceptance by My Trustee

By executing this instrument, my Trustee accepts and agrees to hold the property transferred to the trust as trust property. All property transferred to my trust after the date of this trust must be acceptable to my Trustee. My Trustee may refuse to accept any property. My Trustee shall hold, administer, and dispose of all accepted trust property for my benefit and for the benefit of my beneficiaries, in accordance with the terms of this trust.

Separate Property

Any property transferred to my trust, including the property's income and the proceeds from the property's sale or exchange, will retain its character as separate property during my life.

Section 1.05 Powers Reserved by Me as Grantor

As Grantor, I retain the powers set forth in this Section in addition to any powers that I reserve in other provisions of this instrument.

Action on Behalf of My Trust

Whenever I am serving as Trustee, I may act for and conduct business on behalf of my trust without the consent of any other Trustee.

Amendment, Restatement, or Revocation

I may amend, restate, or revoke this instrument, in whole or in part, for any purpose.

Any amendment, restatement, or revocation must be made in writing and delivered to my then-serving Trustee.

Addition or Removal of Trust Property

I may add property to my trust and may remove any property from my trust at any time. Community property removed from my trust will retain its character as community property.

Control of Income and Principal Distributions

I retain the right to control the distribution of income and principal from my trust. I may direct my Trustee to distribute as much of the net income and principal of the trust property as I consider advisable to me or to other persons or entities. My Trustee may distribute the net income and principal to me or for my unrestricted use and benefit, even to the exhaustion of all trust property. Any undistributed net income is to be added to the principal of my trust.

Approval of Investment Decisions

I reserve the absolute right to review and change my Trustee's investment decisions. But my Trustee is not required to seek my approval before making investment decisions.

Section 1.06 Grantor Trust Status

By reserving the broad rights and powers set forth in 0 of this Article, I intend to qualify my trust as a *Grantor Trust* under Internal Revenue Code Sections 671 to 677. This means that, for federal income tax purposes, I will be treated as the owner of all the assets held in my trust during my lifetime, as if I held them in my individual capacity.

During any period that my trust is a Grantor Trust, the Taxpayer Identification Number of my trust will be my Social Security number, in accordance with Treasury Regulation Section 301.6109-1(a)(2).

(Remainder of page intentionally left blank.)

Article Two Family Information

I am married to Wafa Khan. We were married on March 2, 2006.

I have two children. They are:

Adam Khan, born on March 3, 2008; and
Sarah Khan, born on March 4, 2010.

All references in this document to *my children* are references to these children and any children subsequently born to me.

I have also provided for my mother, Mariam Khan.

(Remainder of page intentionally left blank.)

Article Three Trustee Succession and Trust Protector Provisions

Section 3.01 Resignation of a Trustee

A Trustee may resign by giving written notice to me. If I am incapacitated or deceased, a resigning Trustee must give written notice to the trust's Income Beneficiaries and to any other then-serving Trustee.

Section 3.02 Trustee Succession during My Lifetime

During my lifetime, this Section governs the removal and replacement of my Trustees.

Removal and Replacement by Me

I may remove any Trustee with or without cause at any time. If a Trustee is removed, resigns, or cannot continue to serve for any reason, I may serve as sole Trustee, appoint a Trustee to serve with me, or appoint a successor Trustee.

During My Incapacity

During any time that I am incapacitated, the following will serve as my successor Trustee in this order:

Wafa Khan, then
Mariam Khan

If I am incapacitated, a Trustee may be removed only for cause, and only if a court of competent jurisdiction approves the removal upon the petition of an interested party. This does not limit the authority of a Trust Protector to remove a Trustee under the provisions of 0 of this Article.

My Legal Representative may petition a court of competent jurisdiction to appoint a successor Trustee to fill any vacancy lasting longer than 30 days. The petition may subject the trust to the jurisdiction of the court only to the extent necessary to make the appointment and may not subject the trust to the continuing jurisdiction of the court.

All appointments, removals, and revocations must be by signed written instrument.

Section 3.03 Trustee Succession after My Death

After my death, this Section will govern the removal and replacement of my Trustees.

Successor Trustee

I name the following, in this order, to serve as my successor Trustee after my death, replacing any then-serving Trustee:

Wafa Khan, then
Mariam Khan

Trustees of the Separate Trusts

The Primary Beneficiary of a separate trust created under this instrument, at any time after attaining 25 years of age, may appoint himself or herself as a Co-Trustee of his or her separate trust to serve with the then-serving successor Trustee. Any time the beneficiary is serving as a Trustee of his or her trust, at least one other Trustee must be serving with the beneficiary. If a Trustee vacancy occurs and no designated successor Trustee is available to serve, the vacancy is to be filled as provided in Subsection 0 of this Section.

Removal of a Trustee

A majority of the Income Beneficiaries of any trust created under this instrument may remove a Trustee of the trust at any time, with or without cause.

A Trustee may be removed under this Subsection only if the person having the right of removal appoints an individual or a corporate fiduciary by the effective removal date and the individual or corporate fiduciary simultaneously commences service as Trustee. This appointed Trustee may not be related or subordinate to the person or persons having the right of removal within the meaning of Internal Revenue Code Section 672(c).

The right to remove a Trustee under this Subsection is not to be interpreted as granting the person holding that right any of the powers of that Trustee.

A minor or incapacitated beneficiary's parent or Legal Representative may act on his or her behalf.

Nothing in this Subsection limits the authority of a Trust Protector to remove a Trustee under the provisions of 0 of this Article.

Default of Designation

If the office of Trustee of a trust created under this instrument is vacant and no designated successor Trustee is able and willing to act as Trustee, my Trust Protector may appoint a successor Trustee. If my Trust Protector is unable or unwilling to act, the trust's Primary Beneficiary may appoint an individual or corporate fiduciary that is not related or subordinate to the person or persons making the appointment within the meaning of Section 672(c) of the Internal Revenue Code as successor Trustee.

Any beneficiary may petition a court of competent jurisdiction to appoint a successor Trustee to fill any vacancy lasting longer than 30 days. The petition may subject the trust to the jurisdiction of the court only to the extent necessary to make the appointment and may not subject the trust to the continuing jurisdiction of the court.

A minor or incapacitated beneficiary's parent or Legal Representative may act on his or her behalf.

Section 3.04 Notice of Removal and Appointment

Notice of removal must be in writing and delivered to the Trustee being removed and to any other then-serving Trustees. The removal becomes effective in accordance with its provisions.

Notice of appointment must be in writing and delivered to the successor Trustee and to any other then-serving Trustees. The appointment becomes effective at the time of acceptance by the successor Trustee. A copy of the notice may be attached to this instrument.

Section 3.05 Corporate Fiduciaries

Any corporate fiduciary serving under this instrument as a Trustee must be a bank, trust company, or public charity that is qualified to act as a fiduciary under applicable federal and state law and that is not related or subordinate to any beneficiary within the meaning of Internal Revenue Code Section 672(c).

Section 3.06 Incapacity of a Trustee

If any individual Trustee becomes incapacitated, the incapacitated Trustee need not resign as Trustee. For Trustees other than me, a written declaration of incapacity by the Co-Trustee or, if none, by the party designated to succeed the incapacitated Trustee, made in good faith, will terminate the trusteeship.

Section 3.07 Appointment of Independent Special Trustee

If for any reason the Trustee of any trust created under this instrument is unwilling or unable to act with respect to any trust property or any provision of this instrument, my Trust Protector shall appoint, in writing, a corporate fiduciary or an individual to serve as an Independent Special Trustee as to this property or with respect to this provision. The Independent Special Trustee appointed may not be related or subordinate to any trust beneficiary within the meaning of Internal Revenue Code Section 672(c). My Trust Protector may revoke any appointment of this kind at any time.

An Independent Special Trustee will exercise all fiduciary powers granted by this trust unless expressly limited elsewhere in this instrument or by my Trust Protector in the instrument appointing the Independent Special Trustee. An Independent Special Trustee may resign at any time by delivering written notice of resignation to my Trust Protector. Notice of resignation will be effective in accordance with the terms of the notice.

Section 3.08 Rights and Obligations of Successor Trustees

Each successor Trustee serving under this instrument, whether corporate or individual, will have all of the title, rights, powers, and privileges granted to the initial Trustee named under this instrument. In addition, each successor Trustee will be subject to all of the restrictions imposed upon, as well as to all discretionary and ministerial obligations and duties given to the initial Trustee named under this instrument.

Section 3.09 Provisions for Trust Protector

The function of the Trust Protector is to direct my Trustee in matters concerning the trust, and to assist, if needed, in achieving my objectives as manifested by the other provisions of my estate plan.

Any Trust Protector named or appointed under this Section must be a corporate fiduciary or an individual who is not related or subordinate to me while I am still living or to any beneficiary within the meaning of Internal Revenue Code Section 672(c). Notwithstanding any provision that may seem to the contrary, a Trust Protector shall not act while I am still living unless I am incapacitated.

Designation of Trust Protector

I appoint John Smith to serve as Trust Protector of any trust created under this instrument.

Resignation of Trust Protector

A Trust Protector may resign by giving notice to me. If I am incapacitated or deceased, a resigning Trust Protector must give notice to the trust's Income Beneficiaries and the then-serving Trustee.

A Trust Protector's resignation takes effect on the date set forth in the notice, but never earlier than 30 days after the delivery date of the resignation notice, unless an earlier effective date is agreed to by me or the Trustee. A resigning Trust Protector will not be liable or responsible for the act of any successor Trust Protector.

Removal and Replacement by Me

I may remove any Trust Protector at any time, with or without cause. If a Trust Protector is removed, resigns, or cannot continue to serve for any reason, I may appoint a successor Trust Protector.

Authority of My Trust Protector to Appoint a Successor Trust Protector

Any Trust Protector, including successor Trust Protectors, may appoint a successor Trust Protector in writing. The appointment of a successor will take effect upon the death, resignation, or incapacity of the appointing Trust Protector. If I have named a successor Trust Protector, the appointment of a successor Trust Protector under this Subsection will take effect only if all Trust Protectors that I named fail to qualify or cease to act.

Default of a Designated Trust Protector

If the office of Trust Protector for a trust is vacant and no effectively named successor Trust Protector exists, any beneficiary may petition a court of competent jurisdiction to appoint a successor Trust Protector to fill any vacancy lasting longer than 30 days. The petition may subject the trust to the jurisdiction of the court only to the extent necessary to make the appointment and may not subject the trust to the continuing jurisdiction of the court.

A minor or incapacitated beneficiary's parent or Legal Representative may act on his or her behalf.

Rights of Successor Trust Protectors

A successor Trust Protector has all of the authority of any predecessor Trust Protector, but will not be responsible for the predecessor's acts, omissions, or forbearances.

Power to Remove and Appoint Trustees

During any time I am incapacitated and following my death, my Trust Protector may remove any Trustee of a trust created under this instrument.

If the office of Trustee of a trust is vacant and no successor Trustee is designated, my Trust Protector may appoint an individual or a corporate fiduciary to serve as Trustee.

A Trust Protector may not appoint itself as a Trustee, and may not simultaneously serve as both Trust Protector and Trustee.

Good Faith Standard Imposed

The authority of my Trust Protector is conferred in a nonfiduciary capacity, and my Trust Protector is not liable for any action taken in good faith. My Trust Protector is not liable for any act, omission, or forbearance. My Trust Protector must be reimbursed promptly for any costs incurred in defending or settling any claim brought against it in its capacity as Trust Protector, unless it is conclusively established that the act, omission, or forbearance was motivated by an actual intent to harm the trust beneficiaries, or was an act of self-dealing for personal benefit.

Power to Amend Trust Provisions

During any time I am incapacitated and following my death, my Trust Protector may amend any provision of this instrument as it applies to any trust to which the Trust Protector is serving as Trust Protector to:

> alter the administrative and investment powers of my Trustee;
>
> amend distribution provisions to comply with my intent of adhering to the Islamic law of Inheritance;
>
> reflect tax or other legal changes that affect trust administration. I recognize that the gift, estate, generation-skipping transfer tax, and income tax provisions of the Internal Revenue Code and Treasury Regulations are subject to change. I grant my Trust Protector the authority to amend this trust instrument's terms in this manner as will, in my Trust Protector's sole and absolute

discretion, eliminate or minimize the state and federal taxes payable by my estate, my wife's estate, and provide the maximum benefit to my beneficiaries as expressed in this instrument. This includes dividing the trust property into separate shares or funds;

correct ambiguities, including scrivener errors, that might otherwise require court construction or reformation; and

grant a beneficiary of any trust created under this instrument the testamentary power to appoint all or part of the beneficiary's trust or trust share to the creditors of the beneficiary's estate. As a condition for the beneficiary's exercise of this power, my Trust Protector may require that the beneficiary first obtain the consent of my Trust Protector. Any testamentary power of appointment granted by my Trust Protector must be in writing, and may be revoked by my Trust Protector throughout that beneficiary's lifetime. I suggest that my Trust Protector exercise this authority to subject trust property to estate tax instead of the generation-skipping transfer tax when it appears that it may reduce overall taxes.

My Trust Protector may not amend this instrument in any manner that would result in a reduction in the estate tax marital deduction under Internal Revenue Code Section 2056 or the estate tax charitable deduction under Section 2055 to which my estate would otherwise be entitled. Further, my Trust Protector may not limit or alter the rights of a beneficiary in any trust assets held by the trust before the amendment.

Any amendment made by my Trust Protector in good faith is conclusive on all persons interested in the trust, and my Trust Protector is not liable for the consequences of making or not making any amendment. Any amendment to this instrument made by my Trust Protector must be made in a written instrument signed by my Trust Protector. My Trust Protector must deliver a copy of the amendment to the Income Beneficiaries and my Trustee.

Role of the Trust Protector in Modifying Islamic Inheritance Shares

If, after the signing of this Trust, I have a new relative who may be entitled to inherit under the Islamic Law of Inheritance or if a relative named herein becomes ineligible for inheritance, my Trust Protector shall be obligated to re-calculate the shares of inheritance utilizing guidelines provided herein.

Inquiry into Eligibility

My Trust Protector shall gather a list of all lineal descendants, ascendants as well as any other relatives who may be eligible under the Islamic Law of Inheritance given the circumstances. He or she will then exclude from eligibility any person who has (a) caused my death unlawfully or (b) has left the religion of Islam. My Trust Protector is not obligated to inquire as to any beneficiary's faith tradition. However, if my Trust Protector knows that a potential beneficiary has publicly rejected Islam, the potential beneficiary should be deemed ineligible for inheritance. Determination of inheritance rights under the Islamic Rules of Inheritance is in my Trust Protector's sole and unreviewable discretion.

Calculation

My Trust Protector shall then determine the shares of inheritance and advise of the same to the Trustee in writing in the form of an Amendment to this Trust. The names and shares shall be provided to all beneficiaries by my Trustee at least 30 days before distribution. Beneficiaries shall have 15 days to advise the Trustee of any errors, who will then make any objections known to the Trust Protector. The determination of shares under the Islamic Law of Inheritance is made at my Trust Protector's sole and reviewable discretion.

My Trustee shall, from the trust, indemnify my Trust Protector for any costs and Attorney Fees expended in defending any decision related to this Trust, including decisions concerning the determination of rights to inheritance under the Islamic Law of Inheritance and the specific shares allotted.

Any amendment made by my Trust Protector in good faith is conclusive on all persons interested in the trust, and my Trust Protector is not liable for the consequences of making or not making any amendment. My Trust Protector shall make any amendment to this instrument in writing and signed by my Trust Protector. My Trust Protector must deliver a copy of the amendment to the Income Beneficiaries and my Trustee.

Not a General Power of Appointment

My Trust Protector may not participate in the exercise of a power or a discretion conferred under this instrument that would cause my Trust Protector to possess a general power of appointment within the meaning of Internal Revenue Code Sections 2041 and 2514. Specifically, my Trust Protector may not use these powers for his or her personal benefit, nor for the discharge of his or her financial obligations.

Release of Powers

My Trust Protector, acting on its own behalf and on behalf of all successor Trust Protectors, may irrevocably release, renounce, suspend, or reduce any or all powers and discretions conferred on my Trust Protector by this instrument by a written instrument delivered to my Trustee.

No Duty to Monitor

My Trust Protector has no duty to monitor any trust created under this instrument in order to determine whether any of the powers and discretions conferred by this instrument on my Trust Protector should be exercised. Further, my Trust Protector has no duty to be informed as to the acts or omissions of others, or to take any action to prevent or minimize loss. Any exercise or non-exercise of the powers and discretions granted to my Trust Protector is in his or her sole and absolute discretion, and will be binding and conclusive on all persons. My Trust Protector is not required to exercise any power or discretion granted under this instrument.

Compensation

Though not required to accept, any Trust Protector serving under this instrument is entitled to receive reasonable compensation for services as determined by my Trustee. My Trust Protector is entitled to reimbursement for all expenses incurred in the performance of its duties as Trust Protector, including travel expenses.

Serving in the capacity of Trust Protector does not prevent my Trust Protector from also providing legal, investment, or accounting services on behalf of the trust or the trust beneficiaries. If my Trust Protector is providing professional services, my Trust Protector may charge its typical fees for professional services, and may also be compensated for its services as Trust Protector.

Right to Examine

The books and records of each trust created under this instrument, including all documentation, inventories, and accountings, must be open and available for inspection by my Trust Protector at all reasonable times.

(Remainder of page intentionally left blank.)

Article Four Administration of My Trust during My Incapacity

Section 4.01 Definition of My Incapacity

I will be considered incapacitated during any time when I am unable to effectively manage my property or financial affairs because of age, illness, mental disorder, dependence on prescription medication or other substances, or any other cause.

Section 4.02 Determination of My Incapacity

For purposes of this instrument, I am incapacitated if I am determined to be so under any one of the following Subsections.

Determination by Physicians

I will be considered incapacitated if two licensed physicians have determined my then-existing circumstances fall within the definition of incapacity as provided in 0.

I will be considered restored to capacity if my personal or attending physician signs a written opinion that I can effectively manage my property and financial affairs.

Court Determination

I will be considered incapacitated if a court of competent jurisdiction determines that I am legally incapacitated, incompetent, or otherwise unable to effectively manage my property or financial affairs.

Detention, Disappearance, or Absence

I will be considered incapacitated if I have an unexplained disappearance or absence for more than 30 days, or if I am detained under duress. My disappearance, absence, or detention under duress may be established by an affidavit of my Trustee, or, if no Trustee is then serving under this trust, by the affidavit of any beneficiary of any trust created under this instrument. The affidavit must describe the circumstances of my disappearance, absence, or detention under duress. A third party dealing with my Trustee in good faith may always rely on the representations contained in the affidavit.

I will be considered restored to capacity upon my written notice to the successor Trustee that I can manage my property and financial affairs.

Section 4.03 Trust Distributions during My Incapacity

During any period of time when I am incapacitated, my Trustee shall administer my trust and distribute its net income and principal as provided in this Section.

Distributions for My Benefit

My Trustee shall regularly and conscientiously make appropriate distributions of income and principal for my general welfare and comfort under the circumstances existing at the time each distribution is made.

Appropriate distributions under this Subsection include the payment of any of my enforceable legal obligations and premiums for insurance policies owned by me or by my trust, including life, medical, disability, property and casualty, errors and omissions, and longterm health care policies.

My Trustee is authorized to honor pledges and continue to make gifts to charitable organizations that I have regularly supported in the customarily given amounts.

The examples included in this Subsection are for purposes of illustration only and are not intended to limit the authority of my Trustee to make any distribution for my benefit that my Trustee determines appropriate.

Manner of Making Distributions

My Trustee may make distributions for my benefit in any one or more of the following ways:

> to me, but only to the extent I am able to manage these distributions;
>
> to other persons and entities for my use and benefit;
>
> to an agent or attorney in fact authorized to act for me under a legally valid durable power of attorney executed by me before my incapacity; and
>
> to my guardian or conservator who has assumed responsibility for me under any court order, decree, or judgment issued by a court of competent jurisdiction.

(Remainder of page intentionally left blank.)

Article Five Administration of My Trust upon My Death

Section 5.01 My Trust Becomes Irrevocable

After my death, my trust is irrevocable and my Social Security number may no longer be used to identify the trust. My Trustee may need to apply for a separate Taxpayer Identification Number for the trust.

Section 5.02 Administrative Trust

After my death and before the distribution of trust property as provided in the subsequent Articles of this trust, the trust will be an *administrative trust,* but may continue to be known as the Khan Family Trust. The administrative trust will continue for a reasonable period of time necessary to complete the administrative tasks set forth in this Article.

Section 5.03 Payment of Expenses and Taxes

My Trustee may pay from the trust property:

expenses of my last illness, funeral, and burial;
legally enforceable claims against me or my estate;
expenses of administering the trust and my estate; and
court-ordered allowances for those dependent upon me.

These payments are discretionary with my Trustee. My Trustee may make decisions on these payments without regard to any limitation on payment of the expenses and may make payments without any court's approval. No third party may enforce any claim or right to payment against the trust by virtue of this discretionary authority.

If payment would decrease the federal estate tax charitable deduction available to my estate, my Trustee may not pay any administrative expenses from assets passing to an organization that qualifies for the federal estate tax charitable deduction.

If payment would decrease the federal estate tax marital deduction available to my estate or violate the provisions of Treasury Regulation Section 20.2056(b)-4(d), my Trustee may not pay any administrative expenses from the net income of property qualifying for the federal estate tax marital deduction.

My Trustee shall pay death taxes out of the trust property's principal, as provided in 0. But if a probate estate is opened within six months after the date of my death, my Personal Representative shall pay any outstanding claims and expenses as authorized by the Personal Representative, as well as any death taxes from my probate estate to the extent that the cash and readily marketable assets in my probate estate are sufficient.

Section 5.04 Restrictions on Certain Payments from Retirement Plans

The term *designation date* means September 30 of the calendar year following the year of my death, or another date as established by Treasury Regulations or other tax law authority as the final date for determining whether this trust meets the requirements for treatment of the trust's oldest beneficiary as if the beneficiary was named individually as beneficiary of any qualified retirement plan payable to this trust.

Notwithstanding any other provision of this trust or state law to the contrary, my Trustee may not distribute any qualified retirement benefit payable to a trust created under this trust to or for the benefit of my estate, any charity, or any beneficiary other than an individual, on or after the *designation date*. My intent is that all qualified retirement benefits held by or payable to this trust on or after the designation date be distributed to or held only for individual beneficiaries, within the meaning of Internal Revenue Code Section 401(a)(9).

Qualified retirement benefits payable to the trust may not be used or applied on or after the designation date for payment of my debts, taxes, expenses of administration, or other claims against my estate, or for payment of estate, inheritance, or similar transfer taxes due because of my death, other than those directly attributable to and the legal obligation of a particular qualified retirement plan. This Section does not apply to any bequest or expense that is specifically directed to be funded with qualified retirement benefits.

Section 5.05 Excluding Life Insurance Proceeds from Creditors

Despite anything to the contrary in this instrument, any life insurance proceeds payable to the Trustee under this instrument must never be or become part of my probate or testamentary estate. Nothing in this instrument directs that these life insurance proceeds be used to pay my debts or expenses.

Section 5.06 Payment of Death Taxes

For the purposes of this Article, the term *death taxes* refers to any taxes imposed by reason of my death by federal, state, or local authorities, including estate, inheritance, gift, and direct-skip generation-skipping transfer taxes. For purposes of this Section, *death taxes* does not include any additional estate tax imposed by Internal Revenue Code Section 2031(c)(5)(C) or Section 2032A(c), or any other comparable recapture tax imposed by any taxing authority. Nor does the term include any generation-skipping transfer tax, other than a direct-skip generation-skipping transfer tax.

Except as otherwise provided in this Article or elsewhere in this trust, my Trustee shall provide for payment of all death taxes from the administrative trust without apportionment. My Trustee may not seek contribution toward or recovery of any payments of death taxes from any individual.

Protection of Exempt Property

Death taxes may not be allocated to or paid from any assets that are not included in my gross estate for federal estate tax purposes. To the extent practicable, my Trustee may not pay any death taxes from assets that are exempt from generation-skipping transfer tax purposes.

Protection of the Marital Deduction

Death taxes may not be paid from or allocated to any property that qualifies for the federal estate tax marital deduction.

Protection of the Charitable Deduction

Death taxes may not be paid from or allocated to any assets passing to an organization that qualifies for the federal estate tax charitable deduction, or from any assets passing to a split-interest charitable trust, unless the Trustee has first used all other assets available to pay the taxes.

Property Passing outside of My Trust

Death taxes imposed with respect to property included in my gross estate for death tax purposes but passing outside of the trust are to be apportioned among the persons and entities benefited. The proportion attributed to each person or entity is the taxable value of each person or entity's beneficial interest over the total taxable value of all property and interests included in my gross estate for death tax purposes. The values used for the apportionment are to be the values as finally determined under federal, state, or local law.

QTIP Property

If my Trustee or my Personal Representative waives any right of recovery granted by Section 2207A and corresponding provisions of applicable state law, death taxes may not be apportioned to any property included in my taxable estate will be apportioned to or collected from the assets of the QTIP as provided in Internal Revenue Code Section 2207A.

Section 5.07 Coordination with My Personal Representative

The following provisions are intended to help facilitate the coordination between my Personal Representative and my Trustee. These provisions apply even if the Personal Representative and the Trustee are the same person or entity.

Reliance on Information from My Personal Representative

My Trustee may rely upon the written request of my Personal Representative for payments authorized under this Article and the amounts included in those payments without computing the sums involved. If a payment is made under this Article to my Personal Representative, my Trustee will have no duty to inquire into the application of the payment.

Receipt of Probate Property

My Trustee may accept or decline any distributions of property tendered to my Trustee by my Personal Representative. If my Trustee accepts the property, my Trustee may do so without audit, and will not be required to review the Personal Representative's records.

Discretionary Distributions to My Personal Representative

My Trustee may distribute cash, accrued income, or other trust property to my probate estate as a beneficiary of this trust, to the extent my Trustee determines that doing so is in the best interests of the trust beneficiaries.

Section 5.08 Authority to Make Tax Elections

After my death, my Trustee may make tax elections as provided in this Section. But if a Personal Representative is appointed for my probate estate, the discretionary authority granted to my Trustee as to any tax election will be subordinate to the Personal Representative's statutorily delegated authority.

Tax Elections

My Trustee may make any tax elections necessary for the efficient administration of my estate, including:

valuing assets according to an alternate valuation date;
electing whether to take administration expenses as estate tax deductions or income tax deductions;
allocating my unused generation-skipping exemption to any portion of the trust property;
electing special-use valuation;
deferring payment of all or any portion of any taxes; and
treating any portion of my administrative trust as part of my estate for federal or state income tax purposes, or both.

In addition, my Trustee, in its sole and absolute discretion, may elect to waive, in whole or in part, my right to have my estate reimbursed for any tax paid as a result of the inclusion in my taxable estate of property held in a qualified terminable interest property (QTIP) trust created for me by my wife.

My Trustee may make equitable adjustments between income and principal because of any tax elections made by my Trustee.

Allocation of GST Exemption

My Trustee may elect to allocate or not allocate any portion of the Available GST Exemption under Internal Revenue Code Section 2631, or a counterpart exemption under any applicable state law to any property of which I am considered the transferor for generation-skipping transfer tax purposes. This includes any property transferred by me during my life for which I did not make an allocation prior to death. The exercise of my Trustee's discretion should be based on the transfers, gift tax returns, and other information known to my Trustee, with no requirement that allocations benefit the various transferees or beneficiaries in any particular manner.

Section 5.09 Payment of Charitable Bequests

To the extent possible, my Trustee must make all charitable distributions from property that constitutes *income in respect of a decedent* (IRD) as that term is defined under the U.S. income tax laws. The distribution will qualify for the income tax charitable deduction under Internal Revenue Code Section 642(c)(2), as amended.

(Remainder of page intentionally left blank.)

Article Six Specific Distributions and Disposition of Tangible Personal Property

Section 6.01 Specific Distribution to Lighthouse Mosque

Upon my death, my Trustee shall allocate $10,000 to the Lighthouse Mosque in Oakland, California.

Section 6.02 Distribution of Tangible Personal Property

My Trustee shall distribute my tangible personal property upon my death as provided in the following Articles.

Section 6.03 Definition of Tangible Personal Property

For purposes of this Article, the term *tangible personal property* includes household furnishings, appliances and fixtures, works of art, motor vehicles, pictures, collectibles, apparel and jewelry, books, sporting goods, and hobby paraphernalia. The term does not include any property that my Trustee, in its sole and absolute discretion, determines to be part of any business or business interest owned by me or my trust.

After my death, if my Trustee receives property to be distributed under this Article from my probate estate or in any other manner, my Trustee shall distribute the property in accordance with this Article's terms. The fact that an item of tangible personal property was not received by my trust until after my death does not diminish the validity of the gift. If property to be distributed under this Article is not part of the trust property upon my death and is not subsequently transferred to my Trustee from my probate estate or in any other manner, then the specific distribution of property made in this Article is null and void, without any legal or binding effect.

Section 6.04 Incidental Expenses and Encumbrances

Until property distributed in accordance with this Article is delivered to the appropriate beneficiary or his or her Legal Representative, my Trustee shall pay the reasonable expenses of securing, storing, insuring, packing, transporting, and otherwise caring for the property as an administration expense. Except as otherwise provided in my trust, my Trustee shall distribute property under this Article subject to all liens, security interests, and other encumbrances on the property.

Section 6.05 Residuary Distribution

Any property not distributed under this or prior Articles of this instrument will be distributed as provided in the following Articles.

(Remainder of page intentionally left blank.)

Article Seven Distributions to My Islamic Heirs

My Trustee shall administer and distribute my remaining trust property (not distributed under prior Articles of this trust instrument) under the provisions of this Article to my Islamic heirs. The term "Islamic heirs" shall refer to those individuals who have the right to inherit under the Islamic Law of Inheritance, as defined in Article 13. This group may include, but is not limited to, my lineal descendants of all generations; ancestors, including parents and grandparents; and other, more distant relatives.

Section 7.01 Division of My Trust Property

My Trustee shall divide my remaining trust property into separate shares for my Islamic heirs as provided in the next Section. As of the date of the execution of this Trust Instrument, my Islamic heirs are the following:

Name	Relationship	Share
Wafa Khan	Wife	1/8
Mariam Khan	Mother	1/6
Adam Khan	Son	17/36
Sarah Khan	Daughter	17/72

If any of the individuals listed above predeceases me or we pass away simultaneously or in a manner in which the order of deaths cannot be ascertained, his or her share shall lapse and my Trust Protector shall be responsible for recalculating the shares for each of my Islamic heirs in accordance with the Islamic Law of Inheritance as defined in Article Thirteen.

Section 7.02 Administration of Beneficiaries' Trusts

My Trustee shall administer the trust for each beneficiary as follows:

Distributions of Income and Principal

My Trustee shall distribute to the beneficiary as much of the income and principal of the beneficiary's trust as my Trustee determines necessary or advisable for the health, education, maintenance or support of the beneficiary.

My Trustee shall add any undistributed net income to principal.

Right to Withdraw Principal

When the beneficiary reaches 18 years of age or if, upon the funding of the trust established for the beneficiary, he or she has already reached 18 years of age, the beneficiary may withdraw from the trust at any time amounts, not to exceed in the aggregate 100% of the accumulated trust income and principal as of the date the beneficiary first has the right to exercise this withdrawal right.

The beneficiary may exercise this right at any time by delivering written notice to my Trustee, setting forth the desired withdrawal amount. Upon receiving a notice, my Trustee shall convey and deliver the requested amount to the beneficiary, free of trust. This right of withdrawal is a privilege that may be exercised only by the beneficiary, and is not subject to the claims of any creditor or to legal process, and may not be voluntarily or involuntarily alienated or encumbered. This provision does not limit the beneficiary's exercise of any power of appointment the beneficiary may have.

Distribution upon the Death of the Beneficiary

Subject to the terms of the next paragraph, the beneficiary has the testamentary general power to appoint all or any portion of the principal and undistributed income remaining in the beneficiary's trust at the beneficiary's death among one or more persons or entities and the creditors of the beneficiary's estate. The beneficiary has the exclusive right to exercise this general power of appointment.

The beneficiary may not exercise this power of appointment to appoint to himself or herself, his or her estate, his or her creditors, or creditors of his or her estate from the *limited share* of the beneficiary's trust. For purposes of this power of appointment, the *limited share* of the beneficiary's trust is that portion of the beneficiary's trust that has an inclusion ratio for generation-skipping transfer tax purposes of zero or that, in the absence of the exercise of the power of appointment, would not constitute a taxable generation-skipping transfer at the beneficiary's death. If the generation-skipping tax does not then apply, the limited share is the beneficiary's entire trust.

If any part of the beneficiary's trust is not effectively appointed, my Trustee shall distribute the remaining unappointed balance *in accordance with the Islamic Law of Inheritance.*

(Remainder of page intentionally left blank.)

Article Eight Remote Contingent Distribution

If any of the beneficiaries listed above predeceases me, that beneficiary's share shall lapse and the Trust Protector shall recalculate, in his or her sole discretion, the shares for my beneficiaries in accordance with Islamic Inheritance law as defined in Article Thirteen.

(Remainder of page intentionally left blank.)

Article Nine Distributions to Underage and Incapacitated Beneficiaries

If my Trustee is authorized or directed under any provision of this trust to distribute net income or principal to a person who has not yet reached 18 years of age or who is incapacitated as defined in 0, my Trustee may make the distribution by any one or more of the methods described in 0. Alternatively, my Trustee may retain the trust property in a separate trust to be administered by my Trustee under 0.

I request that before making a distribution to a beneficiary, my Trustee consider, to the extent reasonable, the ability the beneficiary has demonstrated in managing prior distributions of trust property.

Section 9.01 Methods of Distribution

My Trustee may distribute trust property for any beneficiary's benefit, subject to the provisions of this Article in any one or more of the following methods:

My Trustee may distribute trust property directly to the beneficiary.
My Trustee may distribute trust property to the beneficiary's guardian, conservator, parent, other family member, or any person who has assumed the responsibility of caring for the beneficiary.
My Trustee may distribute trust property to any person or entity, including my Trustee, as custodian for the beneficiary under the Uniform Transfers to Minors Act or similar statute.
My Trustee may distribute trust property to other persons and entities for the beneficiary's use and benefit.
My Trustee may distribute trust property to an agent or attorney in fact authorized to act for the beneficiary under a valid durable power of attorney executed by the beneficiary before becoming incapacitated.

Section 9.02 Retention in Trust

My Trustee may retain and administer trust property in a separate trust for any beneficiary's benefit, subject to the provisions of this Article as follows.

Distribution of Net Income and Principal

My Independent Trustee may distribute to the beneficiary as much of the net income and principal of any trust created under this Section as my Independent Trustee may determine advisable for any purpose. If there is no then-serving Independent Trustee, my Trustee shall distribute to the beneficiary as much of the net income and principal of the trust created under this Section as my Trustee determines is necessary or advisable for the beneficiary's health, education, maintenance or support. Any undistributed net income will be accumulated and added to principal.

Right of Withdrawal

When the beneficiary whose trust is created under this Section either reaches 25 years of age or is no longer incapacitated, the beneficiary may withdraw all or any portion of the accumulated net income and principal from the trust.

Distribution upon the Death of the Beneficiary

Subject to the terms of the next paragraph, the beneficiary whose trust is created under this Section may appoint all or any portion of the principal and undistributed net income remaining in the beneficiary's trust at the beneficiary's death among one or more persons or entities, and the creditors of the beneficiary's estate. The beneficiary has the exclusive right to exercise this general power of appointment.

The beneficiary may not exercise this power of appointment to appoint to the beneficiary, the beneficiary's estate, the beneficiary's creditors, or creditors of the beneficiary's estate from the *limited share* of the beneficiary's trust. For purposes of this power of appointment, the *limited share* of the beneficiary's trust is that portion of the beneficiary's trust that has an inclusion ratio for generation-skipping transfer tax purposes of zero or that without the exercise of the power of appointment, would not constitute a taxable generation-skipping transfer at the beneficiary's death. If the generation-skipping tax does not then apply, the limited share will be the beneficiary's entire trust.

Section 9.03 Application of Article

Any decision made by my Trustee under this Article is final, controlling, and binding upon all beneficiaries subject to the provisions of this Article.

The provisions of this Article do not apply to distributions to me or to my wife from any trust established under this trust.

Further, the provisions of this Article do not apply to distributions that are required to be made to a beneficiary under the provisions of 0.

(Remainder of page intentionally left blank.)

Article Ten Retirement Plans and Life Insurance Policies

The provisions of this Article apply to qualified retirement plans and insurance policies owned by or made payable to my trust.

Section 10.01 Retirement Plans

Notwithstanding any contrary provision of this trust, the provisions of this Section apply to qualified retirement plans.

Rights of My Trustee

Subject to the provisions below pertaining to distributions from qualified retirement plans, my Trustee may exercise the right to determine the manner and timing of qualified retirement plan benefit payments permitted under these plans and consistent with the federal income tax rules regarding required minimum distributions under Internal Revenue Code Section 401(a)(9).

My Trustee may make a qualified disclaimer of any qualified retirement benefits or non-qualified annuity benefits payable to my trust.

My Trustee may not be held liable to any beneficiary for any decision regarding the death benefit election or the disclaimer of any qualified retirement benefits payable to my trust.

My Trustee may not change or designate beneficiaries under any retirement plan. Any power extended to my Trustee under the terms of a retirement plan that gives or appears to give my Trustee the power to change the identity or rights of any beneficiaries under the plan is void *ab initio*.

Distributions from Qualified Retirement Plans to Trusts

Unless specifically stated otherwise beginning with the year of my death, if any trust created under this trust, including any administrative trust created under 0, becomes the beneficiary of death benefits under any qualified retirement plan, my Trustee shall annually withdraw from the trust's share of the plan the minimum distribution required under Internal Revenue Code Section 401(a)(9). My Trustee may withdraw additional amounts from the trust's share of the plan as my Trustee deems advisable, but only if the dispositive terms of the trust authorize my Trustee to immediately distribute the withdrawn amount as provided below. My Trustee shall immediately distribute all amounts withdrawn in accordance with the Islamic Law of Inheritance.

Amounts required to be withdrawn and distributed under this Section will reduce mandatory distribution amounts under other provisions of this trust that otherwise require distribution of all the trust's income.

This Section's purpose is to ensure that the life expectancy of the trust beneficiaries may be used to calculate the minimum distributions required by the Internal Revenue Code. This Section is to be interpreted consistent with my intent, despite any direction to the contrary in this trust.

Minimum Required Distribution

In administering my trust, the minimum required distribution for each qualified retirement plan for any year is the greater of:

> the value of the qualified retirement plan determined as of the preceding year end, divided by the applicable distribution period; and
> the amount that my Trustee is required to withdraw under the laws then applicable to the trust to avoid penalty.

If I die before my required beginning date for a qualified retirement plan, the applicable distribution period means the beneficiary's life expectancy. If I die on or after my required beginning date for a qualified retirement plan, the applicable distribution period means the beneficiary's life expectancy, or my remaining life expectancy, if longer.

Notwithstanding the foregoing, if I die on or after my required beginning date for a qualified retirement plan, the minimum required distribution for the year of my death means:

> the amount that was required to be distributed to me with respect to the qualified retirement plan during the year; minus
> amounts actually distributed to me with respect to the qualified retirement plan during the year.

Life expectancy, required beginning date, and other similar terms used in this Subsection are to be determined under Internal Revenue Code Section 401(a)(9).

Section 10.02 Life Insurance Policies

The following provisions apply to life insurance policies owned by or made payable to my trust.

Provisions during My Life

During my life, I reserve all of the rights, powers, privileges, and options, with respect to any insurance policy, annuity, or any other third-party beneficiary contract owned by or made payable to my trust. This includes the rights to designate and change beneficiaries, to borrow money, to surrender the policy, to receive any payments as owner, and to make any available elections.

My Trustee will have no duty to exercise or not exercise any rights, powers, privileges, or options with respect to any insurance policy, annuity contract, or other third-party beneficiary contract. My Trustee will have no obligation to pay premiums or other contractual amounts that may be payable under any policy.

Provisions after My Death

After my death, my Trustee may make all appropriate elections with respect to these policies and may collect all sums made payable to my trust or my Trustee under all these policies or contracts.

My Trustee may exercise any settlement options or other options or rights that may be available under the terms of any policy or contract. My Trustee may not be held liable to any beneficiary on account of any election my Trustee made with respect to any policy or contract.

Section 10.03 Limitation on Liability of Payor

Persons or entities dealing in good faith with my Trustee are not required to see to the proper application of proceeds delivered to my Trustee, or to inquire into any provision of this trust.

A receipt signed by my Trustee for any proceeds or benefits paid will be a sufficient discharge to the person or entity making the payment.

Section 10.04 Collection Efforts

My Trustee shall make reasonable efforts to collect all life insurance policy proceeds and qualified retirement benefits payable to my trust.

My Trustee may commence legal or administrative proceedings to collect any life insurance policy proceeds or qualified retirement benefits to which the trust is entitled. My Trustee need not commence any proceedings until my Trustee is satisfactorily indemnified for any expenses and liabilities my Trustee may incur in connection with the proceeding.

My Trustee may settle any claims with respect to the collection of any life insurance proceeds or qualified retirement benefits to which my trust may be entitled. A settlement made by my Trustee will be binding on all beneficiaries.

Section 10.05 No Obligation to Purchase or Maintain Benefits

Nothing in this trust is to be interpreted as imposing any obligation on me or on my Trustee to purchase, invest, or maintain any qualified retirement plan or life insurance policy.

(Remainder of page intentionally left blank.)

Article Eleven Trust Administration

Section 11.01 Distributions to Beneficiaries

Whenever this trust authorizes or directs my Trustee to make a net income or principal distribution to a beneficiary, my Trustee may apply any property that otherwise could be distributed directly to the beneficiary for his or her benefit. My Trustee is not required to inquire into the beneficiary's ultimate disposition of the distributed property unless specifically directed otherwise by this trust.

My Trustee may make cash distributions, in-kind distributions, or distributions partly in each, in proportions and at values determined by my Trustee. My Trustee may allocate undivided interests in specific assets to a beneficiary or trust in any proportion or manner that my Trustee determines, even though the property allocated to one beneficiary may be different from that allocated to another beneficiary.

My Trustee may make these determinations without regard to the income tax attributes of the property and without the consent of any beneficiary.

Section 11.02 Beneficiary's Status

Until my Trustee receives notice of the incapacity, birth, marriage, death, or other event upon which a beneficiary's right to receive payments may depend, my Trustee will not be held liable for acting or not acting with respect to the event, or for disbursements made in good faith to persons whose interest may have been affected by the event. Unless otherwise provided in this trust, a parent or Legal Representative may act on behalf of a minor or incapacitated beneficiary.

My Trustee may rely on any information provided by a beneficiary with respect to the beneficiary's assets and income. My Trustee will have no independent duty to investigate the status of any beneficiary and will not incur any liability for not doing so.

Section 11.03 Mandatory Payments of a Pecuniary Amount

If any person holds the right to receive a pecuniary amount from my trust upon my death, my Trustee must either:

satisfy the entire pecuniary amount or irrevocably set aside property to satisfy the entire pecuniary amount within 15 months of my death; or

pay appropriate interest, as defined in Treasury Regulations Section 26.2642-2(b)(4)(ii)(B), to the person.

If my Trustee satisfies the pecuniary amount with an in-kind distribution, my Trustee will allocate assets to satisfy the pecuniary amount in a manner that fairly reflects net appreciation or depreciation in the value of the available assets, as measured from the valuation date to the payment date.

Section 11.04 No Court Proceedings

My Trustee shall administer this trust with efficiency, with attention to the provisions of this trust, and with freedom from judicial intervention. If my Trustee or another interested party institutes a legal proceeding, the court will acquire jurisdiction only to the extent necessary for that proceeding. Any proceeding to seek instructions or a court determination may only be initiated in the court with original jurisdiction over matters relating to the construction and administration of trusts. Seeking instructions or a court determination is not to be construed as subjecting this trust to the court's continuing jurisdiction.

I request that any questions or disputes that arise during the administration of this trust be resolved by mediation and, if necessary, arbitration in accordance with the Uniform Arbitration Act. Each interested party involved in the dispute, including any Trustee involved, may select an arbiter and, if necessary to establish a majority decision, these arbiters may select an additional arbiter. The decision of a majority of the arbiters selected will control with respect to the matter.

Section 11.05 No Bond

My Trustee is not required to furnish any bond for the faithful performance of the Trustee's duties unless required by a court of competent jurisdiction, and only if the court finds that a bond is needed to protect the beneficiaries' interests. No surety will be required on any bond required by any law or court rule, unless the court specifies its necessity.

Section 11.06 Exoneration of My Trustee

No successor Trustee is obligated to examine the accounts, records, or actions of any previous Trustee or the Personal Representative of my estate. No successor Trustee may be held responsible for any act, omission, or forbearance by any previous Trustee or of the Personal Representative of my estate. Absent clear and convincing evidence of willful bad faith on the part of my Trustee, my Trustee is exonerated from any liability for the acts, omissions, or forbearances of any Trust Protector and from any liability for my Trustee's own acts, omissions, or forbearances directed by the Trust Protector.

Any Trustee may obtain written agreements from the beneficiaries or their Legal Representatives releasing and indemnifying the Trustee from any liability that may have arisen from the Trustee's acts, omissions, or forbearances. If acquired from all the trust's living beneficiaries or their Legal Representatives, any agreement is conclusive and binding on all parties, born or unborn, who may have or who may later acquire an interest in the trust.

My Trustee may require a refunding agreement before making any distribution or allocation of trust income or principal, and may withhold distribution or allocation pending determination or release of a tax or other lien. This refunding agreement provision will not apply to any distribution that qualifies for the federal estate tax unlimited marital deduction or the federal estate tax charitable deduction.

Section 11.07 Limitations on Trustee Liability

I direct that any individual or corporate fiduciary that serves as my Trustee will not incur any liability for any action, omission, or forbearance made in good faith reliance on information, consent, or directions received from a Trust Protector, except for cases of willful misconduct or gross negligence on the Trustee's part.

Any individual or corporate fiduciary currently serving as a Trustee may expend any portion of the trust assets to defend any claim brought against the Trustee as a result of his or her good faith reliance on any information, consent, or directions received from a Trust Protector, even if my Trustee's defense costs would exhaust the trust's value. Any individual or corporate fiduciary that formerly served as a Trustee is entitled to reimbursement from the trust estate for any expenses, including reimbursement for attorney's fees and litigation costs reasonably incurred as a result of the Trustee's good faith reliance on information, consent, or directions received from a Trust Protector.

Except for cases of willful misconduct or gross negligence on the Trustee's part, any action, omission, or forbearance made in good faith reliance on information, consent, or directions received from a Trust Protector will be considered to have been made in good faith for this Section's purposes.

Section 11.08 Trustee Compensation

An individual serving as Trustee is entitled to fair and reasonable compensation for the services provided as a fiduciary. A corporate fiduciary serving as Trustee will be compensated by agreement between an individual serving as Trustee and the corporate fiduciary. In the absence of an individual Trustee or an agreement, a corporate fiduciary will be compensated in accordance with the corporate fiduciary's current published fee schedule.

A Trustee may charge additional fees for services provided that are beyond the ordinary scope of duties, such as fees for legal services, tax return preparation, and corporate finance or investment banking services.

In addition to receiving compensation, a Trustee may be reimbursed for reasonable costs and expenses incurred in carrying out the Trustee's duties under this trust.

Section 11.09 Employment of Professionals

My Trustee may appoint, employ, and remove investment advisors, accountants, auditors, depositories, custodians, brokers, consultants, attorneys, advisors, agents, and employees to advise or assist in the performance of my Trustee's duties. My Trustee may act on the recommendations of the persons or entities employed, with or without independent investigation.

My Trustee may reasonably compensate an individual or entity employed to assist or advise my Trustee, regardless of any other relationship existing between the individual or entity and my Trustee.

My Trustee may compensate providers of contracted services at the usual rate out of the trust's income or principal, as my Trustee deems advisable. My Trustee may compensate an individual or entity employed to assist or advise my Trustee without diminishing the compensation the Trustee is entitled to under this trust. A Trustee who is a partner, stockholder, officer, director, or corporate affiliate in any entity employed to assist or advise my Trustee may still receive the Trustee's share of the compensation paid to the entity.

Section 11.10 Trust Accounting

Except to the extent required by law, my Trustee is not required to file accountings in any jurisdiction. After my death, my Trustee must provide an annual accounting to the Income Beneficiaries of any trust created under this trust unless waived by the Income Beneficiaries.

The annual accounting must include the receipts, expenditures, and distributions of income and principal and the assets on hand for the accounting period. A copy of the federal fiduciary tax return filed for a trust during the accounting will satisfy this reporting requirement.

In the absence of fraud or obvious error, assent by all Income Beneficiaries to a Trustee's accounting will make the matters disclosed in the accounting binding and conclusive upon all persons, including those living on this date and those born in the future who have or will have a vested or contingent interest in the trust property. In the case of an Income Beneficiary who is a minor or incapacitated, the beneficiary's natural guardian or Legal Representative may give the assent required under this Section.

A beneficiary may object to an accounting provided by my Trustee only by giving written notice to my Trustee within 60 days after my Trustee provides the accounting. Any beneficiary who does not submit a timely written objection is considered to assent to the accounting.

My Trustee must make the trust's financial records and documents available to beneficiaries at reasonable times and upon reasonable notice for inspection. My Trustee is not required to furnish any information regarding my trust to anyone other than a beneficiary. My Trustee may exclude any information my Trustee determines is not directly applicable to the beneficiary receiving the information.

In all events, a beneficiary's Legal Representative may receive any notices and take any action on behalf of the beneficiary as to an accounting. If any beneficiary's Legal Representative fails to object to any accounting in writing within 60 days after my Trustee provides the accounting, the beneficiary's Legal Representative will be considered to assent to the accounting.

Section 11.11 Action of Trustees and Delegation of Trustee Authority

When I am not serving as a Trustee, if two Trustees are eligible to act with respect to a given matter, they must agree unanimously for action to be taken unless the express terms of the Trustees' appointment provide otherwise. If more than two Trustees are eligible to act with respect to a given matter, the Trustees must agree by majority for action to be taken.

If my Trustees are unable to agree on a matter for which they have joint powers, I request that the matter be settled by mediation and then by arbitration, if necessary, in accordance with the Uniform Arbitration Act. Each of my Trustees may select an arbiter and these arbiters may select an additional arbiter, if necessary to establish a majority decision. The decision of a majority of the arbiters will control with respect to the matter.

A nonconcurring Trustee may dissent or abstain from a decision of the majority. A Trustee will be absolved from personal liability by registering the dissent or abstention in the trust records. After doing so, the dissenting Trustee must then act with my other Trustees in any way necessary or appropriate to effect the majority decision.

Subject to the limitations set forth in 0, any Trustee may, by written instrument, delegate to any other Trustee the right to exercise any power, including a discretionary power, granted to my Trustee in this trust. During the time a delegation under this Section is in effect, the Trustee to whom the delegation is made may exercise the power to the same extent as if the delegating Trustee has personally joined in the exercise of the power. The delegating Trustee may revoke the delegation at any time by giving written notice to the Trustee to whom the power was delegated.

Section 11.12 Trustee May Disclaim or Release Any Power

Notwithstanding any provision of this trust to the contrary, any Trustee may relinquish any Trustee power in whole or in part, irrevocably or for any specified period of time, by a written instrument. The Trustee may relinquish a power personally or may relinquish the power for all subsequent Trustees.

Section 11.13 Trustee May Execute a Power of Attorney

My Trustee may appoint any individual or entity to serve as my Trustee's agent under a power of attorney to transact any business on behalf of my trust or any other trust created under this trust.

Section 11.14 Additions to Separate Trusts

If upon my death, or upon the termination of any trust created under this trust, a final distribution is to be made to a person who is the Primary Beneficiary of another trust established under this trust, and there is no specific indication whether the distribution is to be made in trust or outright, my Trustee shall make the distribution to the second trust instead of distributing the property to the beneficiary outright. For purposes of administration, the distribution will be treated as though it had been an original part of the second trust.

Section 11.15 Authority to Terminate Trusts

My Trust Protector may terminate any trust created under this trust at any time, if my Trust Protector determines that administering a trust created under this trust is no longer economical. Once distributed, my Trustee will have no further responsibility with respect to that trust property. My Trustee will distribute the trust property from a terminated trust in this order:

to me, if I am then living;
if I am not then living, to my wife, if then a trust beneficiary;
if I am not then living and my wife is not then a trust beneficiary, to the beneficiaries then entitled to mandatory distributions of the trust's net income, in the same proportions; and then
if none of the beneficiaries are entitled to mandatory distributions of net income, to the beneficiaries then eligible to receive discretionary distributions of the trust's net income, in the amounts and shares my Trust Protector determines.

(Remainder of page intentionally left blank.)

Article Twelve My Trustee's Powers

Section 12.01 Introduction to Trustee's Powers

Except as otherwise specifically provided in this trust, my Trustee may exercise the powers granted by this trust without prior approval from any court, including those powers set forth under the laws of the State of Arizona or any other jurisdiction whose law applies to this trust. The powers set forth in A.R.S. Sections 14-10815 and 14-10816 are specifically incorporated into this trust.

My Trustee shall exercise the Trustee powers in the manner my Trustee determines to be in the beneficiaries' best interests. My Trustee must not exercise any power inconsistent with the beneficiaries' right to the enjoyment of the trust property in accordance with the general principles of trust law.

My Trustee may have duties and responsibilities in addition to those described in this trust. I encourage any individual or corporate fiduciary serving as Trustee to obtain appropriate legal advice if my Trustee has any questions concerning the duties and responsibilities as Trustee.

Section 12.02 Execution of Documents by My Trustee

My Trustee may execute and deliver any written instruments that my Trustee considers necessary to carry out any powers granted in this trust.

Section 12.03 Investment Powers in General

My Trustee may invest in any type of investment that my Trustee determines is consistent with the investment goals of the trust, whether inside or outside the geographic borders of the United States of America and its possessions or territories, taking into account the overall investment portfolio of the trust.

Without limiting my Trustee's investment authority in any way, I request that my Trustee exercise reasonable care and skill in selecting and retaining trust investments. I also request that my Trustee take into account the following factors in choosing investments:

the potential return from the investment, both in income and appreciation;

the potential income tax consequences of the investment;

the investment's potential for volatility; and
the role the investment will play in the trust's portfolio.

I request that my Trustee also consider the possible effects of inflation or deflation, changes in global and US economic conditions, transaction expenses, and the trust's need for liquidity while arranging the trust's investment portfolio.

My Trustee may delegate his or her discretion to manage trust investments to any registered investment advisor or corporate fiduciary.

Section 12.04 Banking Powers

My Trustee may establish any type of bank account in any banking institutions that my Trustee chooses. If my Trustee makes frequent disbursements from an account, the account does not need to be interest bearing. My Trustee may authorize withdrawals from an account in any manner.

My Trustee may open accounts in the name of my Trustee, with or without disclosing fiduciary capacity, and may open accounts in the name of the trust. When an account is in the name of the trust, checks on that account and authorized signatures need not disclose the account's fiduciary nature or refer to any trust or Trustee.

Section 12.05 Business Powers

If the trust owns or acquires an interest in a business entity, whether as a shareholder, partner, general partner, sole proprietor, member, participant in a joint venture, or otherwise, my Trustee may exercise the powers and authority provided for in this Section. The powers granted in this Section are in addition to all other powers granted to my Trustee in this trust.

No Duty to Diversify

Notwithstanding any duty to diversify imposed by state law or any other provision of this trust, my Trustee may acquire or indefinitely retain any ownership interest in or indebtedness of any closely held or nonpublicly traded entity in which the trust, myself, my spouse, my descendants, and the spouses of my descendants have an ownership interest (the *business interests*), and even though any business interest may constitute all or a substantial portion of the trust property. I specifically authorize my Trustee to invest or indefinitely retain all or any part of the trust property in these business interests, regardless of any resulting risk, lack of income, diversification, or marketability. I waive any applicable prudent investor rule, as well as the Trustee's standard of care and duty to diversify with respect to the acquisition or retention of these business interests.

I recognize that the value of a noncontrolling interest in a business entity may be less than the underlying value of the entity's net assets. Nevertheless, I authorize my Trustee to acquire or retain any noncontrolling business interests.

Specific Management Powers

My Trustee has all power and authority necessary to manage and operate any business owned by the trust, whether directly or indirectly, including the express powers set forth in this Subsection. My Trustee may participate directly in the conduct of the business, by serving as a general partner of a limited partnership, a member, manager or managing member of a limited liability company, or a shareholder of a corporation, or may employ others to serve in that capacity.

My Trustee may participate in the management of the business and delegate management duties and powers to any employee, manager, partner, or associate of the business, without incurring any liability for the delegation. To the extent that the business interest held by the trust is not one that includes management powers (such as a minority stock interest, limited partnership interest, or a membership interest in a limited liability company), my Trustee has no obligation to supervise the management of the underlying assets, and no liability for the actions of those who do manage the business.

My Trustee may enter into management trusts and nominee trusts in which my Trustee and the trust may serve as the exclusive manager or nominee of property or property interests on behalf of any limited partnership, limited liability company, or corporation.

My Trustee, individually, or if my Trustee is a corporate fiduciary, then an employee of my Trustee, may act as a director, general or limited partner, associate, or officer of the business.

My Trustee may participate with any other person or entity in the formation or continuation of a partnership either as a general or limited partner, or in any joint venture. My Trustee may exercise all the powers of management necessary and incidental to a membership in the partnership, limited partnership, or joint venture, including making charitable contributions.

My Trustee may reduce, expand, limit, or otherwise adjust the operation or policy of the business. My Trustee may subject the trust's principal and income to the risks of the business for any term or period, as my Trustee determines.

For any business in which the trust has an interest, my Trustee may advance money or other property, make loans (subordinated or otherwise) of cash or securities, and guarantee the loans of others made to the business. My Trustee may borrow money for the business, either alone or with other persons interested in the business, and may secure the loan or loans by a pledge or mortgage of any part of any trust property.

My Trustee may select and vote for directors, partners, associates, and officers of the business. My Trustee may enter into owners' agreements with a business in which the trust has an interest or with the other owners of the business.

My Trustee may execute agreements and amendments to agreements as may be necessary to the operation of the business, including stockholder agreements, partnership agreements, buy-sell agreements, and operating agreements for limited liability companies.

My Trustee may generally exercise any powers necessary for the continuation, management, sale, or dissolution of the business.

My Trustee may participate in the sale, reorganization, merger, consolidation, recapitalization, or liquidation of the business. My Trustee may sell or liquidate the business or business interest on terms my Trustee deems advisable and in the best interests of the trust and the beneficiaries. My Trustee may sell any business interest held by the trust to one or more of the beneficiaries of this trust or to any trust in which a majority of the beneficiaries are beneficiaries of this trust. My Trustee may make the sale in exchange for cash, a private annuity, an installment note, or any combination of those.

My Trustee may exercise all of the business powers granted in this trust even though my Trustee may be personally invested in or otherwise involved with the business.

Business Liabilities

If any tort or contract liability arises in connection with the business, and if the trust is liable, my Trustee will first satisfy the liability from the assets of the business, and only then from other trust property as determined by my Trustee.

Trustee Compensation

In addition to the compensation set forth in 0, my Trustee may receive additional reasonable compensation for services in connection with the operation of the business. My Trustee may receive this compensation directly from the business, the trust or both.

Conflicts of Interest

My Trustee may exercise all of the powers granted in this trust even though my Trustee may be involved with or have a personal interest in the business.

Section 12.06 Contract Powers

My Trustee may sell at public or private sale, transfer, exchange for other property, and otherwise dispose of trust property for consideration and upon terms and conditions that my Trustee deems advisable. My Trustee may grant options of any duration for any sales, exchanges, or transfers of trust property.

My Trustee may enter into contracts, and may deliver deeds or other instruments, that my Trustee considers appropriate.

Section 12.07 Common Investments

For purposes of convenience with regard to the trust property's administration and investment, my Trustee may invest part or all of the trust property jointly with property of other trusts for which my Trustee is also serving as a Trustee. A corporate fiduciary acting as my Trustee may use common funds for investment. When trust property is managed and invested in this manner, my Trustee will maintain records that sufficiently identify this trust's portion of the jointly invested assets.

Section 12.08 Insurance Powers

My Trustee may purchase, accept, hold, and deal with as owner, insurance policies on my life, any beneficiary's life, or any person's life in whom any beneficiary has an insurable interest.

My Trustee may purchase disability, medical, liability, longterm health care and other insurance on behalf of and for the benefit of any beneficiary. My Trustee may purchase annuities and similar investments for any beneficiary.

My Trustee may execute or cancel any automatic premium loan agreement with respect to any policy, and may elect or cancel any automatic premium loan provision in a life insurance policy. My Trustee may borrow money to pay premiums due on any policy, either by borrowing from the company issuing the policy or from another source. My Trustee may assign the policy as security for the loan.

My Trustee may exercise any option contained in a policy with regard to any dividend or share of surplus apportioned to the policy to reduce the amount of a policy, to convert or exchange the policy, or to surrender a policy at any time for its cash value.

My Trustee may elect any paid-up insurance or extended-term insurance nonforfeiture option contained in a policy.

My Trustee may sell any policy at its fair market value to anyone having an insurable interest in the policy, including the insured.

My Trustee may exercise any other right, option, or benefit contained in a policy or permitted by the issuing insurance company.

Upon termination of the trust, my Trustee may transfer and assign the policies held by the trust as a distribution of trust property.

Section 12.09 Payment of Property Taxes and Expenses

Except as otherwise provided in this trust, my Trustee may pay any property taxes, assessments, fees, charges, and other expenses incurred in the administration or protection of the trust. All payments will be a charge against the trust property and will be paid by my Trustee out of income. If the income is insufficient, then my Trustee may make any payments of property taxes or expenses out of the trust property's principal. My Trustee's determination with respect to this payment will be conclusive on the beneficiaries.

Section 12.10 Real Estate Powers

My Trustee may sell at public or private sale, convey, purchase, exchange, lease for any period, mortgage, manage, alter, improve, and in general deal in and with real property in the manner and on the terms and conditions as my Trustee deems appropriate.

My Trustee may grant or release easements in or over, subdivide, partition, develop, raze improvements to, and abandon any real property.

My Trustee may manage real estate in any manner considered best, and may exercise all other real estate powers necessary to effect this purpose.

My Trustee may enter into contracts to sell real estate. My Trustee may enter into leases and grant options to lease trust property, even though the term of the agreement extends beyond the termination of any trusts established under this trust and beyond the period that is required for an interest created under this trust to vest in order to be valid under the rule against perpetuities. My Trustee may enter into any contracts, covenants, and warranty agreements that my Trustee deems appropriate.

Section 12.11 Residences and Tangible Personal Property

My Trustee may acquire, maintain, and invest in any residence for the beneficiaries' use and benefit, whether or not the residence is income producing and without regard to the proportion that the residence's value may bear to the trust property's total value, even if retaining the residence involves financial risks that Trustees would not ordinarily incur. My Trustee may pay or make arrangements for others to pay all carrying costs of any residence for the beneficiaries' use and benefit, including taxes, assessments, insurance, maintenance, and other related expenses.

My Trustee may acquire, maintain, and invest in articles of tangible personal property, whether or not the property produces income. My Trustee may pay for the repair and maintenance of the property.

My Trustee is not required to convert the property referred to in this Section to income-producing property, except as required by other provisions of this trust.

My Trustee may permit any Income Beneficiary of the trust to occupy any real property or use any personal property owned by the trust on terms or arrangements that my Trustee determines, including rent free or in consideration for the payment of taxes, insurance, maintenance, repairs, or other charges.

My Trustee is not liable for any depreciation or loss resulting from any decision to retain or acquire any property as authorized by this Section.

Section 12.12 Digital Assets

My Trustee has the authority to access, modify, control, archive, transfer, and delete my digital assets.

Digital assets include my sent and received emails, email accounts, digital music, digital photographs, digital videos, gaming accounts, software licenses, social-network accounts, file-sharing accounts, financial accounts, domain registrations, Domain Name System (DNS) service accounts, blogs, listservs, web-hosting accounts, tax-preparation service accounts, online stores and auction sites, online accounts, and any similar digital asset that currently exists or may be developed as technology advances.

My digital assets may be stored in the cloud or on my own digital devices. My Trustee may access, use, and control my digital devices in order to access, modify, control, archive, transfer, and delete my digital assets—this power is essential for access to my digital assets that are only accessible through my digital devices. Digital devices include desktops, laptops, tablets, peripherals, storage devices, mobile telephones, smartphones, and any similar hardware that currently exists or may be developed as technology advances.

Section 12.13 Retention and Abandonment of Trust Property

My Trustee may retain any property constituting the trust at the time of its creation, at the time of my death, or as the result of the exercise of a stock option, without liability for depreciation or loss resulting from retention. My Trustee may retain property, notwithstanding the fact that the property may not be of the character prescribed by law for the investment of assets held by a fiduciary, and notwithstanding the fact that retention may result in inadequate diversification under any applicable Prudent Investor Act or other applicable law.

My Trustee may hold property that is not income producing or is otherwise nonproductive if holding the property is in the best interests of the beneficiaries in the sole and absolute discretion of my Trustee. On the other hand, my Trustee will invest contributions of cash and cash equivalents as soon as reasonably practicable after the assets have been acquired by the trust.

My Trustee may retain a reasonable amount in cash or money market accounts to pay anticipated expenses and other costs, and to provide for anticipated distributions to or for the benefit of a beneficiary.

My Trustee may abandon any property that my Trustee considers of insignificant value.

Section 12.14 Securities and Brokerage Powers

My Trustee may buy, sell, trade, and otherwise deal in stocks, bonds, investment companies, mutual funds, common trust funds, commodities, and other securities of any kind and in any amount, including short sales.

My Trustee may place all or any part of the securities held by the trust in the custody of a bank or trust company. My Trustee may have all securities registered in the name of the bank or trust company or in the name of the bank's nominee or trust company's nominee. My Trustee may appoint the bank or trust company as the agent or attorney in fact to collect, receive, receipt for, and disburse any income, and generally to perform the duties and services incident to a custodian of accounts.

My Trustee may employ a broker-dealer as a custodian for securities held by the trust, and may register the securities in the name of the broker-dealer or in the name of a nominee; words indicating that the securities are held in a fiduciary capacity are optional. My Trustee may hold securities in bearer or uncertificated form, and may use a central depository, clearing agency, or book-entry system, such as The Depository Trust Company, Euroclear, or the Federal Reserve Bank of New York.

My Trustee may participate in any reorganization, recapitalization, merger, or similar transaction. My Trustee may exercise or sell conversion or subscription rights for securities of all kinds and descriptions. My Trustee may give proxies or powers of attorney that may be discretionary and with or without powers of substitution, and may vote or refrain from voting on any matter.

Section 12.15 Settlement Powers

My Trustee may settle any claims and demands in favor of or against the trust by compromise, adjustment, arbitration, or other means. My Trustee may release or abandon any claim in favor of the trust.

Section 12.16 Limitation on My Trustee's Powers

All powers granted to Trustees under this trust or by applicable law are limited as set forth in this Section, unless explicitly excluded by reference to this Section.

An Interested Trustee Limited to Ascertainable Standards

An Interested Trustee may only make discretionary decisions when they pertain to a beneficiary's health, education, maintenance, or support as described under Internal Revenue Code Sections 2041 and 2514.

Interested Trustee Prohibited from Acting

Whenever this trust specifically prohibits or limits an Interested Trustee from exercising discretion or performing an act, then any Interested Trustee serving as my Trustee is prohibited from participating in the exercise of that discretion or performance of that act. If there is no Trustee serving who is not an Interested Trustee, then an Independent Special Trustee may be appointed under the provisions of 0 to exercise the discretion or perform the act.

Exclusive Powers of My Independent Trustee

Whenever a power or discretion is granted exclusively to my Independent Trustee, then any Interested Trustee who is then serving as my Trustee is prohibited from participating in the exercise of the power or discretion. If there is no Independent Trustee then serving, then an Independent Special Trustee may be appointed under the provisions of 0 to exercise the power or discretion that is exercisable only by my Independent Trustee.

No Distributions in Discharge of Certain Legal Obligations

My Trustee may not exercise or participate in the exercise of discretion with respect to the distribution of income or principal that would in any manner discharge a legal obligation of my Trustee, including the obligation of support.

If a beneficiary or any other person has the power to remove a Trustee, that Trustee may not exercise or participate in the exercise of discretion with respect to the distribution of income or principal that would in any manner discharge a legal obligation of the person having the power to remove the Trustee, including that person's obligation of support.

(Remainder of page intentionally left blank.)

Article Thirteen General Provisions

Section 13.01 Maximum Term for Trusts

Notwithstanding any contrary provisions or unless terminated earlier under other provisions of this trust, each trust created under this trust document will terminate 21 years after the death of the last to die of the descendants of my paternal and maternal grandparents and the descendants of my wife's paternal and maternal grandparents who are living at the time of my death.

At that time, the remaining trust property will vest in and be distributed to the persons entitled to receive mandatory distributions of the trust's net income, in the same proportions. If no beneficiary is entitled to mandatory distributions of net income, the remaining trust property will vest in and be distributed to the beneficiaries entitled to receive discretionary distributions of the trust's net income, in equal shares.

Section 13.02 Spendthrift Provision

No beneficiary may assign, anticipate, encumber, alienate, or otherwise voluntarily transfer the income or principal of any trust created under this trust. In addition, neither the income nor the principal of any trust created under this trust is subject to attachment, bankruptcy proceedings or any other legal process, the interference or control of creditors or others, or any involuntary transfer.

This Section does not restrict a beneficiary's right to disclaim any interest or exercise of any power of appointment granted in this trust.

Section 13.03 Contest Provision

If any person attempts to contest or oppose the validity of this trust or any amendment to this trust, or commences, continues, or prosecutes any legal proceedings to set this trust aside, then that person will forfeit his or her share, cease to have any right or interest in the trust property, and will be considered to have predeceased me for purposes of this instrument.

Section 13.04 Survivorship Presumption

If any beneficiary is living at my death, even momentarily, they shall be entitled to inherit from me pursuant to the Islamic law of Inheritance.

Section 13.05 Changing the Governing Law and Situs of Administration

At any time, my Trust Protector may change the governing law of the trust; change the situs of the administration of the trust; and remove all or any part of the property from one jurisdiction to another. My Trust Protector may elect, by filing an instrument with the trust records, that the trust will then be construed, regulated, and governed by the new jurisdiction's laws. My Trust Protector may take action under this Section for any purpose my Trust Protector considers appropriate, including the minimization of any taxes in respect of the trust or any trust beneficiary.

If considered necessary or advisable by my Trust Protector, my Trust Protector may appoint an Independent Trustee to serve as Trustee in the new situs.

If necessary and if my Trust Protector does not appoint an Independent Trustee within 30 days of my Trust Protector's action to change the governing law or situs of the trust, the beneficiaries entitled to receive distributions of the trust's net income may appoint a corporate fiduciary in the new situs by majority consent. If a beneficiary is a minor or is incapacitated, the beneficiary's parent or Legal Representative may act on the beneficiary's behalf.

Section 13.06 Antilapse Statutes

Whether existing now or enacted later, no *antilapse* statute of Arizona or any other jurisdiction will be applied in construing any provision of this trust.

Section 13.07 Definitions

For purposes of this trust, the following terms have these meanings:

Descendants

The term *descendants* means persons who directly descend from a person, such as children, grandchildren, or great-grandchildren. The term *descendants* does not include collateral descendants, such as nieces and nephews.

Education

The term *education* is intended to be an ascertainable standard under Internal Revenue Code Sections 2041 and 2514 and includes:

enrollment at private elementary, junior, and senior high school, including boarding school;
undergraduate and graduate study in any field at a college or university;
specialized, vocational, or professional training or instruction at any institution, as well as private instruction; and
any other curriculum or activity that my Trustee considers useful for developing a beneficiary's abilities and interests including athletic training, musical instruction, theatrical training, the arts, and travel.

The term *education* also includes expenses such as tuition, room and board, fees, books, supplies, computers and other equipment, tutoring, transportation, and a reasonable allowance for living expenses.

Good Faith

For the purposes of this trust, a Trustee has acted in good faith if:

an action or inaction is not a result of intentional wrongdoing;
the Trustee did not make the decision to act or not act with reckless indifference to the beneficiaries' interests; and
an action or inaction does not result in an improper personal benefit to the Trustee.

Further, all parties subject to the provisions of this trust will treat any action or inaction made in reliance on information, consent, or directions received from the Personal Representative of my estate as made in good faith for the purposes of this Section, except for cases of willful misconduct or malfeasance on the Trustee's part.

Grantor

Grantor has the same legal meaning as *Settlor, Trustor* or any other term referring to the maker of a trust.

Incapacity

Except as otherwise provided in this trust, a person is considered incapacitated in any of the following circumstances.

The Opinion of Two Licensed Physicians

An individual is considered to be incapacitated whenever two licensed physicians give the opinion that the individual is unable to effectively manage his or her property or financial affairs, whether as a result of age; illness; use of prescription medications, drugs, or other substances; or any other cause. If an individual whose capacity is in question refuses to provide necessary documentation or otherwise submit to examination by licensed physicians, that individual will be considered incapacitated.

An individual is considered restored to capacity whenever the individual's personal or attending physician provides a written opinion that the individual is able to effectively manage his or her property and financial affairs.

Court Determination

An individual is considered incapacitated if a court of competent jurisdiction has declared the individual to be disabled, incompetent, or legally incapacitated.

Detention, Disappearance, or Absence

An individual is considered to be incapacitated whenever he or she cannot effectively manage his or her property or financial affairs due to the individual's unexplained disappearance or absence for more than 30 days, or whenever he or she is detained under duress.

An individual's disappearance, absence, or detention under duress may be established by an affidavit of my Trustee, or by the affidavit of any beneficiary if no Trustee is then serving. The affidavit must describe the circumstances of the individual's disappearance, absence, or detention, and may be relied upon by any third party dealing in good faith with my Trustee.

Income Beneficiary

The term *Income Beneficiary* means any beneficiary who is then entitled to receive distributions of the trust's net income, whether mandatory or discretionary.

Unless otherwise provided in this trust, the phrase *majority of the Income Beneficiaries* means any combination of Income Beneficiaries who would receive more than 50% of the accrued net income if that income were distributed on the day of a vote. For purposes of this calculation, beneficiaries who are eligible to receive discretionary distributions of net income receive the imputed income in equal shares.

References to a *majority* refer to a majority of the entire trust collectively until my Trustee allocates property to separate trusts or trust shares. After my Trustee allocates property to separate trusts or trust shares, references to a *majority* refer to a majority of each separate trust or trust share.

Income in Respect of a Decedent (IRD)

The term *income in respect of a decedent* (IRD) means income received after a decedent's death that would have been taxable to the decedent if the income had been received by the decedent during the decedent's lifetime. For example, payments under qualified retirement plans and other deferred compensation arrangements are IRD. For purposes of this trust, IRD means any income that would be classified as IRD under Internal Revenue Code Section 691(a).

Independent Trustee

The term *Independent Trustee* means any Trustee who is not an Interested Trustee as defined in Subsection 0 and includes an Independent Special Trustee appointed under the provisions of 0.

Instrument

The term *this instrument* means this trust, and includes all trusts created under the terms of this trust.

Interested Trustee

The term *Interested Trustee* means a Trustee who:

is a transferor or beneficiary;
is related or subordinate to a transferor or beneficiary;
can be removed and replaced by a transferor with either the transferor or a party who is related or subordinate to the transferor; or
can be removed and replaced by a beneficiary with either the beneficiary or a party who is related or subordinate to the beneficiary.

For purposes of this Subsection, *transferor* means a person who transferred property to the trust during that person's lifetime, including a person whose disclaimer resulted in property passing to the trust. A person is only a transferor during his or her lifetime. *Beneficiary* means a person who is or may become eligible to receive income or principal from the trust under the terms of the trust, even if this person has only a remote contingent remainder interest in the trust, but not if the person's only interest is as a potential appointee under a power of appointment. *Related or subordinate* is used as defined in Internal Revenue Code Section 672(c).

Internal Revenue Code and Treasury Regulations

References to the *Internal Revenue Code* or to its provisions are to the Internal Revenue Code of 1986, as amended, and any corresponding Treasury Regulations. References to the *Treasury Regulations,* are to the Treasury Regulations under the Internal Revenue Code in effect. If a particular provision of the Internal Revenue Code is renumbered or the Internal Revenue Code is superseded by a subsequent federal tax law, any reference is considered to be made to the renumbered provision or to the corresponding provision of the subsequent law, unless to do so would clearly be contrary to my intent as expressed in this trust. The same rule applies to references to the Treasury Regulations.

Islamic Law of Inheritance

The Islamic Law of Inheritance is derived from verses of the Quran and Hadith of the Prophet Muhammad (peace be upon him) and provides a set of rules to determine who is entitled to inherit from a decedent's estate. In the event any of the heirs listed in Section 4.04 predecease me or if we die in a simultaneous death situation, I instruct my personal representative to recalculate the shares of inheritance based upon the following rules which are based upon the Hanafi school of jurisprudence.

Under these rules, Quranic heirs inherit first and receive fixed portions from the estate. If any assets remain in the estate, residuary heirs receive their share next. If there are no Quranic or residuary heirs, the estate passes to distant kindred.

Quranic Heirs (Dhawil Furood)

There are twelve *Dhawil Furood,* or Quranic heirs (four male and eight female), entitled to receive predetermined shares as specified in the Quran. However, not all the heirs may inherit, as some may be excluded by the presence of other heirs. The terms "high" and "low" refer to ascendants and descendants.

1. **Father:** A father inherits in one of three ways:
   a. A father receives a 1/6 share of the estate if the decedent is survived by a son or grandson through a son, however low.
   b. A father receives a 1/6 share of the estate as a Quranic heir plus the residue of the estate if the decedent is survived by at least one daughter or a daughter from a son, however low.
   c. A father converts to a residuary heir if the decedent is not survived by children or grandchildren, however low.
2. **Paternal Grandfather:** The paternal grandfather or great-grandfather, however high, will take the place of the father if the decedent's father is deceased. According to the *Hanafi* school of jurisprudence, the presence of a paternal grandfather will cause siblings to be excluded.
   a. A paternal grandfather receives a 1/6 share of the estate if the decedent is survived by at least one son or grandson through a son, however low.
   b. A paternal grandfather receives a 1/6 share of the estate plus any residue if the decedent is survived by at least one daughter or a daughter from a son, however low.
3. **Husband (Widower):** A widower always inherits from his late wife.
   a. A widower receives a 1/4 share of his late wife's estate if she is survived by any children or son's children, however low.
   b. A widower receives 1/2 his late wife's estate if she is not survived by any children or son's children, however low.
4. **Wife (Widow):** A widow always inherits from her late husband.
   a. A widow receives a 1/8 share of her late husband's estate if he is survived by any children or son's children, however low.
   b. A widow receives a 1/4 share of her late husband's estate if he is not survived by any children or son's children, however low.
5. **Daughter:** A daughter will always inherit in one of the following three conditions:
   a. If the decedent is survived by one daughter and no sons, the daughter receives 1/2 the [gross] estate.
   b. If the decedent is survived by two or more daughters and no sons, the daughters will split 2/3 of the [gross] estate equally.
   c. If the decedent is survived by one or more sons and one or more daughters, all the children shall be converted into residuary heirs and the sons receive twice the daughters' share.

6. **Granddaughter from Son:** In the absence of living children, a son's daughter is treated like a daughter.
   a. If the decedent is not survived by children or a grandson from a son, but is survived by one granddaughter from a son, the granddaughter receives 1/2 the estate.
   b. If the decedent is not survived by children or a grandson from a son, but is survived by more than one granddaughter from a son, the granddaughters will split 2/3 of the estate equally.
   c. If the decedent is survived by one daughter and a granddaughter from a son, but no son and no grandson from a son, the granddaughter receives a 1/6 share.
   d. If the decedent is survived by more than one daughter and no sons, and is survived by a granddaughter from a son, the granddaughter would be excluded unless the decedent was also survived by a grandson from a son.
7. **Mother**
   a. If the decedent is not survived by any children or two or more siblings, the mother receives a 1/3 share of the estate.
   b. If the decedent is survived by children or grandchildren, or two or more siblings, the mother receives a 1/6 share of the estate.
8. **Grandmother** (paternal and maternal)
   a. A paternal grandmother receives a 1/6 share of the estate if the decedent is not survived by a mother, father, or maternal grandmother.
   b. A paternal grandmother receives a 1/12 share of the estate if the decedent is not survived by a mother or father, but is survived by a maternal grandmother.
   c. A maternal grandmother receives a 1/6 share of the estate if the decedent is not survived by a mother, father, or paternal grandmother.
   d. A maternal grandmother receives a 1/12 share of the estate if the decedent is not survived by a mother or father, but is survived by a paternal grandmother.
9. **Full Sisters**
   a. If the decedent is survived by one full sister, but not by offspring, male paternal ancestors, or full brothers, the sister receives 1/2 the estate.
   b. If the decedent is survived by two or more full sisters, but not by offspring, male paternal ancestors, or full brothers, the sisters will split 2/3 of the estate equally.

10. **Agnate Sisters** (Paternal Half-Sisters)
    a. If the decedent is survived by one agnate sister, but not by offspring, male paternal ancestors, or full brothers or sisters, the agnate sister receives 1/2 the estate.
    b. If the decedent is survived by more than one agnate sister, but not by offspring, male paternal ancestors, or full brothers or sisters, the agnate sisters will split 2/3 of the estate equally.
    c. If the decedent is survived by one or more agnate sisters and by one full sister, but not by offspring, male paternal ancestors, or full brothers, the agnate sisters will split 1/6 of the estate equally.
11. **Uterine Brother** (Maternal Half-Brother): A uterine brother is excluded if the decedent is survived by a child or a son's child, however low, or a father, or paternal grandfather, however high.
12. **Uterine Sister** (Maternal Half-Sister): A uterine sister is excluded if the decedent is survived by a child or a son's child, however low, or a father, or paternal grandfather, however high.
    a. If the decedent is survived by one uterine sibling, but not by an offspring or male paternal ancestors, the uterine sibling receives a 1/6 share of the estate.
    b. If the decedent is survived by two or more uterine siblings, but not by an offspring or male paternal ancestors, the uterine siblings will split 1/3 of the estate equally. (Note that the traditional rule that males receive double the share of females is not applicable in this context.)

Once all the Quranic heirs receive their shares, the remainder of the estate is distributed to the *Asabah*, or residuary heirs. If there are no living *asabah*, the remainder of the estate is redistributed proportionally to the Quranic heirs under the doctrine of return, or *Radd* (with the exception of the spouse) before any residuary is distributed to the *Dhawil Arham*, or distant kindred.

Residuary Heirs (Asabah)

After Quranic heirs receive their shares, the rest of the estate should be distributed to the residuary heirs. The Prophet Muhammad instructed his companions, "Give the portion of the inheritance to the Quranic heirs, and whatever is left should go to the closest male relative of the deceased." Residuary heirs typically are male relatives, or are related to the decedent through the paternal lineage, and are divided into several groups. Three important rules apply with respect to distribution to residuary heirs:

1. The presence of any member of a higher group (see Table 1) excludes anyone in a lower group from inheriting with two exceptions:
   a. A son can never cause a father to be excluded.
   b. The *Shafi*, *Maliki*, and *Hanbali* schools of jurisprudence hold that a paternal grandfather excludes neither full nor half-siblings while the *Hanafi* school holds that a paternal grandfather excludes agnate siblings.
2. Within a group, an individual who is nearer in degree to the decedent excludes the more remote from inheriting.
3. Full-blood relatives take priority over half-blood relatives of the same degree.

Women who would otherwise be categorized as primary heirs become residuary heirs in the presence of a brother, as described in Table 2 below. In such cases, females will receive half the share of their brothers based on the Quranic injunction, "For males is twice the share of females." Only the decedent's daughter, son's daughters, full sister, agnate sister, and mother (in only one scenario) can become female residuary heirs through this process. The presence of a female residuary heir does not change any of the distribution rules described above.

Table 1. Male Residuary Heirs (*Asabah*)

Groups	**Members of Group**
Group 1 — Descendants	Son Son's male descendants
Group 2 — Ascendants	Father Father's male ascendants
Group 3 — Brother and Male Issue	Full Brother Agnate Brother Full Brother's Son Agnate Brother's Son Descendants of Group 3
Group 4 — Paternal Uncle and Male Issue	Full Paternal Uncle Agnate Paternal Uncle Full Paternal Uncle's son Agnate Paternal Uncle's Son Descendants of Group 4

Table 2. Female Residuary Heirs

Relation to Decedent	Converted to Residuary Heirs Only If . . .
Daughters	they have brothers
Son's Daughters	they have brothers or cousins of equal rank
Full Sisters	the decedent is survived by full brothers
Agnate Sisters	the decedent is survived by agnate brothers

There is only one scenario in which a sister can become a residuary heir in the absence of a brother: when the deceased is not survived by brothers but is survived by a daughter or son's daughter. In such a scenario, all the distribution rules stated above are applicable and the sister is treated as a male in Table 1.

If there are no residuary heirs, the remainder will be re-distributed proportionally to the primary heirs under the doctrine of *Radd* – with the exception of the spouse –whose share cannot be increased through *Radd* as she is not related to the decedent by blood but through marriage.

Distant Kindred **(Dhawil Arham)**

If there are any assets in excess of shares distributed to Quranic and residuary heirs, they are to be distributed among the distant kindred—all the decedent's remaining relatives who are not categorized as Quranic or residuary heirs. There are four categories of distant kindred, identified in order below. Two basic rules govern distribution to distant kindred: (1) The presence of any members of a higher category excludes all members of any category below from inheriting, and (2) within each category, the presence of any individuals in a higher class excludes all members of the classes below from inheriting.

Legal Representative or Personal Representative

As used in this trust document, the term *Legal Representative* or *Personal Representative* means a person's guardian, conservator, executor, administrator, Trustee, attorney in fact under a Durable Power of Attorney, or any other person or entity representing a person or the person's estate. In the case of a minor beneficiary, the beneficiary's parent or another adult with custody of the beneficiary, except for any transferor to a trust created under this instrument, will be considered the beneficiary's Legal Representative for purposes of this trust.

Table 3. Distant Kindred

Category 1—Descendants Who Are Not Quranic Heirs or Residuary Heirs	Class 1— Daughter's Children Class 2— Son's Daughter's Children Class 3— Daughter's Children's Children
Category 2—Ascendants Who Are Not Quranic Heirs or Residuary Heirs	Class 1— Maternal Grandfather Class 2— Father's Maternal Grandfather Mother's Paternal Grandfather Mother's Maternal Grandfather Mother's Maternal Grandmother
Category 3—Nieces and Nephews Who Are Not Quranic Heirs or Residuary Heirs	Class 1— Sister's Children Paternal Half-Sister's Children Maternal Half-Sister's Children Brother's Daughters Paternal Half-Brother's Daughters Maternal Half-Brother's Children Class 2— Brother's Son's Daughters Paternal Half-Brother's Son's Daughters Maternal Half-Brother's Son's Children Brother's Daughter's Children Paternal Half-Brother's Daughter's Children Maternal Half-Brother's Daughter's Children Sister's Son's Children Paternal Half-Sister's Son's Children Maternal Half-Sister's Son's Children Sister's Daughter's Children Paternal Half-Sister's Daughter's Children Maternal Half-Sister's Daughter's Children

(continued on next page)

Table 3. Distant Kindred *(continued)*

Category 4—Aunts, Uncles, and Cousins Who Are Not Quranic Heirs or Residuary Heirs	Class 1(a)—Father's Sister Father's Paternal Half-Sister Father's Maternal Half-Sister Father's Maternal Half-Brother Class 1(b)—Mother's Brother Mother's Sister Mother's Paternal Half-Brother Mother's Paternal Half-Sister Mother's Maternal Half-Brother Mother's Maternal Half-Sister Class 2(a)—Paternal Uncle's Daughters Paternal Aunt's Children Father's Paternal Half-Brother's Daughters Father's Paternal Half-Sister's Children Father's Maternal Half-Brother's Children Father's Maternal Half-Sister's Children Class 2(b)—Maternal Uncle's Children Maternal Aunt's Children Mother's Paternal Half-Brother's Children Mother's Paternal Half-Sister's Children Mother's Maternal Half-Brother's Children Mother's Maternal Half-Sister's Children Class 3(a)—Father's Paternal Aunt Father's Father's Paternal Half-Sister Father's Father's Maternal Half-Brother Father's Father's Maternal Half-Sister Class 3(b)—Father's Maternal Uncle Father's Maternal Aunt Father's Mother's Paternal Half-Brother Father's Mother's Paternal Half-Sister Father's Mother's Maternal Half-Brother Father's Mother's Maternal Half-Sister Class 3(c)—Mother's Paternal Aunt Mother's Father's Paternal Half-Sister Mother's Father's Maternal Half-Brother Mother's Father's Maternal Half-Sister Class 3(d)—Mother's Maternal Uncle Mother's Maternal Aunt Mother's Mother's Paternal Half-Brother Mother's Mother's Paternal Half-Sister Mother's Mother's Maternal Half-Brother Mother's Mother's Maternal Half-Sister

Primary Beneficiary

The *Primary Beneficiary* of a trust created under this trust is that trust's oldest Income Beneficiary, unless some other individual is specifically designated as the Primary Beneficiary of that separate trust.

Qualified Retirement Benefits

The term *qualified retirement plan* means a plan qualified under Internal Revenue Code Section 401, an individual retirement arrangement under Section 408 or Section 408A, or a tax-sheltered annuity under Section 403. The term *qualified retirement benefits* means the amounts held in or distributed pursuant to a plan qualified under Section 401, an individual retirement arrangement under Section 408 or Section 408A, a tax-sheltered annuity under Section 403, or any other benefit subject to the distribution rules of Section 401(a)(9).

Shall and May

Unless otherwise specifically provided in this trust or by the context in which used, I use the word *shall* in this trust to impose a duty, command, direct, or require, and the word *may* to allow or permit, but not require. In the context of my Trustee, when I use the word *shall* I intend to impose a fiduciary duty on my Trustee. When I use the word *may* I intend to empower my Trustee to act with the Trustee's sole and absolute discretion unless otherwise stated in this trust. When I use the words *may not* in reference to my Trustee, I specifically mean my Trustee *is not permitted to.*

Trust

The terms *this trust, this document, instrument,* and *this trust document* refer to this trust and all trusts created under the terms of this trust.

Trustee

The terms *my Trustee* and *Trustee* refer to the Initial Trustee named in Article One and to any successor, substitute, replacement, or additional person, corporation, or other entity that ever acts as the Trustee of any trust created under the terms of this trust. The term *Trustee* refers to singular or plural as the context may require.

Trust Property

The term *trust property* means all property acquired from any source and held by a Trustee under this trust.

Section 13.08 General Provisions and Rules of Construction

The following general provisions and rules of construction apply to this trust.

Multiple Originals; Validity of Paper or Electronic Copies

This trust may be executed in any number of counterparts, each of which will be considered an original.

Any person may rely on a paper or electronic copy of this trust that the Trustee certifies to be a true copy as if it were an original.

Singular and Plural; Gender

Unless the context requires otherwise, singular words may be construed as plural, and plural words may be construed as singular. Words of one gender may be construed as denoting another gender as is appropriate within the context. The word *or*, when used in a list of more than two items, may function as both a conjunction and a disjunction as the context requires.

Headings of Articles, Sections, and Subsections

The headings of Articles, Sections, and Subsections used within this trust are included solely for the convenience of the reader. They have no significance in the interpretation or construction of this trust.

Governing State Law

This trust is governed, construed, and administered according to the laws of Arizona, as amended except as to trust property required by law to be governed by the laws of another jurisdiction and unless the situs of administration is changed under 0.

Notices

Unless otherwise stated, any notice required under this trust will be in writing. The notice may be personally delivered with proof of delivery to the party requiring notice and will be effective on the date personally delivered. Notice may also be mailed, postage prepaid, by certified mail with return receipt requested to the last known address of the party requiring notice. Mailed notice is effective on the date of the return receipt. If a party giving notice does not receive the return receipt but has proof that he or she mailed the notice, notice will be effective on the date it would normally have been received via certified mail. If the party requiring notice is a minor or incapacitated individual, notice will be given to the parent or Legal Representative.

Severability

The invalidity or unenforceability of any provision of this trust does not affect the validity or enforceability of any other provision of this trust. If a court of competent jurisdiction determines that any provision is invalid, the remaining provisions of this trust are to be interpreted as if the invalid provision had never been included.

I have executed this Trust on January 1, 2019. This trust instrument is effective when signed by me, whether or not now signed by a Trustee.

____

Abdullah Khan, Grantor and Trustee

STATE OF ARIZONA)
) ss.
COUNTY OF MARICOPA)

This instrument was acknowledged before me on January 1, 2019, by Abdullah Khan, as Grantor and as Trustee.

[Seal]

____

Notary Public

My commission expires: January 1, 2020

Schedule A

____

____

____

____

____

____

____

____

____

____

____

____

____

APPENDIX

F

Sample Property Agreement

Marital Property Agreement

This is an important document and may affect your rights, including those of your estate beneficiaries. Please make sure that you understand the issues presented in this document before executing it.

Adam Khan and Sarah Khan enter into this agreement this date ______.

Recitals and Terms

History

On August 1, 1998, Adam Khan (referred to as *Husband* after this) and Sarah Khan (referred to as *Wife* after this) were married. We may refer to Husband and Wife collectively as the *Parties* or individually as a *Party*.

Property Covered

By entering into this agreement, we intend to clarify the status of our joint and separate property as identified in the attached schedules.

Estate Plan

On January 1, 2019, we created an estate plan by establishing the Khan Family Trust and separate pour-over wills.

Separate and Community Property Estate

The term Separate Property Estate refers to any property in which each spouse individually has present and existing interest as defined in Schedules B and C.

The term *Community Property Estate* refers to any and all property in which Husband and Wife have present and existing interests as defined in Schedule A

Estate Planning Objectives

We desire to enter into a comprehensive agreement concerning the following estate planning objectives:

> to conclusively establish the status of our various property interests;
> to confirm our intention that our respective assets should pass to our heirs in accordance with our faith of Islam and the Islamic Law of Inheritance;
> to expressly waive all rights including any elective share rights upon the death of either of us;
> to allow a *non pro rata* division of our Community Property Estate when the community terminates on the death of either of us;
> to clarify that Retirement Accounts are to be deemed and treated as the separate property of the named account holder;
> to agree and pledge among ourselves that if either of us receives a share of the deceased spouse's separate property estate or our community property estate that exceeds the surviving spouse's entitlement under the Islamic law of Inheritance, as defined in the Khan Family Trust, the surviving spouse shall compensate the Trustee of the deceased spouse's trust with his or her separate property in order to ensure that each of our beneficiaries receive their rightful shares under the Islamic law of Inheritance;
> to allow a basis adjustment under Internal Revenue Code Section 1014 for the surviving spouse in the entire interest of each Community Property asset.

Agreement

In order to give effect to our intent, we agree as follows:

Identification of Community Property

We both mutually agree and confirm that all assets and real, personal, and business property identified in Schedule A which is attached and incorporated to this agreement, whether the property has been titled in the name of one or more of us and whether the property has been held in joint tenancy or as tenants in common shall be treated as Community Property during our lifetime and upon the death of the first of us to die, unless otherwise transmuted by us in writing.

We further agree that each of us owns an undivided one-half interest in the total aggregate value of our Community Property Estate rather than an undivided one-half interest in each community property asset the Trustee of the Khan Family Trust or the Personal Representative of each Party's estate may divide the community property on a *non pro rata* basis to achieve our estate planning objectives.

Any assets or property that are subsequently acquired by us and titled in both of our names or in the Khan Family Trust that are not expressly identified as the separate property of either spouse shall be deemed and treated as community property.

Identification of Separate Property

We both mutually agree and confirm that all assets and real, personal, and business property identified in Schedules B and C as well as any future property that either spouse acquires by gift or inheritance or that is titled solely in one spouse's name shall be deemed and treated as the separate property of that spouse, unless otherwise transmuted by us in writing.

Separate Property of Husband

Husband's separate property is described on Schedule B and is attached and incorporated into this agreement.

Wife's additions to the Separate Property of Husband are quitclaimed and gifted to Husband from Wife, and become the sole and separate property of the Husband.

Separate Property of Wife

Wife's separate property is described on Schedule C and is attached and incorporated into this agreement.

Husband's additions to the Separate Property of Wife are quitclaimed and gifted to Wife from Husband, and become the sole and separate property of the Wife.

Intent to Distribute Assets in Accordance with Islamic Inheritance Law

We desire to distribute our assets upon our death to our heirs in accordance with our faith of Islam and the Islamic law of Inheritance. Accordingly, if either of us is named as the primary beneficiary of a retirement account or life insurance policy or automatically becomes the sole owner of an asset through a right of survivorship in a manner that causes the survivor to receive an aggregate share that is greater than what he or she is entitled to receive under the Islamic law of Inheritance, we agree to compensate the trustee of the deceased spouse's trust through our separate property estate in order to ensure that the deceased spouse's heirs receive their rightful shares under Islamic law.

Waiver of Elective Shares

We understand and acknowledge that our share of inheritance under the Islamic Law of Inheritance as defined in our respective living trusts may be smaller than a state-designated elective share, if applicable. Nonetheless, we both expressly waive any right to an elective share under any state statute.

Written Modifications

This agreement can only be modified or revoked by a written instrument that refers explicitly to this agreement and is executed by both of us.

Execution of Other Instruments

We both agree that on the request of the either of us or our respective successors or assigns, either of us or our respective successor or assigns shall execute, deliver, and properly acknowledge any deeds or documents necessary to give effect to this agreement.

Applicable Law

Arizona law will govern all matters pertaining to the validity, construction, interpretation, and effect of this agreement.

Representation by Counsel

We have consented to joint representation by [Attorney Name] for purposes of drafting and reviewing the contents of this agreement. Given the possibility of conflicting legal and property interests between us, each of us is aware of his or her right to obtain independent counsel to advise him or her concerning this agreement, and each of us has knowingly waived the right to independent counsel.

Severability

If a court of competent jurisdiction finds any provision or part of a provision of this agreement to be void or unenforceable, the remainder of the agreement will remain valid and enforceable.

We execute and accept this Marital Property Agreement on this date of January 1, 2019.

____

Adam Khan

____

Sarah Khan

STATE OF ARIZONA)

) ss.

COUNTY OF MARICOPA)

This instrument was acknowledged before me on January 1, 2019, by Adam Khan and Sarah Khan.

[Seal]

____

Notary Public

My commission expires: ______________________

Schedule A

Community Property

Schedule B

Husband's Separate Property

Schedule C

Wife's Separate Property

Glossary

Asabah, residuary heirs.

Ayat, verses of the Quran.

Awl, the equitable doctrine of increase.

Bait al-maal, public treasury.

Dhawil Arham, distant kindred.

Dhawil Furood, Quranic heirs.

Eid al-Fitr, the Feast of Celebration. One of the two major Islamic holidays.

Faraid, mandatory distributions under Islamic inheritance law.

Fard kifayah, communal obligation.

Fidyah, penalty.

Fiqh, the schools of Islamic jurisprudence.

Gharar, excessive speculation.

Hadith, normative traditions of the Prophet Muhammad.

Hajj, once-in-a-lifetime pilgrimage to Mecca for Muslims who are financially and physically able to. One of the five pillars of Islam.

Halal, dietary restrictions in Islam.

Hanafi, one of the four Sunni orthodox schools of jurisprudence, or *Fiqh*.

Hanbali, one of the four Sunni orthodox schools of jurisprudence, or *Fiqh*.

Haram, prohibited.

Hiba, gift. Under Islamic law, this means an immediate and unconditional transfer of the ownership of some property or of some right, without any consideration.

Iddah, a waiting period for a woman after her husband dies or in the case of a revocable divorce.

Idtirar, the affirmation that necessity renders the forbidden permissible.

Ijab, a proposal as carried out in a marriage ceremony.

Ijma, scholarly consensus on a matter.

'Ilm al-Fara'id, the knowledge of predetermined shares, or Islamic inheritance law.

Islam, lit. "submission to God."

Ja'fari, one of the two Shia schools of jurisprudence, or *Fiqh*.

Mafqood, a missing person. This individual is presumed to be alive with regard to his or her estate and deceased with regard to the estate of others.

Mahr, equivalent to a Western dower. A gift to the bride.

Mahr mu'akhar, the deferred portion of *mahr* that is paid upon divorce or death.

Maliki, one of the four Sunni orthodox schools of jurisprudence, or *Fiqh*.

Manf'ah, usufruct of a property.

Maqasid, goals and principles.

Maradul maut, the "final illness," a period of time in which a person is on his or her deathbed and is unable to perform routine daily functions, or when a healthy person is facing the possibility of imminent death.

Mawarith schedules, charts and schedules that practitioners may choose to attach to trusts to instruct successor trustees on determining fixed shares for specific beneficiaries.

Maysir, forms of gambling.

Muslim, lit. "one who submits to the will of God."

Munasakha, when a beneficiary dies before receiving his or her distribution.

Mut'a, a temporary marriage. A couple agrees to sexual union for a stated period of time, after which the "marriage" is null.

Nikkah, a valid Islamic marriage ceremony. Also known as *kitab.*

Nisab, a threshold amount of wealth used when determining *zakat.*

Qabool, the acceptance of one party to a proposal (*ijab*) from the other party in an Islamic marriage ceremony.

Qiyas, a process of analogical deduction that Muslim scholars use to derive Islamic legal rulings for new developments.

Quran, the Muslim holy scripture.

Radd, doctrine of return.

Riba, interest.

Rushd, intellectual maturity.

Sadaqah, voluntary almsgiving or charity.

Sadaqah jariya, ongoing charity. A special type of charity that continues to benefit others even after the donor's death.

Salah, prayer. Muslims pray five times a day: before sunrise, around noon, in the afternoon, after sunset, and in the late evening. One of the five pillars of Islam.

Shafi, one of the four Sunni orthodox schools of jurisprudence, or *Fiqh.*

Shahada, testimony of faith for a Muslim. One of the five pillars of Islam.

Sharia, lit. "a way to the watering place" or "a path to seek felicity and salvation." The term is often used interchangeably with "Islamic law."

Shia, one of the two major sects of Islam.

Shura, mutual consultation.

Siyam, fasting during the Muslim holy month of Ramadan. Every Muslim who is physically able to must fast. One of the five pillars of Islam.

Sunnah, the normative tradition of the Prophet Muhammad.

Sunni, one of the two major sects of Islam.

Surah, chapter of the Quran.

Ta'awun, the Islamic concept of mutual assistance.

Takaful, lit. "solidarity," an Islamically permissible form of cooperative insurance.

Waqf, an endowment or trust that owns a property/asset and is not subject to the Islamic Law of Inheritance. These assets are donated, bequeathed, or purchased for the purpose of being held in perpetual and irrevocable trust as an ongoing charity or for a general or specific cause that Islam regards as socially beneficial. Plural is *awqaf*.

Wasiyah, a discretionary bequest. A Muslim may dispose of up to one-third of his or her estate through a *wasiyah* to anyone who is not entitled to inherit as an Islamic heir, any charitable institution(s), or any combination thereof.

Zaidi, one of the two Shia orthodox schools of jurisprudence, or *Fiqh*.

Zakat, lit. "purification" or "increase"; almsgiving or charity that is mandatory for every financially able Muslim. One of the five pillars of Islam.

Index

M

N

O

P

U

W

Z